W9-BWG-094

Availability

This text is available
in a variety of formats—
print and digital. Check your
favorite digital provider for
your eText, including **Coursesmart**,
Kindle, **Nook**, and more.
To learn more about our
programs, pricing options and
customization, visit

Rhetorical Public Speaking

Second Edition

NATHAN CRICK

Louisiana State University

PEARSON

Boston Columbus Indianapolis New York San Francisco Upper Saddle River
Amsterdam Cape Town Dubai London Madrid Milan Munich Paris Montreal Toronto
Delhi Mexico City São Paulo Sydney Hong Kong Seoul Singapore Taipei Tokyo

Editor-in-Chief: Ashley Dodge
Senior Acquisitions Editor: Melissa Mashburn
Editorial Assistant: Megan Hermida
Project Manager: Clara Bartunek
Executive Marketing Manager: Kelly May
Marketing Coordinator: Theresa Rotondo
Digital Editor: Lisa Dotson
Art Director, Cover: Jayne Conte
Full-Service Project Manager: Sudha Balasundaram/S4Carlisle Publishing Services
Compositors: S4Carlisle Publishing Services
Cover Designer: Karen Noferi
Cover Photo: Alamy
Printer/Binder: STP Courier

"Quintilian, quoted in THE PHILOSOPHY OF RHETORIC, in THE RHETORICAL TRADITION: READINGS FROM CLASSICAL TIMES TO THE PRESENT, ed. Patricia Bizzell and Bruce Herzberg (Boston: Bedford Books of St. Martin's Press, 1990), 329."

Library of Congress Cataloging-in-Publication Data
Crick, Nathan.
    Rhetorical public speaking / Nathan Crick, Louisiana State University.—Second Edition.
      pages cm
    Includes index.
    ISBN 978-0-205-86936-7
    1. Business communication—Handbooks, manuals, etc.   2. Business writing—Handbooks,
    manuals, etc.   3. Public speaking—Handbooks, manuals, etc.   I. Title.
    HF5718.C75 2013
    808.5'1—dc23
                                                              2012042686

1 2 3 4 5 6 7 8 9 10

ISBN-13: 978-0-205-86936-7
ISBN-10:   0-205-86936-X

CONTENTS

PREFACE

The purpose of this book is to give students a practical understanding of how public speaking can function as a rhetorical intervention—as an act of persuasion designed to alter how other people think about and respond to public affairs that affect their lives. The audience for this book is the **engaged citizen**—that individual who is an active participant in the democratic process of debate, deliberation, and persuasion as it relates to issues of public concern.

NEW TO THIS EDITION

This new edition has been updated and expanded to provide students with the tools they need to be effective public speakers. The following lists specific changes to the new second edition:

- Updated examples of rhetorical artifacts from historical social movements and contemporary popular culture to show public speaking in action
- An introduction to media theory that articulates the relationship of rhetoric to written, electronic, and oral communication
- A succinct definition of rhetoric as the art of giving form to a situation through the action of an audience
- A comprehensive presentation of the Five Canons of Rhetoric that allows you to master the basics of public speaking in the first few weeks of class
- The addition of a chapter on eloquence to challenge advanced public speakers to raise their skills to a higher level

The guiding rationale for this book is that the success or failure of democratic social life depends on the cultivation of engaged citizens, each of whom has the capacity to act rhetorically in the public sphere. In other words, democracy suffers when we base our educational system on the naïve faith that individuals instinctively possess the skills of public advocacy. The reality is that citizens are made, not born. Part of that educational process involves instilling in people the belief that free speech is their right and individual expression is their duty. The other part of the process is to give them the knowledge, skill, and confidence to perform that duty and to judge the performances of others when the situation demands it. One unique function of a class in public speaking is to provide a structured and supportive environment in which to develop these skills in preparation for an active life. This textbook is designed to facilitate that process by providing the tools—understood as methods—that promote the creative expression of engaged citizens.

The speaker in rhetorical public speech is therefore something more than just a person who says words in the presence of others. A rhetorical public speaker is called a **rhetor**, meaning a conscious instigator of social action who uses persuasive discourse to achieve his or her ends. Being *conscious* implies that a rhetor is not simply one whose speech happens to have consequences. All acts of communication have the potential to influence people and events, but rhetorical public speech is unique in having been created specifically for that purpose. That is what makes it an art rather than a product of luck. Being an *instigator* means that a rhetor intentionally behaves in such a manner as to cause others to think and feel in new and different ways. We instigate not only when we prompt, originate, and begin something, but also when we do so in the presence of others who may be reluctant to follow. An instigator makes people act in ways they might not otherwise have done if not prodded to do so. Finally, what is instigated is a *social action*, meaning that the effects of a rhetor's persuasive discourse are determined by how they alter and impact the behaviors of other people with respect to some end, or some goal or interest that functions in response to an exigence. A rhetor thus represents a person willing to stir, motivate, challenge, and even confront audiences in order to make them think and act in such a way that addresses a shared problem.[1]

It is from this methodological and pedagogical perspective that examples have been chosen which represent strategies for generating social change within certain historical moments of crisis. Methodologically, a historian of public speaking finds the most interesting examples of rhetoric on the margins of culture. Understandably, this does *not* mean that these strategies were particularly *effective* or *virtuous;* it means only that the strategy was explicitly and creatively employed in such a way that makes it useful for the purpose of elaboration. Instructors and students who do not find their own views expressed in the examples of the book should bring them to the table during the span of the course to generate productive discussion through engagement.

The controversial nature of these speeches also provides an opportunity to discuss the ethics of rhetoric. By "ethics," I do not refer to whether a speaker's beliefs match up to some formal catechism or obey some polite convention. The **ethics of rhetoric** are determined by how well the speaker has fully considered the broader consequences of his or her actions beyond the immediate moment and has acted conscientiously with respect to that evaluation. Part of the responsibility of rhetorical theory is to make speakers aware of just how much impact a single speech might have in a complex and interconnected world in which "good intentions" are not enough to produce desired consequences. The ethical study of public speech helps people to avoid getting trapped into such a situation by providing the tools to survey a broader social environment before acting. Based on this "holistic" ethical ideal, a large part of what distinguishes this book from other texts on public speaking is its continual emphasis on the speaker as a part of a larger social whole.

I have tried, in this book, to reconnect public speaking with the rhetorical and wholly democratic tradition of eloquence—of the act of appearing before others to express one's truth with beauty and excellence. Toward this end, I have emphasized that aspect of public speaking which is often quickly passed over by textbooks in haste to present the latest in flowcharts and moral catechisms—the act of appearing before others. Throughout this book, I will emphasize public speaking

---

[1]For the relationship between rhetoric and citizenship, see Robert Asen, "A Discourse Theory of Citizenship," *Quarterly Journal of Speech* 90, no. 2 (2004), 189–211.

as an action that occurs in the company of others who share experience on matters of common concern. Although rhetorical public speaking is arguably about the act of persuasion, it is more importantly an action of gathering together people to appear before one another in a shared space of their common world. Nonetheless, a few examples are analyzed in this book that appeared in print and were meant to be read. I have selected them because they perfectly exemplify a specific persuasive strategy and because they highlight an important figure in history. As much as I am able, I will emphasize how the written form changes the delivery and organization of the argument in order to make clear the difference between the written and spoken word.

Finally, the book emphasizes that public speaking is an art. As an art, it is learned through practice. Nothing replaces the pure experience of simply talking in front of others. This experience cannot be quantified or measured. The value of any conceptual material, therefore, must be judged with respect to how it enriches and broadens the experience of the student in the act of speaking. The Roman rhetorician Quintilian wrote, "An art consists of perceptions consenting and cooperating to some end useful to life" and involves "a power working its effects by a course, that is by method;" consequently, "no man will doubt that there is a certain course and method in oratory."[2] A successful course in public speaking will seek to educate students in a method of channeling the power of the spoken word toward ends that are useful in life.

Those who have used earlier editions of this book in the past will find this edition to be far more lucid, accessible, and practical. The challenge of writing this textbook has been to integrate complex theoretical concepts and rich historical material into a practical teaching manual. Trial and error have revealed which concepts should be forefront and what examples speak to the diverse experiences of students. One effect of this has been to streamline the conceptual material. This version of the textbook has eliminated an entire chapter on the psychology of motivation and has reduced considerably the discussion of the rhetorical background, folding relevant material into a single chapter on the rhetorical situation. Furthermore, it has altered a chapter originally titled "Style" so that it focuses instead on "eloquence," and by doing so has reduced six poetic categories to three—the heroic, the comic, and the tragic. Another effect has been to alter the makeup of the historical examples, requiring (with two exceptions) all of the examples to be originally delivered orally. Third, the entire body of text has been completely rewritten in order to make it more readable and accessible to students while also reinforcing dominant themes of the book. Finally, the extended treatment of a single speech by Martin Luther King, Jr. (that originally occupied the summary sections in each chapter) has been replaced by more focused summaries that simply show how all of the conceptual material relates to each other. The result is a book that I believe has identified the core concepts that are absolutely essential for the mastery of public speaking presented in a way that challenges and engages students.

---

[2]Quintilian, quoted in *The Philosophy of Rhetoric*, in *The Rhetorical Tradition: Readings from Classical Times to the Present*, ed. Patricia Bizzell and Bruce Herzberg (Boston: Bedford Books of St. Martin's Press, 1990), 329.

INTRODUCTION

The goal of rhetorical public speaking is the transformation of a collection of disparate individual hearers into a common and committed audience through the power of the spoken word. Every metaphor, every gesture, and every argument must be directed toward this act of turning the many into the one, at least for a moment. This basic fact was recognized by nineteenth-century orator and philosopher Ralph Waldo Emerson, who wrote more than one essay on the subject of "eloquence." Of the orator, he says the following:

> That which he wishes, that which eloquence ought to reach, is not a particular skill in telling a story, or neatly summing up evidence, or arguing logically, or dexterously addressing the prejudice of the company,—no, but a taking sovereign possession of the audience. Him we call an artist who shall play on an assembly of men as a master on the keys of the piano,—who, seeing the people furious, shall soften and compose them, shall draw them, when he will, to laughter and to tears. Bring him to his audience, and, be they who they may,— coarse or refined, pleased or displeased, sulky or savage, with their opinions in the keeping of a confessor, or with their opinions in their bank-safes,—he will have them pleased and humored as he chooses; and they shall carry and execute that which he bids them.[3]

Although Emerson's language expresses something of a tyrannical tenor ("Do my bidding!"), he nonetheless emphasizes the essential characteristic that sets public speaking apart from other mediated forms of communication, such as writing or video—the fact that experience of being in the same place at the same time to listen to a single person speak can be a very powerful experience indeed. This is because, as Walter Ong later pointed out, "spoken words are always modification of a total, existential situation, which always engages the body. . . . In oral verbalization, particularly public verbalization, absolute motionless is itself a powerful gesture."[4] When we watch someone on a screen or read his or her words on paper, silence may bore us and we can always turn our attention to other things; but when we are present together to listen to a speech that captures our attention, we commit ourselves completely to the experience.

However, it is natural to ask whether Emerson would have had held oratorical eloquence in such high regard if he lived in our modern technological age of the Internet, television, smartphones, digital video, photography, movie, radio, and all the other technologies from the past hundred years. Indeed, one might argue that modern technology will soon make the art of oratory obsolete altogether. Why,

---

[3]Ralph Waldo Emerson, "Eloquence," http://oll.libertyfund.org/?option=com_staticxt&staticfile=show.php%3Ftitle=86&chapter=104478&layout=html&Itemid=27 (accessed 15 Dec. 2011).

[4]Walter Ong, *Orality and Literacy*, 67.

after all, give an informative speech about the history of the civil rights movement when one can forward a PDF file? Why bother making introductory speeches to every person in a new workplace when one can send a group e-mail? And why get everyone in the same room to hear a sales pitch when they can do it by videoconferencing? In an age where communication via electronic technology is the first choice for most people in their busy lives, one must have a clear reason for gathering people together in the same space at the same time to hear a speech. Consequently, any book that purports to teach public speaking as oratory must address the unique quality of oral performance that makes it something to take seriously despite the pervasiveness and attractiveness of new media.

The best place to find evidence of the continued vitality of the oratorical tradition is simply one's everyday experience. On the one hand, it is undeniable that new media have effectively challenged or even replaced many communicative interactions that previously had relied on face-to-face contacts. One can imagine a time when the university classroom, the corporate boardroom, and the local merchandise store will all go the way of the door-to-door salesperson and the colonial-era town hall meeting, and when a "friend" will refer simply to a relationship one has with a digital picture and associated text messages. On the other hand, the science fiction projections of a time when human beings will be content simply sitting alone in a room surrounded by video screens and constant chatter are really meant as amplifications of isolated tendencies in society rather than serious predictions based on human nature. For the fact remains that despite our ability to communicate through media as never before, there is a very basic need in every human being for intimate human contact that comes from simply being with others in the same place at the same time and recognizing and welcoming one another's presence. There is simply no way that any form of media will replace the necessity to be present together at births and at deaths, during weddings and wakes, in celebration and in tragedy, and to achieve communion and to resolve crisis. In short, even as the amount of time spent communicating through new media increases mathematically, the importance of those moments when we must come together and share the experience of eloquence increases geometrically. We may not speak to one another in person as much as we had in the past, but that only means that we must be prepared to do so with passion and with power when the moment calls.

Moreover, although the inventions of our time are certainly new additions to the world, the challenge of adapting our forms of communication to new technology is a very ancient one. In the age of Classical Greece in the fifth century B.C.E., the new technology was writing and the new media was papyrus. We might think this an archaic media by our standards, but at the time it was highly disruptive to the traditional oral community. In the *Phaedrus*, Plato complained that writing will "introduce forgetfulness into the soul of those who learn it: they will not practice using their memory because they will put their trust in writing, which is external and depends on signs that belong to others, instead of trying to remember from the inside, completely on their own. . . . And they will imagine that they have come to know much while for the most part they will know nothing."[5] Although a writer

---

[5]Plato, *Phaedrus*, 275b.

himself, Plato wanted to limit the scope and influence of writing because he believed it would interfere with the pursuit of wisdom through what he called "dialectic," which was a method to use face-to-face dialogue to seek out truths of both the world and of the soul through living speech. For him, writing threatened to replace that which was real and vibrant with that which was artificial and mechanical.

But just as every first generation has its Plato, whose job it is to warn us of the dangers of being seduced by new technology, every second generation has its Aristotle, whose job it is to adapt our method of communication to our available mediums. Although a student of Plato, Aristotle did not look upon writing with such anxiety. He simply recognized that each medium required its own unique form, and that "each kind of rhetoric has its own appropriate style."[6] In his mid-fourth-century B.C.E. treatise *Rhetoric*, Aristotle gives us perhaps the first extended treatment of the differences between the written and spoken word:

> The written style is the more finished: the spoken better admits of dramatic delivery—alike the kind of oratory that reflects character and the kind that reflects emotion. Hence actors look out for plays written in the latter style, and poets for actors competent to act such plays . . . [However, speeches made to hear spoken] look amateurish enough when they pass into the hands of a reader. This is because they are so well suited for an actual tussle, and therefore contain many dramatic touches, which, being robbed of all dramatic rendering, fail to do their own proper work and consequently look silly. Thus strings of unconnected words, and constant repetitions of words and phrases, are very properly condemned in written speeches: but not in spoken speeches—speakers use them freely, for they have a dramatic effect.[7]

Aristotle points out perhaps the most essential quality of the spoken word—its unique suitability to capture the emotional character of a situation with only a few words or gestures, and to do so in such a way that powerfully brings an audience together through shared experience. Whereas writing must reproduce every single aspect of a situation through words, thus necessitating lengthy and detailed narration and argumentation, oral performance can accomplish the same task with a simple turn of phrase or wave of the hand. And even perhaps more important, Aristotle recognizes that the spoken and written word are not in competition; each is suited for its own unique purpose and has its own unique form.

The difference between these two mediums was emphasized again much later by philosopher John Dewey in the twentieth century, who made an effort to recover the importance of the face-to-face community that he felt was being threatened by rapid changes in both transportation and mass communication. At the time, many people were arguing that the only way to sustain democratic life was to abandon the oral tradition and instead concentrate on disseminating massive amounts of print material that would inform citizens about every single aspect of the world so that they could make educated decisions about matters of political and economic affairs. What Dewey recognized was that although the written word was certainly

---

[6]Aristotle, *Rhetoric*, 1413b5.

[7]Aristotle, *Rhetoric*, 1413b1020.

important to deal with complex matters, it was not sufficient to sustaining democratic life. He wrote:

> Signs and symbols, language, are the means of communication by which a fraternally shared experience is ushered in and sustained. But the winged words of conversation in immediate intercourse have a vital import lacking in the fixed and frozen words of written speech. Systematic and continuous inquiry into all the conditions which affect association and their dissemination in print is a precondition of the creation of a true public. But it and its results are but tools after all. Their final actuality is accomplished in face-to-face relationships by means of direct give and take. . . .The connections of the ear with vital and out-going thought and emotion are immensely closer and more varied than those of the eye. Vision is a spectator; hearing is a participator. Publication is partial and the public which results is partially informed and formed until the meanings it purveys pass from mouth to mouth.[8]

For Dewey, written speech has a linear pattern and logical coherence that makes it suitable for effectively arranging and disseminating complex ideas, whereas oral speech tends to emphasize the total quality of shared experience that makes it more suitable to sustain relationships and to create connections among diverse groups of people. Written speech highlights the power of language to create a network of causal relationships, to weave together a web of meanings, and to project possibilities into the future based on knowledge of the present and past.

In effect, written speech gives order to a complex world, as exemplified in the scope and power we grant to the discourses of science, religion, economics, and history. He thus relates writing to "vision" not only because one has to literally look at the words, but also because it creates the experience of being an observer from a distance. By contrast, by connecting via the ear, oral speech tends to create the experience of being surrounded by and immersed within an environment. Oral speech made in the presence of others brings ideas and possibilities to life within the objects, people, and events of one's surroundings. When successful, oral speech draws people together to share what is created in that moment, an effect that is often associated with ritual ceremonies and celebrations. In short, genuine community can only exist within the spoken word. Dewey's democratic ideal would therefore strike a balance between the two mediums. A harmonious relationship between written and oral speech would bring about the best of both "spectator" and "participant" experiences, thereby allowing people to stand outside a situation and contemplate it from a distance while also, periodically, immersing themselves in the shared life of a community.

The introduction of even newer electronic media of communication has not refuted this ideal as much as supplemented it. The phrase "electronic media" is taken from Canadian media theorist Marshall McLuhan, who used it to denote any technology of communication that used any form of electricity to disseminate messages immediately across a potentially global field and/or reproduce auditory sounds or visual images with great accuracy and the potential for playback. The

---

[8]John Dewey, *The Public and Its Problems* (Athens: Ohio University Press, 1954).

term *electronic media* therefore includes both traditional "mass media" such as the television and radio as well as newer "digital media"—everything accessible through modern computers, such as e-mail, the Internet, and digital photography and video. Starting with the telegraph in the nineteenth century and extending up to and beyond modern smartphones, electronic media far surpasses the invention of the printing press and introduces the utopian possibility of immersing ourselves in the total life of the planet in a single moment. This creates opportunities for expanding the horizon of one's experience to distances unheard of a century ago. Social networking sites and global communication systems now create the possibility of reaching thousands if not millions of people instantaneously.

Yet despite all of this, we still demand the detached solitude of the literate life and the tactile experience of partaking in the spoken word. Each medium serves its own function and must be appraised by that function. In order to guide judgments about what medium of communication is appropriate for what types of situations, this introduction will define three different speech contexts: the context for written speech, the context for online communication, and the context for public speaking.

THE CONTEXT FOR WRITTEN SPEECH

Written speech, as it is used here, refers to the primary media of a print rather than handwriting insofar as print privileges sequential ordering of parts, a specific point of view, an explicit logical progression, a complex arrangement of information, and a spirit of objective detachment. According to McLuhan, printed speech is marked by isolation, reflection, distance, specialization, and fragmentation. In writing, one does not participate together in a shared moment; one composes or reads in private, taking each word and each sentence at a time, and threading together a total sequential narrative that often has a sense of past, present, and future. McLuhan observes that "writing tends to be a kind of separate or specialist action in which there is little opportunity or call for reaction. The literate man or society develops the tremendous power of acting in any matter with considerable detachment from the feelings or emotional involvement that an illiterate man or society would experience."[9] By "acting without reacting," McLuhan means the ability to reflect on ideas or situations—not with just an overt, physical response—but by quietly writing down one's thoughts in logical or poetic form.

Writing, that is to say, makes possible the monk, the poet, the scientist, and the philosopher. Written speech refers to those objects that we wish to study in private, to dwell over and reflect upon, to use as a reliable guide for judgment. Objects of written speech include annual business reports, scientific journal articles, the Bible, handwritten letters, diaries, legal judgments, novels, the U.S. Constitution, technical manuals, poetry anthologies, new procedural guidelines, to-do lists, biographies, economic projections, and philosophies. Because of the nature of the medium, the context for written speech tends to be of a much broader scope than that of oral or electronic communication. A written document takes time to compose and to publish in the promise that the message it contains will retain relevance for some time to

---

[9]Marshall McLuhan, *Understanding Media: The Extensions of Man* (Boston: MIT Press, 1994), 79.

come. For instance, sometimes it is better to provide a written manual rather than to explain a procedure, to print out an article rather than send it by e-mail, or to document the reasons for a judgment rather than argue them in a public setting. To put it succinctly, written speech is the best response when we wish to give an audience material to "take home and study." Whenever we want someone to reflect upon a message in private and be able to return to it later, written speech is the ideal medium.

Perhaps the paradigmatic case of written speech as a rhetorical response to a complex and enduring problem is the publication of "reports" produced by research committees and commissioned by government or industry to provide frameworks for action based on a careful research into the current situation. Ideally, these reports are then studied by relevant authorities, after which time they present their judgments on how to act. "Reports" are the way that specialist groups such as scientists, judges, economists, theologians, and historians actually function rhetorically in the broader political environment. Even though their intention may not have been specifically to "persuade," the publication of their research acts to guide judgments about public affairs in a powerful and convincing way. From a rhetorical perspective, situations that call for a persuasive response through written speech tend to possess the following qualities:

- A pervasive problem that endures across durations of time and breadth of space
- Sufficient time to deliberate upon a proper response without the need for immediate action
- Significant resources to draw upon in analyzing the problem
- An audience with the willingness and capacity to deliberate over a period of time upon a single issue

Given this type of situation, rhetoric that takes the form of written speech generally attempts to accomplish the following goals:

- Provide a distinct perspective on a situation that offers a useful point of view
- Give order and coherence to a disordered and chaotic condition
- Replace short-sighted fears and desires with far-sighted judgment
- Replace overheated involvement with cooler forms of detachment
- Encourage delayed individual reflection over immediate group response

Discussion: The best way to understand the unique character of written speech as a print form is to compare the same text presented in two different media types. What is the difference, for instance, between checking out a book from the library and reading it as a PDF file online? What is the difference between writing and receiving a handwritten letter and just sending an e-mail? And when do you feel you need to "send a card" with writing inside of it versus simply sending an e-card?

THE CONTEXT FOR ELECTRONIC COMMUNICATION

Although electronic forms of communication include many technologies of the mass media, most of us will primarily make use of online forms of electronic communication, such as e-mail, teleconferences, website postings, and text messaging. **Online communication** is thus meant to refer to text, image, audio, and video messages sent and received by individuals on computer-aided technologies and capable of being received simultaneously by an infinite number of users, and also being recalled by those users at any time. As indicated by McLuhan's analysis, online communication tends to foster mobility and decentralization and at the same time create a sense of constant feeling of being "in touch" with other people. In addition, it tends to favor messages that have an iconic or mosaic form over those that feature more primarily linear narratives or arguments more fitting to written speech.

There are several specific features of online communication that make it unique. First, it allows for multiple messages to be sent and received simultaneously and at rapid speed. This creates an enormous competition for time, as it creates an almost permanent backlog of messages awaiting consideration. In this environment, messages are naturally developed to capture one's immediate attention and be received and understood in a short amount of time. Second, the capability of multimedia messaging further heightens the competition for attention, such as a simple e-mail might be supplemented with embedded images, attached files, and background graphics or sound. Third, it creates a situation of receiving a message in private at the same time that it is capable of being broadcast to a group. This reduces the sense of "privacy" that written speech tends to produce while at the same time allowing a message to be freed from its situational context. Fourth, the capability of saving and resending messages allows them to spread widely and rapidly, thereby allowing both successes and mistakes to be immediately broadcast to all members of a group, from a group of friends to a global audience. Fifth, it creates the possibility of anonymity if the message is sent with a blind or disguised sender, thereby liberating the message not only from context but from authorship.

The majority of our online communication tends to be informal in quality—despite the intended content. Even in organizational settings, official e-mails are often laced with personal observations, jokes, compliments, or complaints that have a conversational tone. E-mail, in particular, fuses composition and production in one function, thereby fostering a type of discourse that is loose and impromptu rather than formal and reflective. In addition, online communication makes ease and entertainment permanent features of its use. Even governmental websites are designed to be appealing to the eye. On the one hand, this makes online communication ideal for situations that require readily accessible information or the rapid dissemination of striking ideas, events, or images. Whereas websites are there to present information or perform a function for anyone who needs it at any time, e-mails and text messages allow individuals to send specific messages to anyone in an instant. On the other hand, online communication tends to lack durability. As quickly as messages are produced, they are destroyed or replaced. Also, online communication tends to lack a sense of shared or situated context. Whereas even a book needs to be read somewhere, online communication has the sense of being received everywhere and nowhere.

But does electronic communication dominate every aspect of our lives simply because it is available? That question can only be answered by looking more closely at the unique qualities of each type of media. If we take the writing of Marshall McLuhan as a guide, the Internet exaggerates all the characteristics of previous electronic media, such as the telegraph, radio, movie, and television, which appear to eclipse the function of both written and oral speech. McLuhan writes that "it is the speed of electric involvement that creates the integral whole of both private and public awareness. We live today in the Age of Information and of Communication because electric media instantly and constantly create a total field of interacting events in which all men participate."[10] McLuhan associates the following qualities with the electronic age: **decentralization**, or the ability for organizations or groups to operate without any central organizing structure; **implosion**, or the impression that everything far away can be brought close to you in an instant; **mosaic form**, or a mode of presentation that places multiple things next to each other simultaneously, as in a hyperlinked website; and **immersion**, the sense that everybody is deeply involved in everyone else's lives and activities all at once.

However, whatever the utopian hopes and terrifying fears generated by the appearance of the Internet, little indicates that online communication has made the book and the speech obsolete. The Internet has certainly created that sense of being a "global village" that McLuhan prophesized, breaking down the stark divisions among peoples by creating a sense of being connected as a whole. However, although the rise of electronic communication has permanently affected almost every aspect of our personal, cultural, and political lives, it has not obliterated (except with a few exceptions, like papyrus and the telegraph) older forms of communication. For instance, despite the ability to reach the whole nation online, political candidates still spend ever-increasing time and money speaking at rallies, community centers, and special events where supporters eagerly gather to listen. Televangelists have been around for decades, yet millions of Americans still travel to places of worship every week to gather together in shared praise. Commemorative events like the Fourth of July or the presidential inaugural address are now streamed online at any time, and yet people will even endure harsh natural elements to be able to say that they were there in person. And while telecommuting and teleconferencing have increased the scope and efficiency of business, the rituals of the board meeting, the national convention, the interview, and the sales pitch remain staples of corporate culture.

Once again, nothing denies that online communication may also transmit complex information that functions similarly to written speech in certain contexts. It only indicates that the medium is more suitable to respond to more immediate situations. Rhetorically, online communication plays a particularly significant role within social movements, both in terms of its organizational capacity during rallies and protests as well as in terms of maintaining an actively interested support based on mass e-mails, videos, text messages, and other media that keep relevant "current events" in the consciousness of the audience. Online communication has made organized movements possible that are of global scale and that can act almost immediately anywhere in the world. As with the written word, then, there are particular situations that are suitable for online communication and those that are not. Rhetorical situations that call for a persuasive response through online communication thus possess the following qualities:

- Dealing with an event that is of short duration and requires immediate response
- Widespread interest in that event, which produces heightened emotional tensions seeking expression

---

[10]McLuhan, *Understanding Media*, 248.

- A rapidly changing situation that makes people desire the latest information
- Little time to dwell upon the complexities of the situation or reflect upon its past or future
- A communication environment where many messages are competing for attention

Rhetoric that takes the form of online communication generally attempts to accomplish the following goals:

- To communicate with individuals in a diverse population across a wide area
- To signal, or call attention to, a specific event, object, person, or quality
- To direct action in the immediate present, often in the form of a command
- To stimulate the senses and satisfy emotional cravings
- To generate a common interest in a particular subject matter

Discussion: When have you been without access to online forms of communication for an extended length of time? What did you feel you were missing? What functions did you feel unable to perform? Did that give you a sense of peace or were you actually more anxious? What does this experience tell you about your relationship to online communication?

THE CONTEXT FOR PUBLIC SPEAKING

If written speech tends to invite individual cognitive reflection in solitude while online communication heightens the feeling of collective immersion in an immediate event, public speaking generates an atmosphere of shared experience within a dramatic situation. For **public speaking** is not so much about the words spoken as the fact that they are spoken *publicly*—which is to say, spoken within a shared space that includes both the words and the total environment in which they are uttered. Public speaking is different from mass communication. **Mass communication** disseminates a message, but it is received in a different environment than that in which it was produced. It reaches a "public," as an organized body of acting citizens, but it is not a *public* speech. A **public speech** is an oral communication delivered by an individual to a public audience gathered in a shared physical environment to listen collectively and respond to that message in the present.

Even a speech videotaped and rebroadcast is not the same as the speech heard by those physically present. A public speech is a shared event that often has a past and a future. The speech includes all the events that led up to it (including the travel required for people to reach the same place, the time it takes to gather together and to wait, and any preceding events that introduced it) and the actions that follow it (including conversation with others about the speech, any proceeding events, and the final departure of the guests). The public speech is not separate from its history. It *requires* its history to be meaningful. Those who watch a speech on television may remember certain words or phrases used, and perhaps an image of the audience flashed before the screen, but their memory of watching the speech is tied up with the physical context of where it is watched—a living room, a bar, a classroom, and the like. For the people actually present, the speech is an event that is a part of a larger drama, even if it includes merely the conversation with co-workers before and after the boardroom meeting.

For McLuhan, the dominant aspect of the spoken word is therefore the creation of "audience participation," not just in the understanding of the words but in the comprehension of the total speech situation that "involves all of the senses dramatically." In oral speech, "we tend to react to each situation that occurs, reacting in tone and gesture even to our own act of speaking." When we speak, we are not just conveying information; we are forming relationships between ourselves and the audience, the audience members with each other, and everyone with the total environmental context. At each word spoken, one must manage a delicate process of adjusting to constant **feedback**, or the return messages that are constantly being sent by the other people involved in the communicative process. Oral communication is thus a means of inviting people to participate in a shared, **tactile** experience that involves what McLuhan calls the profound and unified "interplay of the senses."[11] In other words, being present at an oral performance is a whole-body experience that we feel "in touch with" in a way that cannot compare to the experience of watching the same speech on a video recording (and this includes even speeches that are incredibly boring; nothing makes you more intimately aware of your chair as a bad speech).

What makes it so difficult for those versed in the language of written or online communication to appreciate the uniqueness of public speaking is the habit of isolating the message from its context and judging it as if it were just a pamphlet or an e-mail. But the unique thing about public speaking is not the content or even the style of the words; it is the fact that the words are spoken in the company of others in a common, shared space. This almost intangible quality is more easily experienced than explained. It is the difference between being part of a graduation ceremony and receiving the diploma in the mail, between going to a place of worship to hear a sermon and reading a religious text at home, between making a toast at a wedding and sending a card of congratulations, between hearing an inspirational speech before a big game and receiving an e-mail of that speech, or between announcing the birth of a child before one's family at Thanksgiving and distributing a video of that speech online.

The fact is that public speaking is a unique and complex experience that cannot be reduced to the simple content of the message. For instance, despite the fact that written communication allows for more complicated factual and logical argumentation and online communication makes possible more sophisticated multimedia presentation, McLuhan observes that oral communication tends to be far more complex in terms of its ability to comprehend and bring together a diverse number of environmental elements into a coherent whole. He notes that dominantly oral communities "are made up of people differentiated, not by their specialist skills or visible marks, but by their unique emotional mixes."[12] Therefore, although oral communication is certainly less capable of precise diagnosis than written speech and is more restricted in scope than online communication, it is far more powerful in situated settings to bring about a feeling of meaningful group participation in a dramatic moment. These kinds of settings often are more capable of producing distinctly memorable events with the possibility of generating lasting relationships and commitments. Although occasions for public speaking may occur less

---

[11]McLuhan, *Understanding Media*, 77–79, 314.

[12]McLuhan, *Understanding Media*, 50.

frequently than occasions for written or online communication, they are far more capable of producing monuments of shared experience that act as a firm ground on which further written or online communication is built.

Perhaps the best way to appreciate the unique functions of a public speech is by experiencing the opposite—speeches that attempt to perform functions better performed by written or online communication. Particularly in organizational settings, so-called informative speeches are often given that really just summarize what is already written on paper. One has, during these speeches, the feeling that the speaker should have just "sent a memo on that." Alternatively, people often launch into speeches that try to re-create the experience of seeing a movie or a video that is better shared by simply being forwarded electronically. The reaction to such speeches is the proverbial, "I guess I needed to be there." A public speech should never be used as a replacement for a medium of communication that can do the job better. But the inverse is also true. Given the ease of sending e-mails, we often assume that a quick message can perform the job that oral communication should do. But there are many times when we need to address people in person, either in a conversation or in a speech. Knowing *what* to say is important, but even more important is knowing *how* to say something. So what is the context for rhetorical public speaking? It includes the following characteristics:

- An issue that is forefront in the consciousness of a public or publics
- A speech situation that occurs within a larger dramatic context with a past and a future
- The necessity or desire to make a judgment in a timely fashion
- The lack of time to wait until further inquiry, which mandates drawing on the best available information
- The ability for members of an audience to gather in a shared space
- The need to establish common understanding and closer relationships among members of the audience

Rhetoric that takes the form of public speaking generally attempts to accomplish the following goals:

- Establish or reinforce relationships between members of the audience
- Encourage dialogue in the audience subsequent to the speech's conclusion, which contributes to shared understanding and solidarity
- Make listeners more attentive to the significance of their physical and social surroundings
- Provide a dramatic narrative that projects and clarifies long-term goals
- Highlight the importance of the most important available means to attain those goals
- Create a unified emotional response capable of moving and inspiring an audience

Discussion: Think of a public speech you attended with friends or family. In that memory, what stands out about the experience as separate from the content of the speech itself? How did the event of being there affect your interpersonal interaction before, during, and after the speech? Last, what was the most memorable moment of that experience: the speech itself or the situation surrounding the speech?

SUMMARY

The easiest way to conceptualize the relationships between these three mediums of communication is by considering how they actually function in multilayered persuasive campaigns in marketing, politics, and religion. All three types of campaigns make use of each medium, although in different ways and in different ratios. Marketing campaigns rely heaviest on electronic media, relying on humorous, seductive, or shocking spectacles to attract attention to a product or issue. Print media, usually in the form of take-home pamphlets, provide more detailed information to interested parties. Yet despite the millions spent on electronic and print advertising, the spoken word remains important both in "closing the deal" (particularly with big-ticket items such as cars and houses) as well as in sparking interest in products through various forms of guerrilla marketing, such as paying college students to wear products and talk about them to other students without disclosing the fact that they are being paid.

Campaigns for political candidates rely even more heavily on the spoken word. On the one hand, we often talk about candidates being "packaged" and "sold" like products precisely because they use the exact same strategies as marketing by paying for television and radio advertisements and disseminating print material to explain their platforms. However, any viable candidate knows that he or she must commit to hundreds of speaking engagements, often addressing only several dozen people at a time in local communities without significant press coverage, in order to solidify support from those communities. In addition, campaigns for higher offices such as Congress or the presidency require a significant staff of volunteers who "canvas" neighborhoods by knocking on doors and speaking individually to hundreds and thousands of people. What makes this type of canvassing worthwhile is not because volunteers actually speak to everyone in a voting precinct but because each person they do persuade usually then speaks to his or her own family and friends about the candidate, thus creating a word-of-mouth network of supporters.

Last, religious campaigns rely heaviest on the spoken word precisely because they are long-term affairs that ask for a lifetime commitment from audience members. This is not to say they do not make use of print or electronic media. In fact, most religions feature an established sacred "text" that can be taken home and studied by adherents in their solitude, and excerpts from this text are almost always included in various pamphlets that can be widely disseminated. And there is a long tradition of various religious faiths using televangelists, billboard campaigns, and television advertisements to deliver their messages. Yet the basic medium of any religious community is the spoken word, delivered either in a sacred space to a whole congregation or in the home with members of an immediate family. This is because the spoken word is a powerful unifying medium that brings people together with a common message that forms emotional bonds not only between speaker and audience but between audience members themselves. It is hardly surprising, therefore, that orators like Emerson speak of eloquence in religious terms, such that "words" which are spoken with truth and passion become the way to realize the "Word" of some higher power.

One does not have to import any such religious understanding of public speaking to appreciate its unique capacity, amongst all forms of communication, to produce the type of shared experience capable of creating both commitment and community. Therefore, when I refer to rhetorical public speaking as "the art of the engaged citizen," I do so not because writing or electronic communication are of less significance to democracy; I do so because it is the most universal form of communication that has the greatest potential to make a change at the local level insofar as it speaks directly to an intimate audience about affairs that directly impact their lives and communities. In an age that requires significant resources to produce and disseminate messages through print or electronic media in a way that will actually reach a wide and influential audience, it is naïve to think that mere access to the Internet somehow equalizes the playing field against well-funded institutions, corporations, and government agencies that can easily overwhelm the national and international media with a well-planned agenda and multilayered yet concentrated message. The fact remains that although print and electronic communication are essential to sustain democratic movement of any kind, they nonetheless must be grounded in the power of the spoken word, which allows individual citizens to confront the power grounded in control of resources with the power of collective commitment grounded in shared experience that is constituted and made conscious by rhetorical public speech.

Of course, the value of public speech is not only found in the political sphere. Public speaking is also the art of the loving family member, the dedicated coach, the charismatic business leader, the persuasive salesperson, the inspirational teacher, the prophetic preacher, and the successful lawyer. Public speaking continues to justify its existence whenever people gather together in the same space to have a chance to hear what everyone else hears, to feel what everyone else feels, to consider what everyone else has considered, and to potentially act together in the knowledge that all present have all heard, felt, and considered the same thing. There is no written or electronic substitute for a story told by a grandmother to her grandchildren in the living room, the halftime speech in the locker room, the confrontational challenge by the chief executive in the boardroom, the witty banter that goes on in an automobile showroom, the Socratic give-and-take that occurs in the classroom, or the pathos-written appeal delivered by a lawyer in the courtroom. These are moments that demand the spoken word, and they are the moments for which this book has been written.

EXERCISES

1. Select a passage from a famous speech and a partner for this exercise. Type the text of your passage as an e-mail and send it to your partner. For the next class period, print out the passage in an elegant font and give it to your partner. Next, actually deliver this passage orally to your partner. Which presentation did your partner find to be most powerful? What differences can you note in how you received each of your partner's messages?

2. Locate a social movement website and analyze its content. Does it use a mosaic form? What iconic images are present? Next, find a speech made by someone connected to the movement, and compare this content with the website. What differences do you note in how information is presented and experienced? Do certain aspects of either seem more effective in delivering the intended message?

3. Think of a moment in American history when a major catastrophic event happened in the past (such as the assassination of JFK) or more recently (such as the World Trade Center attacks). Now consider learning of this news through a face-to-face conversation, through print, and through television. What difference would this make in how we receive the information? Do we often seek out other media after our initial encounter?

4. Select a short public speaking passage and a partner for this exercise. Deliver your speech for your partner while he or she records it, and then switch roles. Listen to the recordings. In both cases, each partner delivers the same speech to the same audience, but in a different medium. What differences do you note? What stands out in each media?

The Canons of Rhetoric

This chapter introduces the basic techniques of public speaking that provide the general framework and methods for putting together any public speech. These include the five canons of rhetoric: invention, arrangement, style, memory, and delivery, which comprise specific guidelines for delivery, appearance, writing your thesis, introductions, conclusions, structuring your points, finding sources, doing searches, citation style, visual aids, outlines, notecards, and methods of dealing with speaking anxiety. Mastering all of these techniques will clearly require extensive practice. However, this chapter will provide the basic methods that should then be applied in giving form to the conceptual strategies and persuasive substance explained in subsequent chapters.

In the Western world, rhetoric didn't appear as a discrete art until a rudimentary democracy, modeled on the earlier Athenian model, came to the Greek colony of Sicily around 466 B.C.E. At that time, the tyrants had been overthrown and the citizens had to find a way to properly and justly redistribute the property that the former leaders had unlawfully confiscated. Their novel solution was to have citizens argue their cases in courts of law. Because these courts required ordinary citizens to speak on their own behalf, techniques for argumentation became a marketable commodity. As a result, the first "handbook" for rhetoric was produced around that time, providing instruction in the basics of speech composition and delivery for a fee.[1]

As democracy spread through the Greek world, particularly in Athens, and expanded from the law courts into political and social forums, instruction in the art of rhetoric flourished and became progressively formalized, first by the development of a class of itinerant teachers called the Sophists and later by the more institutional education provided by the schools of Plato and Aristotle. This is not to say that rhetorical practice in Greece was an egalitarian enterprise. Access to education was restricted to those with financial resources, and the ability to even participate in politics was restricted to a relative minority of male citizens—women and slaves being two major groups excluded from public life. The birth of rhetoric thus did not lead to a "Golden Age" for everyone. Many of the powerless remained powerless, in part because they were denied both access to the political forum and the artful tools necessary to influence others.

---

[1]George A. Kennedy, *Aristotle, On Rhetoric: A Theory of Civic Discourse,* 2nd ed. (Oxford: Oxford University Press, 2007).

Nonetheless, rhetoric and democracy contributed to each other's development because both were concerned with facilitating the process of collective judgment, even if for a relatively small—if expanding—group of free citizens. The more the burdens of advocacy and judgment were placed upon the shoulders of individual citizens, the more urgent that training in rhetoric became; and the more citizens became skilled in rhetoric, the more they craved and demanded participation in the decision-making processes of governance. It was thus in Greece that rhetoric established its position as an *art*—not in the sense of being a form of creative self-expression, but in the sense of being a practical skill based on a body of knowledge, much as we think of engineering or architecture.

A DEFINITION OF RHETORIC

This book is thus oriented toward the cultivation of public speaking as a rhetorical art much in the way that the Greeks understood it to be. The modifier "rhetorical" is meant to distinguish the subject from the broader category of public speaking, which involves any situation in which one speaks in a public setting.

Rhetorical public speaking *is the art of addressing pressing public concerns by employing deliberate persuasive strategies before a public audience at a specific occasion in order to transform some aspect of a problematic situation by encouraging new forms of thought and action.* In other words, rhetoric involves us in the social and political struggle over **meaning**, and, hence, over power. It is about how people use language and symbols to transform the way a society or community thinks, feels, and behaves. Rhetoric is ultimately about how people act as agents of social change, using whatever symbolic power they can harness to move people from this place to that place.

This definition can be broken down into the following parts:

1. *The art:* Referring to rhetoric as an art distinguishes it from a mere instinctual or unreflective talent. *Art* thus does not mean an intuitive creativity or genius lacking in method. Quite the opposite, art requires the application of rational concepts and methods in the creative process of guiding situated judgment.

2. *of addressing pressing public concerns:* Except for matters of idle curiosity, the only reason we voluntarily expose ourselves to rhetorical discourse is because it speaks to a shared concern that is in the forefront of our consciousness. We listen to rhetoric with the hope that the person speaking might be able to suggest a path out of our current predicament or a solution to our current problem.

3. *by employing deliberate persuasive strategies:* Persuasion is often accidental or a product of sheer luck. This does not alter its *function* as a persuasive message, but it does change how we evaluate it in terms of *art*. In contradistinction to rhetorical criticism, which can evaluate anything that strikes us as persuasive, the productive art of rhetoric concerns itself with improving how something is produced, and one cannot improve accident or luck.

4. *before a public audience:* The *public* character of the audience means that it addresses an audience of relative strangers who come together to address areas of common concern. Persuading an audience of friends may still employ

rhetoric, but that rhetoric generally appeals to the unique bonds of those friends rather than their shared characteristics as part of a larger public.

5. *at a specific occasion:* This aspect addresses the situated character of rhetoric *as a form of public speaking* and not simply a genre of persuasion. One can, of course, create rhetorical discourse in the form of a written or visual medium. The use of the Internet has certainly led to an explosion of attempts at long-distance persuasion. But rhetorical *public speech* more narrowly refers to rhetoric delivered in the physical presence of others.

6. *in order to transform some aspect of a problematic situation:* Rhetoric seeks to change some aspect of the natural or social environment that is *felt* to be problematic by members of a public. This shared experience of uncertainty, anxiety, and urgency focuses people's attention on a speech and thus gives it a unique power. Absent such a situation, the same speech might be experienced not as rhetoric, but as a form of poetry, news, or entertainment. It is not the speech itself that determines its character, but the total **context** in which it is spoken.

7. *by encouraging new forms of thought and action:* The means by which rhetoric transforms that environment is by symbolic persuasion—by the use of symbols which encourage other people to change their attitudes toward objective things in the world. Rhetoric is thus an indirect form of action. It makes changes by changing what people think and do with hope that their behaviors might resolve some shared problem.

Because rhetoric becomes rhetoric only within urgent contexts of judgment, rhetorical public speech is a fundamentally *ethical* activity insofar as it forces one to take a stand about what "good" we should pursue and how we should pursue it. Paradoxically, however, the very problematic aspect of the rhetorical situation often throws into question the conventional ethical standards that had guided previous action. Thus, rhetorical public speakers must do more than seek mere tactical "success"; they must also determine what success would look like in such a situation and then justify that vision on the basis of a reflective ethical judgment. And to do that successfully means constructing an argument using the tools of reason (*logos*), credibility (*ethos*), emotion (*pathos*), and style (*lexis*) capable of challenging and transforming some aspect of public sentiment in the face of opposition.

Discussion: One of the most enduring rhetorical moments following the terror attacks of 9/11 was the image of President George W. Bush standing atop World Trade Center rubble, addressing an audience of workers with a bullhorn. How did this particular speech fit the definition of rhetoric? What aspect of the speech do you think was the most (and least) artistic?

THREE ETHICAL ATTITUDES TOWARD RHETORIC

Just as today, not everyone in Ancient Greece valued this art equally. In the fifth and fourth centuries B.C.E., there arose three distinct perspectives on rhetoric that are still useful in understanding the broader relationship between rhetoric and democracy: the Sophistical, the Platonic, and the Aristotelian. The most controversial perspective was held by the Sophists, who were teachers of rhetoric who professed to be able to have the ability of making the weaker argument the stronger. The Greek **Sophists** arose in the fifth century B.C.E. in Classical Greece when political conditions brought about the need and opportunity for citizens to acquire the skills to participate in the new democratic empire. In providing education in *logos* (meaning reason, argument, and critical thinking) for a fee, the Sophists acted as traveling universities. The Sophistical attitude was thus one of supreme confidence in the creative power of the persuasive word in the hands of the citizens. In this way, the Sophists were the first *humanists*. Rhetoric, for them, was a way of trying to bring about better experiences in the world which benefited both the speaker and the audience in the present. Consequently, they tended to emphasize creativity and experimentation in language in the hope that the best ideas would win out in the end by producing happiness.

The Sophists' boast that they could turn the weaker argument into the stronger was often interpreted to mean that they intended to undermine traditional ethics through false reasoning. However, as John Poulakos points out, the literal translation of the Greek leads to a far more conventional interpretation. It simply takes "weaker" (*to hetton*) to refer "to that argument or position which commands less power because the majority shuns it or is not persuaded by it," and "stronger" (*to kreitton*) to refer "to that argument or position which is dominant because the majority has found it more persuasive than other alternatives." From such a perspective, the function of sophistical rhetoric is to "reverse in some measure the established hierarchy of things" by employing "the resources of language and its surrounding circumstances to move what is regarded as weaker to a position of strength."[2] In this sense, to argue that slavery is a violation of human rights would have been a relatively "weak" argument in eighteenth century America, one that was then made stronger in part through the efforts of rhetorical public speakers such as Sarah and Angelina Grimke, William Lloyd Garrison, and Frederick Douglass. For the Sophists, what allowed these individuals to invert these traditional hierarchies was not only their courage and creativity but also their rhetorical initiative to grasp the right moment to speak.

However, some saw that those who employed rhetoric often did so for personal gain in neglect of the larger public good. **Plato**, in particular, accused rhetoric of being the use of "empty words" to distract us from "reality" and deceive us about the truth in the pursuit of narrow pleasures. Plato, in other words, was an *idealist,* but not in the sense we use it today to mean a sort of youthful and naïve optimism about the future. Plato was an Idealist because he believed that only "Ideals" were real and that our everyday existence in the world was but a shadow of that reality. Consequently, he emphasized our duty to search for, comprehend, and then convey the nature of the Ideal to those in a fallen world in order to bring it closer to the true reality that exists in the word of a rational God. For Plato, rhetoric was a kind of "pastry baking" that makes sweet-sounding speeches without any nutritional value. Consequently, he saw the Sophists—who were paid teachers in public speaking, much as are modern-day professors of communication—as a breed of social parasites. Plato's

---

[2]John Poulakos, *Sophistical Rhetoric in Classical Greece* (Columbia: University of South Carolina Press, 1995), 65.

ultimate solution was thus two-pronged. On the one hand, he wished to ban all rhetoric that was not based on prior philosophical inquiry into the nature of the fixed ideals of the Good, the Beautiful, and the True. On the other hand, he encouraged a form of rhetoric that could inspire people to pursue genuine virtue and thereby liberate themselves from bodily pleasures. In his *Gorgias*, Plato asked,

> What of the rhetoric addressed to the Athenian people and other free peoples in various cities—what does that mean to us? Do the orators seem to you always to speak with an eye to what is best, their sole aim being to render the citizens as perfect as possible by their speeches, or is their impulse also to gratify the citizens, and do they neglect the common good for their personal interest and treat the people like children, attempting only to please them, with no concern whatever whether such conduct makes them better or worse?[3]

Like many of critics today who see the political sphere populated with demagoguery and irrational appeals to personal bias and self-interest, Plato understood rhetoric to be a method of flattery that told the ignorant that they were smart and the greedy that they were virtuous. Consequently, he called for a rhetoric that would educate rather than debase an audience, lifting it up by speaking the truth beautifully and eloquently.

If the Sophists were rhetorical humanists and Plato a rhetorical idealist, Plato's student **Aristotle** was a rhetorical realist. Aristotle was educated at a time when the heights of the Classical era of Sophistical optimism was long past and when the devastating Peloponnesian War that had produced Plato's skepticism of political rhetoric had finally come to an end. Aristotle's Athens was a democracy, but no longer an empire; it was a city filled with intellectuals trying to make sense of a long, complex, and tragic history. His goal was neither to inaugurate radical changes nor inspire a revolution; it was simply to find a way for people to live together in harmony for as long as possible. Aristotle thus understood rhetoric through a historical lens, seeing it as an experimental tool for determining the best judgment through the exchange of ideas, good or bad, in the public sphere. Thus, he wrote,

> We must be able to employ persuasion, just as strict reasoning can be employed, on opposite sides of a question not in order that we may in practice employ it in both ways (for we must not make people believe what is wrong), but in order that we may see clearly what the facts are, and that, if another man argues unfairly, we on our part may be able to confute him.[4]

The goal for Aristotle was not to praise or condemn rhetoric, but to acknowledge its limitations and identify the situations in which it was useful and necessary for making collective judgments in a practical democracy. Aristotle was therefore a *realist* in the sense that he started with the facts on the ground and simply tried to make the most out of the resources we humans were given.

---

[3]Plato, *Gorgias,* 502e.
[4]Aristotle, *The Rhetoric and the Poetics of Aristotle,* trans. Roberts, W. Rhys, ed. Edward P. J. Corbett (New York: The Modern Library, 1984), 1355a30.

These three attitudes toward rhetoric—the Sophistical, the Platonic, and the Aristotelian—still thrive within contemporary culture, and each carry with them important ethical considerations. The Sophistical attitude emphasizes the importance of *kairos,* or "timeliness," which means that a speaker has the responsibility to speak at the right moment to make a rhetorical intervention. For the Sophists, good intentions meant nothing if one was always too late or too early for the party. Being a responsible citizen meant being in the midst of things and being aware of subtle nuances in every situation. Plato, however, would be annoyed by the cacophony of noise emitted by the contemporary news media. For Plato, the genuine orator did not concern himself with the passing issues of the day. His mind was concerned with, "tracking down by every path the entire nature of each whole among the things that are, and never condescending to what lies near at hand."[5] For him, an ethical speaker first and foremost had to be knowledgeable and to always speak the truth based on prior inquiry and thoughtful reflection. Last, Aristotle reminds both of his predecessors that because human beings are fallible and make judgments based on limited resources, no amount of prior research or an intuitive sense of timeliness will guarantee success. Certainly, ethical speech was timely and based on knowledge, but most of all it was speech that helped sustain civic life by respecting the norms of the deliberative process in the faith that truth, beauty, and goodness will reveal themselves in the long term despite bumps along the road. In other words, Aristotle demanded of us first and foremost to be good citizens, striving always to live in the Golden Mean between extremes, knowing that the maintenance of a healthy civic life was far more important than the success or failure of any particular speech. These three virtues of **Sophistical initiative,** **Platonic wisdom,** and **Aristotelian temperance** remain essential for any public speech.[6]

Discussion: Consider the range of popular celebrities and commentators on the various news shows on television (both "serious" and "fake" news). Whom would you consider to be a Sophist? A Platonist? An Aristotelian? How does a person's type of response to a contemporary controversy determine his or her attitude?

THE FORM OF RHETORIC

It is one thing to praise or condemn rhetoric; it is another thing to actually understand how it functions. Perhaps the most common misunderstanding about public speaking is that it is mostly concerned with conveying "information." From this perspective, one might think of public speaking much as one thinks of a standard news article, whose business is to convey the latest happenings of the world as truthfully and as sensationally as possible. The underlying set of assumptions behind this perspective is that the most powerful methods of maintaining interest are surprise and suspense, **surprise** meaning that which appears suddenly,

---

[5]Plato, *Theaetetus,* 174a.
[6]On the comparison between the three perspectives on rhetoric, see Everett Lee Hunt, "Plato and Aristotle on Rhetoric and Rhetoricians," *Reading on Rhetoric,* 100–159.

unexpectedly, and shockingly (like a surprise party), and **suspense** meaning that which has been promised to appear but whose actual qualities have been kept secret (like a birthday gift). From this perspective, rhetoric is about how to convey specific facts, details, events, or beliefs by packaging them correctly and delivering them at the right time.[7]

Although this type of perspective certainly applies to press conferences, dramatic announcements, water-cooler conversations, and blockbuster films, it has only minimal relevance to understanding rhetorical persuasion. This is because persuasion requires a kind of *movement* from one place to another, a mental journey that begins at a familiar place and sojourns toward somewhere new; and no amount of isolated facts, however surprising or suspenseful, ever really moves us anywhere. Such facts merely startle us by suddenly appearing out of nowhere. This is all to say that to understand rhetoric one must adopt a different psychology, a "psychology of form," meaning a state of mind that is less interested in gazing passively at already completed objects and more interested in participating in how something comes together over time. Following Kenneth Burke, **form** is not an empty space waiting to be filled in with content, but rather an entire arc of temporal experience with an artifact that first arouses and then fulfills desires and appetites in an audience. For him, not everything has form in this sense. Rather, a work has form insofar one part of the work arouses interest in what follows and then provides gratification.

In rhetoric, form is thus achieved when the end of the speech satisfies the desires that are aroused at its beginning, thereby generating a feeling of movement ending in a powerful emotional consummation; both necessary for people to come to new beliefs and attitudes. For instance, when Martin Luther King Jr. announces that he has a dream, makes us desire to observe the meaning of that dream, and then places that dream before us in a way that brings about feelings of hope, belonging, and unity—that is form. By contrast, a speech that merely declares the content of a dream and then provides a list of supporting facts has only minimal form, as it relies instead on the audience's intrinsic interest in the facts themselves to capture and keep their attention. In other words, for a speech to have form, the audience must feel as if they are being carried forward on a wave while swimming toward a destination, meaning that the speech's words propel them forward (the wave) but also encourage them to participate in the movement itself (the swimming). Without this active participation by the audience to reach a destination with the speaker, persuasion is impossible because everybody stands still. Form is therefore not a quality of the speech itself in isolation; it is an accomplishment that occurs when a speech "works" with an audience to move them to a new place.

At all times, therefore, one must keep in mind that no specific technique or combination of techniques can ever amount to "form." Form is only attained when a speech conveys what John Dewey calls a "sense of qualitative unity" that comes about when one arranges "events and objects with reference to the demands of

---

[7] See Kenneth Burke, *Counter-Statement* (Chicago: University of Chicago Press, 1931), 33.

complete and unified perception."[8] By **qualitative unity**, Dewey means the feeling that one can sum up that entire arc of experience within a single term, as when one associates *exhilarating* with climbing a mountain, *tragic* with the death of a loved one, *joyous* with the family reunion at a holiday, or *inspiring* at the conclusion of a passionate speech. A speaker always wants someone to leave a speech feeling "That was a ____ speech!" in which the blank is filled with some single dominating quality that lingers with the listener even after the specific facts may have been forgotten. Although mastering the individual techniques is essential to becoming an eloquent speaker, one should never allow attention to the parts (the "matter") to distract one from attending to the whole (the "form").

Perhaps one of the best efforts to translate this notion of form into a concrete rhetorical technique is **Monroe's Motivated Sequence**. Alan Monroe was a professor of speech at Purdue University who developed a special sequence designed for policy speeches that encourage immediate action. Although its "method" is simply made up of basic public speaking strategies, Monroe's sequence incorporates the strategies into a form that is explicitly based on arousing the audiences' desires and then moving them, through the use of visual narrative, toward a promised satisfaction that results in concrete judgment and action. The five steps of attention, need, satisfaction, visualization, and action therefore follow neatly Burke's understanding of form and conclude with Dewey's understanding of qualitative unity.

1. *Attention:* Like any good introduction, get the attention and interest of your audience: "Little Margaret was an otherwise happy child. She liked television, she liked ice cream, and she liked to play with dolls. She also was six years old and weighed over one hundred pounds."

2. *Need:* Another word for "problem," *need* establishes the necessity to address some issue by graphically articulating why we "need" to act: "Childhood obesity is becoming a national epidemic. Over 30 percent of children under the age of eight are now considered obese. This leads to poorer school performance and chronic health problems."

3. *Satisfaction:* Another word for "solution," *satisfaction* lays out what is required to be done in order for audience members to feel that their needs have been satisfied: "We need to implement an aggressive health campaign in this nation that brings healthy lunches and active gym classes to the schools and also delivers a targeted marketing campaign to parents to encourage healthy eating and exercise."

4. *Visualization:* This step relies on heightening emotions by visualizing the wonderful state of affairs that will occur after satisfaction: "With such steps, Little Margaret could achieve a more active and energetic lifestyle in which she and other children leave the couch to play outside in the fresh air and sun."

5. *Action:* Now that the audience has been suitably inspired, this step tells them what they can do to help by laying out specific things to be done: "These changes must come from you. Become an active member in your school

---

[8]John Dewey, *Art as Experience* (New York: Perigree Books, 1934), 142.

board and advocate changes at a local level while writing your congressional representative to support new health initiatives."

Because of the simplicity and clarity of the steps, there is almost no better method to start with than Monroe's Motivated Sequence to begin to understand the importance of form to rhetorical persuasion. It is a method that applies not only to politics and social action but also to our everyday interpersonal interactions in which we try to motivate our friends to choose a college major, our family to go on vacation to a certain place, or our colleagues to support a new office policy that will increase sales and morale.

The rest of this chapter will look at some of the most common techniques employed by the speaker to arouse and fulfill the desires of an audience by organizing them under the "Five Canons of Rhetoric." These canons were formalized in the Roman work *Rhetorica ad Herennium*, written anonymously in the first century B.C. but generally credited to be the work of Cicero, a Roman orator and senator. These canons represented the five essential methods necessary to employ in creating a successful speech. Subsequent teaching of rhetoric, up to the present day, largely follows this organization. The author writes:

> The speaker, then, should possess the faculties of Invention, Arrangement, Style, Memory, and Delivery. Invention is the devising of matter, true or plausible, that would make the case convincing. Arrangement is the ordering and distribution of the matter, making clear the place to which each thing is to be assigned. Style is the adaptation of suitable words and sentences to the matter devised. Memory is the firm retention in the mind of the matter, words, and arrangement. Delivery is the graceful regulation of voice, countenance, and gesture.[9]

These canons effectively summarize the basic rules of the game, and any student of rhetoric—no matter how naturally talented—must follow them to achieve success beyond accident or luck. Yet these rules are merely a precondition for participation, not a guarantee of success. Just as knowing the rules of baseball does not make one a good player, knowing the technique to "be humorous" in an introduction does not mean that one knows how to be funny to particular audiences in particular circumstances. The hard work comes in finding out what, exactly, is funny to whom and when, but this requires a great deal of wit, situational understanding, and insight into human nature. Handbooks can tell us where we might find these things, but they do not tell us what we will find or what to make of them.

Discussion: To understand the relationship between rhetoric and form, consider the traditional "romantic" way that movies and television portray marriage proposals made by men to women. The suitor puts one knee down, holds up the ring, and then gives a short speech in which he describes how they first met, how he fell in love, and how he wants to spend the rest of his life with the lucky woman.

---

[9]*Rhetorica ad Herennium* (Loeb Classical Library, 1954). Available from the University of Chicago <http://penelope.uchicago.edu/Thayer/E/Roman/Texts/Rhetorica_ad_Herennium/1*.html> (accessed 16 April 2010).

How does this follow the structure of form? And how do comedies often violate the structure? What are the consequences when form does not come to its anticipated conclusion?

THE CANONS OF RHETORIC

The First Canon: Invention

When Aristotle defined rhetoric as the capacity for discovering the available means of persuasion in each case, he defined rhetoric as an inventional art. Derived from the Latin word *invenire*, "to find," **invention** refers to the act of finding something to say that lends support to the speaker's position. It is not surprising that the scientific-minded Aristotle would place such emphasis on invention; for it is precisely invention that provides a public speaker with the resources and knowledge that gives a speech its substance and value. Without invention, a speaker is left simply repeating the same statement over and over again. Consequently, the author of *Rhetorica ad Herennium* says that "Of the five tasks of the speaker Invention is the most important and the most difficult."[10] The reason it is difficult is because invention requires us to exert a great deal of time and effort not only trying to think of the type of resources that might be helpful to defend a claim but also trying to find them. One of the most common reasons for a speech's failure is neglect of invention, usually in the assumption on the part of the rhetor that his or her claim is so obviously true and persuasive that it needs no further backing by extensive research and creative argumentation. But as the Sophists long ago pointed out, with effort, a good speaker can make the weaker argument the stronger just as easily as a poor speaker can make the stronger argument the weaker. More often than not, both of these reversals come about as a result of success or failure of invention.

With respect to rhetorical form, however, the materials of invention should not be considered the "core" of a speech that are only later conveyed to an audience through "style" any more than tubes of paint are the "core" of a painting only later given "style" by the hand of the painter. The "core" of the speech, as for a painting, is the qualitative unity in thought and in feeling that is produced in an audience after having experienced it. The materials of invention are merely resources to be used by the speaker to construct a message capable of producing that effect. The act of invention, therefore, should be thought of as the act of gathering things together and spreading them out on a table. As the creative work of composition ensues, some of that material finds a central place in the speech, while other material is made peripheral or not used at all. What is important is not what percentage of possible material is used in a speech, but that the speaker feels confident that what has been selected is the best choice of all available options. In other words, the best speakers leave many potential resources on the "cutting room floor" as evidence that they have selected only the most fitting material.

---

[10]Ibid.

Resources for Invention   One of the best resources to draw from when beginning a speech is that collective resource known as public memory. **Public memory** represents the storehouse of social knowledge, conventions, public opinions, values, and shared experiences that a speaker can appeal to within that speech and be confident that they will resonate meaningfully with that audience. For example, William West says of memory:

> The study of memory encompasses not just ideas of memory at a particular historical moment, but entire regimes of memory, ways of privileging certain types of knowledge, certain values, certain ideas, beliefs, symbols—in short, and entire cultural ethnography coalesces around the apparently innocuous ability to remember the past. Memory serves as the locus of personal history and individual identity.[11]

Public memory represents those memories that are handed down from generation to generation, usually through stories and phrases and rituals that attempt to preserve the past in the present. In a political environment that moves at such a rapid pace as ours, creating such a lasting object in the public memory is a rare and significant accomplishment. In this way, public memories of this type can act as a reservoir of feelings, images, and stories from which a rhetor can draw. Especially if a rhetor shares common memories with his or her audience, the appeal to collective memory can be very powerful in gaining interest and focusing attention.

Rhetorically, public memory is a resource for what is called social knowledge. **Social knowledge** signifies a culture's conventional wisdom and practical judgment as expressed in maxims, generally held beliefs, and value judgments.[12] In other words, social knowledge represents what we might call "common sense." Social knowledge tells us what is better and worse, what the acknowledged facts of the world are, and thereby represents something of a cultural "second nature." Social knowledge thus signifies an attitude that is almost universally held by a wide number of people and has been passed down through generations and reaffirmed throughout history. Consequently, social knowledge is the most durable and most hard to change of any of the qualities of the public. It represents the collective judgments of a social group that are the result of past experience and that guide beliefs and behaviors in future situations. Consequently, social knowledge and public memory are vast storehouses of resources that a rhetor can select from when beginning to compose a speech.

What are we trying to find as we go through the process of invention? Any good speech will draw from seven basic categories of resources available to the public speaker to persuade an audience—**maxims, facts, statistics, testimony, examples, narratives,** and **topics.** Gathering together material from each of these categories

---

[11]William West, "Memory," in *Encyclopedia of Rhetoric,* ed. Thomas Sloan (Oxford, UK: Oxford University Press, 2001), 483.
[12]Thomas Farrell, "Knowledge, Consensus, and Rhetorical Theory," in *Contemporary Rhetorical Theory: A Reader,* ed. John Louis Lucaites, Celeste Michelle Condit, and Sally Caudill (New York: The Guilford Press, 1999), 147.

will provide a wealth of resources from which to draw upon to construct a speech that is complex and powerful.

1. **Maxims:** A maxim is a short, pithy statement expressing a general truth or rule of conduct that is commonly accepted by culture and used to justify a variety of beliefs and actions. We often encounter maxims in the form of proverbs ("A tree is known by its fruit") and clichés ("The early bird catches the worm"). All cultures at all times have made use of maxims to bind together a community through shared principles and rules. The key for the speaker is to know which maxims speak to the unique culture of the audience while also being fitting to the situation and the argument.

2. **Facts:** A fact is a condensed empirical claim that tells us about some facet of the world that we can rely upon to be true. Most of the facts that we know come from everyday experience, such as "heavy objects fall" or "the sun sets at night." Other facts are derived from scientific research and are based on our trust in expertise, such as "objects are weightless in space" or "the earth goes around the sun." A speaker can use both types of facts to support claims, drawing on everyday facts to make a claim seem supported by common sense while also appealing to the facts of scientific research to make the case for more specific and controversial claims that might challenge common sense.

3. **Statistics:** Statistics are different from facts because they do not deal with specific assertions about concrete objects but are mathematical generalizations that help us make predictions about certain types of objects or events. They do not tell us what something *is* but rather what we can probably *expect* of it. For instance, direct use of numeric facts and statistics is helpful to either show the magnitude of something ("Over 90 percent of the colonists now support a revolution.") or the probability of something ("Given the number of British warships in Boston Harbor, it is likely that war shall come."). In other words, statistics let us know that if we were to encounter an American colonist, there is a good chance that he or she would support a revolution, just as if we were to see British warships in Boston Harbor, then it is likely that we will see a war. Particularly when we are concerned with the outcomes of our potential judgments, statistics that tell us the likelihood of certain outcomes are very persuasive, provided that the statistics come from respected sources and are not distorted by partisan influences.

4. **Testimony:** Testimony consists of direct quotations from individuals who can speak with some authority on a certain state of affairs. Testimony can come in various forms. **Lay testimony** derives from ordinary people who have had relevant experience with some issue. Such testimony can prove that something exists or has happened by drawing on the personal experience ("I have seen warships in Boston Harbor.") or it can give a "human touch" to a story by using colorful quotes to exemplify some point ("I saw the young man bleeding to death in my arms."). **Expert testimony** comes from individuals who may not have directly experienced something but who know a considerable amount about the subject matter due to extensive research. Such testimony is used to challenge or override competing explanations by appealing to

the authority of knowledge ("According to General Nash, 'There is no conceivable reason other than war for so many ships to be in Boston Harbor.'"). Last, **prestige testimony** comes from famous and well-respected individuals who may have nothing directly to do with an issue but whose words provide inspiration and insight. ("So I say we should pursue revolution against the King of England, for as John Locke wrote, 'In transgressing the law of nature, the offender declares himself to live by another rule than that of reason and common equity.'")

5. **Examples:** These include descriptions of actual or hypothetical events, people, objects, or processes that can embody an idea or argument in a concrete form so that audiences can "see" what it means ("If one wants to know the nature of tyranny, go to Boston. There, the streets are filled with armed men, the courts have been abolished, and young men are killed in the streets."), and/or that can act as evidence to prove the existence or define the nature of something ("War is upon us, as evidenced by the battle of Concord and the presence of British troops marching through our countryside."). Examples can be drawn from newspapers, history, biographies, science, or personal experience. They are crucial in embodying abstract claims within concrete visual images that bring to life the causes and consequences of certain actions and beliefs.[13] There are two main kinds of examples: actual examples and fictional examples, as follows:

   a. **Actual examples** are descriptions of real things that exist or have existed, that happen or have happened. The main sources of actual examples are history, the news, personal experience, or science. Thus, one could use the Salem witch trials to exemplify intolerance, a feature story about a New Orleans family to exemplify the struggles after Hurricane Katrina, a personal story about one's immigrant grandfather to exemplify personal courage, or a scientific discovery of an Egyptian tomb to exemplify ancient wisdom. Actual examples are important for making speeches appear thoroughly researched and backed by evidence rather than simply being expressions of personal opinion. Actual examples thus function both to *prove* one's point as well as to demonstrate it.

   b. **Fictional examples** are descriptions of events that are only imagined to have happened in the past, present, or future. There are two kinds of fictional examples: third-person examples (referring to "he" or "she") and second-person examples (referring to "you"). **Third-person fictional examples** describe the actions of other people as if they actually happened until usually revealing at the end that it is just a story. For example, one might say "Joe was an aspiring actor until he started doing drugs and then had an overdose and died. Joe is not a real person, but there are thousands of people like Joe every day." The most effective third-person examples come from stories taken from literature or other popular forms of art that are commonly known by an audience. The other kind of example is a

[13]For more on the persuasive use of examples, see Scott Consigny, "The Rhetorical Example," *Southern Speech Communication Journal* 41 (1976), 121–134.

second-person fictional example, which places the audience in a hypothetical situation that asks them to envision doing something. For example, one might say "Imagine you were walking down the street and saw a homeless man being beaten. Would you rush to save him or walk away?" Second-person examples usually offer the audience some choice in order to get them thinking about the problem that the speech then proceeds to address. Fictional examples can be helpful in demonstrating the meaning of a speech, but being pure fabrications, they generally lack the authenticity and power of actual examples. As a general rule, a speaker should choose actual examples over fictional examples whenever possible.

6. **Narratives:** A narrative is a dramatic story that is more complex than an example, and that captures and holds the attention of an audience by promising that, through the unfolding of the plot and character, something new and satisfying will be produced at the end. Narratives are excellent ways of conveying complex states of affairs in ways that are meaningful and memorable for an audience. It is important to note that stories are not "irrational" components of speeches that are to be opposed with facts and statistics. Quite the opposite, when faced with competing narratives, an audience must decide which narrative is more "rational" to follow. According to Walter Fisher:

> Rationality is determined by the nature of persons as narrative beings—their inherent awareness of *narrative probability,* what constitutes a coherent story, and their constant habit of testing *narrative fidelity,* whether the stories they experience ring true with the stories they know to be true in their lives."[14]

In other words, **narrative fidelity** refers to how accurately a narrative represents accepted facts, such as newspaper reports of Paul Revere's ride printed days after the event. **Narrative probability** refers to the coherence of the narrative as a story apart from the actual facts, such as the poem "The Midnight Ride of Paul Revere" written by Henry Wadsworth Longfellow in 1860, almost a century later. The most effective narrative from a rhetorical standpoint should have both high narrative probability *and* high narrative fidelity. By presenting an argument in a form of a story that accurately represents reality in a coherent, engaging, and powerful manner, a speaker invites an audience to vicariously participate in a new vision of reality. Especially when narratives are broad in scope, they can completely alter an audience's basic worldview. The narratives we tell of our common histories have particular power in structuring our social organizations, our self-conceptions, and our relationships with other groups.

7. **Topics:** The last resource for invention is not a particular "thing" but rather a way of relating things together. These are called "topics of invention"

---

[14]Walter Fisher, "Narration as a Human Communication Paradigm: The Case of Public Moral Argument," in *Contemporary Rhetorical Theory: A Reader,* ed. John Louis Lucaites, Celeste Michelle Condit, and Sally Caudill (New York: The Guilford Press, 1999), p. 247. See also Walter Fisher, *Human Communication as Narration: Toward a Philosophy of Reason, Value, and Action* (Columbia: University of South Carolina Press, 1987).

(in Greek, "*topoi,*" which means "places"). **Topics of invention** therefore represent specific ways of placing material into relationships that ideally bring about new questions and new insights. If one imagines all of the previous material for invention spread out on a table, topics represent certain places on the table that make the material look different when placed within their circle, much as placing objects under different microscopes or lenses makes them disclose new characteristics. Topics therefore serve the function of invention by encouraging a rhetor to experiment with different ways of asking questions about the subject matter to find out if anything interesting is produced by the different lenses. Here are four such topics:

1. *Definition:* The topic of definition simply asks something to define itself properly. Often, a speaker persuades simply by providing a more correct and precise definition of a situation, object, person, or action. For instance, the Founding Fathers often distinguished between a "democracy" (which was direct majority rule by the people) and a "republic" (which was indirect representative government by elected leaders). Demanding proper definitions often can challenge unspoken preconceptions about things and invite people to inquire about their real natures.

2. *Division:* Division either takes something that seems to be a "whole" and breaks it into its constituent parts ("A republic requires fair elections, a parliamentary body, separation of powers, and the rule of law.") or combines disparate parts into a whole ("I may be a New Yorker, and you might be a Virginian, but we are all Americans."). Division tells us either what something is made of (by breaking it up) or how to make something (by putting it together).

3. *Comparison:* Comparison takes two different things and puts them side by side to show their similarities and differences. Sometimes comparison can be used to make something seem more valuable ("Those who died in the Boston Massacre are akin to the Greeks who died at Thermopylae, sacrificing themselves for the sake of freedom."), to make it seem less valuable ("The British soldiers are merely well-dressed thieves"), or simply to identify it properly ("I call it a massacre because like other massacres in history it featured an armed force killing unarmed innocents.").

4. *Relationship:* A relationship puts two or more things in causal relationship to one another in order to understand how something was produced. Unlike comparison, which simply shows how two things are similar or different, relationship asks how one thing influenced another thing. Relationships can either be described in terms of physical cause and effect ("Oppressive taxation of the colonies has led to revolt.") or in terms of historical lineage ("The colonists are the children of the English king.").

Sources   The power of invention often derives from the integrity and breadth of one's **sources**. Finding sources that are respected by your audience is paramount to persuading them that you are both informed of the situation and sympathetic to their attitudes and concerns. Except in special circumstances, most people generally tend to respect the same sources—usually those coming from representatives of some established public or private institution such as a university, a news organization, or research bureau. Generally, specific strategies for finding sources can be found at any university library, and there are dozens of websites that maintain updated links to helpful databases, including the following:

University of California–Berkeley:
http://www.lib.berkeley.edu/instruct/guides/primarysources.html

Duke University:
http://library.duke.edu/research/finding/primarysource.html

Here are some general considerations about how to go about finding sources:

1. *Websites:* As a general rule, independent websites that are not affiliated with a professional institution such as a university, newspaper, or government agency are notoriously poor sources for information, particularly those websites that sell themselves as being dedicated to a specific issue. More often than not, these websites are themselves acting as forms of rhetorical advocacy in some way or another. Consequently, they are usually only valuable when they are themselves examples of rhetoric, for instance as one might do a paper on an ongoing debate in the public sphere using competing advocacy sites as examples. By contrast, sites like Wikipedia can offer a good overview of a topic and provide a basic framework of understanding that allows you to narrow your focus on more particular aspects of the subject. For general knowledge that does not need citation, Wikipedia can be valuable. However, is should only be considered a means of familiarizing yourself with a topic before delving into more detailed research. Whenever possible, speakers should get in the habit of looking elsewhere then the Internet for material for invention, for even when the material found is not invalid, it more often than not is commonplace and overused.

2. *Newspapers, magazines, or other journalistic sources:* These serve four purposes. First, they are excellent sources for getting first-person quotations from ordinary people about events of public interest. Nothing livens up a speech better than hearing what everyday people have to say about things that happened to them directly. Second, they provide quotations from various "experts" in a highly condensed and lively form that saves a speaker from having to delve through densely written academic material. Third, they usually provide the necessary facts to understand any issue, thus orienting a speaker to the situation. Fourth, journalistic writing is especially helpful in finding examples to use in introductions and conclusions, as newspaper articles are written with a similar incentive to "get attention and interest." A note of caution is in order, however. Like websites, newspapers and magazines are notoriously "slanted" toward specific audiences and therefore tend to pick and choose certain facts, certain experts, and certain stories in order to appeal to the stereotypes of their audiences. A reliable speaker will cross-reference numerous articles from respected news sources in order to determine which facts are accepted and which matters are in dispute.

3. *Books written about your subject by respected authors:* These generally provide a wealth of primary material as well as interpretative resources to help back up your claims. Books by university presses are generally more respected than books by popular presses, although they can be more dense and time

consuming to search through. For books that appear only in print, a good strategy is to first go to the index to see whether your particular interest is represented by a category entry. Often, a quick index search in a biography or history book will give you a wealth of details that could give your speech character. However, many books are now available online through Google Books. It is generally a good idea to first do a search on Google Books in order to see if there is any quotable material easily accessible online before having to spend hours flipping through pages in the library.

4. *Academic journal articles:* The best electronic database for essays from communication and rhetorical scholars is the Communication and Mass Media Complete database, accessed via the EBSCO search engine. The database includes all the essays from journals such as *Quarterly Journal of Speech* and *Philosophy and Rhetoric*. These usually present a very specific argument about an aspect of your case studies from either a scientific or a theoretical perspective. Even if they may not be directly relevant to your argument, they often provide good models for how to critically analyze objects for the purposes of drawing meaningful conclusions.

5. *Government documents:* Documents prepared and distributed by government agencies are often very useful when looking for data or analysis on general social conditions that can be measured by some objective standard. In general, the value of government documents is found in statistics.

Doing Proper Searches. When using electronic database searches, particularly newspaper and magazine databases, you need to try many different strategies. First, you should always avoid relying on general terms alone, such as "global warming" or "civil rights." You should always try to pair general terms with specific terms to narrow the search. Try adding specific names, places, dates, or "catchwords" that will call up more relevant searches—for instance, "Global warming Gore documentary controversy," or "intelligent design Dover 2006 debate," or "Malcolm X violence social change." Second, once you find one source, you should also scan it for more keywords that might be unique and helpful. Last, always check the bibliographies of articles and books to find new sources. Even if they are not immediately helpful, these new sources might, in turn, cite other articles and books in their own bibliographies that are helpful. This is a useful source for search tips:

> *Finding It Online: Web Search Strategies:*
> http://owl.english.purdue.edu/owl/resource/558/04/

Writing Your Thesis   The culmination of the process of invention is the development of a concrete goal—its **specific purpose**—as well as something to say to achieve that goal—a **thesis**. A specific purpose is the answer to the question, "What is this speech trying to do?" whereas a thesis is the answer to the question, "What is this speech trying to say?" Especially for beginning speakers, the quality of a speech stands or falls with how well the thesis helps to achieve the specific purpose. The thesis is the center around which every aspect of a speech revolves. Conveying a thesis to the audience gives a speaker a concrete focus necessary to create a logical and coherent message and provides an audience reference point to understand the speech.

1. **Specific Purpose:** A specific purpose is an expression of an interest in a particular goal that the speaker finds interesting and that may have value for an
   audience. It involves four characteristics, as follows:
   a. the kind of speech one is giving (Chapter 2)
   b. the audience to which this speech is delivered (Chapter 5)
   c. the occasion for the speech (Chapter 3)
   d. the effect on the audience that the speech is supposed to have (Chapter 4)
   Examples of specific purposes might include "to persuade my parents over
   dinner to buy me a car" or "to commemorate the Battle of Normandy during
   Memorial Day in front of a public audience to make them remember the sacrifices of veterans" or "to persuade the school board to support school uni-
   forms during the monthly school board meeting." For a speech delivered in a
   public speaking class, the audience can be the actual class or some imagined
   situation, depending on the decision of the instructor. In general, however,
   speeches given to actual audiences (the class) generally have more value because one can gauge an actual rather than a hypothetical response.

2. **Thesis:** A thesis is the specific argument that seeks to achieve the specific
   purpose. It is usually a single sentence that sums up what the entire speech is
   arguing, including a claim and reasons in support of that claim. Whereas a
   specific purpose is written for the speaker in order to help to *develop* a concrete idea during the writing process, a thesis is the *product* of that process.
   Thus, for the specific purpose "to persuade my parents over dinner to buy
   me a car," a thesis would be "You should purchase me a car because I have
   proved myself responsible, I require transportation to and from my job, and I
   need a car if I am ever to get a date." A thesis should:
   a. *Be specific.* A thesis should be specific. Vague and generic thesis state-
      ments always lead to speeches that are vague, confused, and lack impact.
      The more specific you can make a thesis, the more focused your speech
      will become and the greater impact it will have on an audience. Instead of
      "Our country should fight for peace," one could write "The U.S. should
      negotiate a settlement with country X by sacrificing interest Z."
   b. *Focus on a single topic.* Avoid including too many topics in a speech. An
      audience can only follow a few lines of reasoning in a sitting, and a speech
      that attempts to go too many places will lose them. Too many topics also
      generally lead to superficial arguments that do not get to the "heart" of an
      issue.
   c. *Be audience centered.* Consistent with the definition of rhetoric, any
      topic should be developed only with respect to the situated interests of an
      audience.
   d. *Make a clear claim.* A thesis should always have a single, clear argumenta-
      tive claim being made (e.g., "We should build this bridge."; "This person is
      noble."; "This policy works."; "The universe is infinite."). The claim is usu-
      ally a restatement of the overarching goal of the specific purpose.
   e. *Present reasons/details.* Following the claim should either be *reasons* in
      support of the claim or *details* about how it will be elaborated. The claim
      "We should build this bridge . . ." is generally followed by reasons like "be-
      cause it will ease traffic, create a scenic walkway, and stop litter." But the

claim "The universe is infinite . . ." should be followed by details like "and I will show how it expands in all directions, has no center, and possesses infinite possibility." A thesis might also have some combination of both reasons and details.

Documenting Sources   Through the invention process, make sure you keep a careful document of your sources. A simple model is the Modern Language Association (MLA) citation style. Use this in recording your sources in an outline, making sure also to retain the page numbers:

1. *Journal or magazine article:* Paroske, Marcus. "Deliberating International Science Policy Controversies: Uncertainty and AIDS in South Africa." *Quarterly Journal of Speech* 95.2 (2009): 148–170.
2. *Newspaper article:* Mitchell, Gordon. "Scarecrow Missile Defense." *Pittsburgh Post-Gazette* 8 July 2001: E-1.
3. *Book:* Danisch, Robert. *Pragmatism, Democracy and the Necessity of Rhetoric.* Columbia: University of South Carolina Press, 2007. Print.
4. *Book article or chapter:* Keränen, Lisa Belicka. "Girls Who Come to Pieces: Shifting Ideologies of Beauty and Cosmetics Consumption in the *Ladies' Home Journal,* 1900–1920." *Turning the Century: Essays in Media and Cultural Studies.* Ed. Carol A. Stabile. Boulder, CO: Westview Press, 2000. 142–165. Print.
5. *Website:* Furness, Zack. "My Dad Kicked Ass for a Living." *BadSubjects. com.* Oct. 2001. Web.

When citing a source in a written paper or outline, you should put the last name of the author and the page number in parentheses at the end of the sentence where the material was cited. This allows you to avoid accusations of plagiarism and also shows your paper to be well researched and documented. A useful guide is found at the Indiana University website (http://www.indiana.edu/~citing/MLA.pdf).

Discussion: Often, the term *invention* is used as a synonym for *magic*, or to create something from nothing. But as all magicians know, there is a lot of labor behind the illusion. Based on your own experience with other arts (music, dance, painting, poetry, etc.), how does "invention" work in these arts as a kind of method for "finding," like it does in rhetoric? What did you find, and how did you learn what to look for?

The Second Canon: Arrangement

After going through the process of invention, a speaker now must organize the various materials gathered together into a coherent speech structure that has a beginning, middle, and end. **Arrangement** represents the step of giving order to a speech in anticipation of giving it "form." Consequently, resources for arrangement generally consist of templates that indicate where certain types of things should go and in what sequence, much as one would think of instructions of how to run a board meeting or how to throw a surprise party. For instance, in Classical Roman oration, the arrangement was quite rigid and required a speaker to begin with an Introduction (*exordium*) to state the speech's purpose and establish credibility, then proceed through a Statement of Facts (*narratio*) to provide an overview of the situation, Division (*partitio*) to outline what is to follow and specify main point, Proof (*confirmatio*) to present arguments and supporting facts, Refutation (*refutatio*) to refute counterarguments, until ending up with the Conclusion (*peroratio*), which summed up claims and reinforced them with emotional appeal. Any speaker who wished to have an influence in the political sphere of the Roman Republic had to follow this arrangement, or else be ignored.

However, just as simply following mechanical instructions does not guarantee a successful meeting or an enjoyable party, no amount of rhetorical templates can ensure that a speech achieves the level of "form" that arouses and satisfies an audience's appetites. More often than not, strict obedience to the rules of arrangement results in superficially competent but largely barren and uninspiring speeches that put an audience to sleep. The following techniques should therefore be considered more like experimental suggestions for getting started. The techniques of arrangement provide several different frameworks that can give an initial order to the chaos of material gathered together through invention. But the final arbiter of success is not how well the speech conforms to rigid rules and formulas; it is how effectively the arrangement captures the attention and interest of the audience and then moves them through the body of the speech until they reach a satisfying conclusion.

Introductions

1. *Function:* An **introduction** should arouse some desire or appetite in the audience to hear the remainder of the speech. An introduction is therefore a kind of promise. It tells the audience what they are going to hear and promises that if they stick around they will have an enriched experience. Introductions should thus be clear and interesting, ideally combining elements of argument and narrative that tell an audience that they will be hearing a well-informed argument as well as some interesting stories along the way. Broken down into specifics, the functions are as follows:

   a. *Capture audience's attention.* Making an audience interested in listening to what you have to say is *the* most important function of an introduction. If they are not interested, then nothing else you say will matter because they won't hear it (see following "Strategies" section).

   b. *State topic of the speech and purpose.* Once you capture attention, you must retain it. You do so by making clear what your speech will be about so the audience will be prepared to sit through a more formal argument that may not be as "flashy" as your introduction. State your thesis as succinctly as you can.

   c. *Relate the topic to your audience.* No topic is intrinsically interesting. Maintaining an audience's attention usually requires that they feel invested in what you have to say. Relating a topic to the interests and experiences of an audience creates this feeling of investment because what you say has value for *them*.

   d. *Set a tone.* Letting an audience know whether you intend to be serious, ironic, funny, critical, or deferential is what it means to "set a tone." Doing so puts your audience in a frame of mind so that they know what to expect, just as audiences prepare themselves for a different "tone" at a comedy club than at a graduation ceremony or a funeral.

e. *Preview main points*. Although not always necessary, laying out the basic sequence of arguments can be helpful, especially when making a fairly complex or lengthy speech. However, previews are generally inappropriate for commemorative or introductory speeches because they are too formal.

f. *Provide a transition to the body of the speech*. Always let your audiences know when the introduction is over and the actual body of the speech has begun. This encourages them to listen with a different set of expectations. Because they have committed themselves to listening to the speech, they no longer need speakers to "get their attention." They now want to hear the details. A transition lets them know when this shift has occurred.

2. *Strategies:* The following are some helpful techniques to "get attention and interest" before stating your thesis and moving to the body.

a. *Use a quote*. Everyone enjoys hearing interesting quotes from famous people. Quotes should be relatively short and easy to understand and drawn from a person readily recognizable to and respected by the audience. These quotes should then be relevant to your own topic and preferably your argumentative claim as well.

b. *Startling fact*. Stating some dramatic fact either reveals some problem in graphic form (like the fact that thousands of people die from some disease every day) or it demonstrates the relevance of your topic (like the fact that the amount of candy eaten in a year, when stacked on a pile, would reach the moon). Speakers then proceed from this startling fact to argue the less exciting details that are necessary to understand and give meaning to that fact.

c. *Begin with a question*. To ask a question is to put your audience in the position of judgment. What would they do if such a thing occurred? What would they think about this or that idea? The intention of this strategy is to generate perplexity that your speech presumably would resolve. A poor question has an obvious answer, such as "If you had a choice, would you abolish cancer?" A good question actually raises some moral issue, such as "If your family was hungry, would you steal bread?"

d. *Refer to a current event*. Usually drawn from news stories, current events demonstrate why your topic is relevant to everyday contemporary life. These events may be *shocking* (like a child imitating violent video games in real life), *inspiring* (like a person who struggled to overcome cancer), or simply *odd* (like a man who thinks he is the king of Canada). In either case, they are used to show how violent video games, cancer cures, or psychological disorders, for example, are relevant issues to talk about.

e. *Tell a story*. A story in an introduction functions a lot like a fable. For instance, the "Boy Who Cried Wolf" conveys a lesson about trust. A story is a way of embodying some message by using plot and character as symbolic of a larger theme. Stories can come from personal experience, news, or history, or can be completely made up. However, completely fictional stories of the hypothetical variety are generally ineffective because the audience does not take them seriously. A good story relates some actual event, even if that event is your grandfather telling you a fictional story as a child.

f. *Perform a demonstration.* A technique with only very narrow applications, performing a demonstration involves actually doing some physical action to make a point. Anyone who has taken physics knows the typical kind of science demonstration meant to demonstrate how Newton's laws function. A demonstration can also be *entertaining* (like doing a magic trick), or *controversial* (like showing how a condom works). In either case, it catches attention through actions rather than just words.

g. *Refer to literary material.* This strategy combines the strategy of quoting and telling a story. This is the one case in which fictional stories are effective because they derive from literature rather than just your imagination. The best source, of course, should be familiar to and appreciated by your audience, especially when it has acknowledged cultural significance for a larger community.

h. *Use humor.* As anybody who has ever attended a religious service knows, humor is not always reserved for "light" topics. Humor can be effectively used in any situation. It takes a very sensitive touch to use humor when the "tone" of the speech is not a humorous one, but when done well it can be an effective way to "break the ice" with an audience.

i. *Create suspense.* Also a variation on telling a story, to create suspense you must set up conditions that may lead to some potential climax, thereby keeping your audience members on the edge of their seats. This suspense can be created through narrative or through demonstration. The risk of this strategy is that if the climax is not very interesting, then audiences feel let down. Also, suspense implies that you are not telling the full story, leading to the possibility that audiences may not know what you are actually speaking about until it is too late.

Main Points   If the primary function of the introduction is to arouse interest, the primary function of the main points is to progressively move an audience toward satisfaction one step at a time. The **main points** are the most important claims made by the speech that are intended to support the main thesis. In fact, most of the time, the thesis itself indicates what the main points will be. Take, for example, this thesis: "We should establish more national parkland because it preserves wildlife, creates more opportunities for outdoor adventure, and connects people to the natural environment." The main purpose of the speech is to argue for the establishment of more national parks. The main points are then specific assertions, usually consisting of topic sentences at the beginning of each major section, that are intended to support this main purpose. For instance, these three main points might be written as follows:

- First, the survival of many species of large predators, such as wolves and mountain lions, depends on having free range in a wide expanse of undeveloped land.
- Second, national parks provide a destination for the many outdoor enthusiasts who desire to use the space for recreation.
- Third, national parks are the best means of creating a sense of stewardship with the environment, an attitude that is necessary for the health of the planet.

Main points can be thought of narratively like acts in a play or structurally like the rooms in a house. In both cases, each main point has its own separate purpose and character and yet only exists to support the construction of a whole work. Moreover, the house analogy should not be interpreted to mean that the rooms have only physical proximity to one another; a house is primarily made to live in, and rooms are constructed so that each room leads naturally to the next. A poor speech, like a badly designed house, will simply place things next to each other that shouldn't go together, like putting the main bathroom next to the kitchen and the dining room on the second floor. Likewise, a poor speech, like a badly written play, will introduce characters in the first act only to never mention them again and will jump from scene to scene without properly demonstrating their connection. In contrast, a good speech will feel like a guided house tour that reveals every aspect of the building's design and a dramatic three-act play in which all the major plot points are resolved in the final scenes. It will present the audience with a clear progression of ideas that they can easily follow so that they know what is coming. If a speech does not fit into any of these orders, then it is likely that the speech will be too disconnected to be effective. These are the basic ways of structuring main points:

1. *Chronological:* Speeches that involve some process of time are suitable for chronological order that describes something from beginning to end. For example, chronological order is useful when doing biographies (the life of Martin Luther King Jr.), events (the Pamplona running of the bulls), or processes (how life may have developed on Mars).

2. *Geographical:* Whereas chronological order deals with differences across time, geographical order deals with differences across space. The classic geographical speech is a kind of "world tour" in which the speaker shows the different manifestations of something in different regions, whether the subject matter is language, culture, science, economics, history, war, or art. But geography can also be used in a more general sense of describing anything spatially, whether it is a microchip, a crime scene, a state capital, or the universe.

3. *Cause–Effect:* The cause-and-effect order almost always deals with speeches concerned with informing an audience about factual knowledge needed to address some problem. Consequently, such speeches almost always deal with issues of process (like the ways AIDS is transmitted or how smoking causes cancer), because a process is by definition something that causes change over time.

4. *Pro–Con:* The pro–con order is the counterpart of the cause–effect order in that it deals with the analysis of solutions that respond to problems. A pro–con order examines a particular solution to some problem and articulates its positive and negative qualities in order to provide an audience with sufficient objective knowledge to make a decision (like the potential environmental benefits of regulating carbon dioxide emissions compared with its economic downsides).

5. *Topical:* The most general organizational structure is "topical," which simply means a series of related qualities or characteristics of your subject matter. Examples are "The four unique aspects of Louisiana cooking," "The

hierarchies of English feudalism," and "Varieties of world religions." These do not fit into any of the previously described orders but still are speeches with thematic connections.

6. *Problem–Solution:* Quite simply, this speech lays out the problem and then addresses that problem by presenting a clear solution. It can also incorporate the pro–con format within its structure.

7. *Comparative Advantage:* Also a variation on the pro–con structure, the comparative advantage puts two competing solutions side by side, and shows how one has more advantages than the other.

As stated earlier, these methods of arrangement should be thought of as different ways of putting the same material together to produce different effects. Although there are exceptions, for the most part almost any general topic can be arranged using any of these methods. For instance, let us say you are interested in giving an enrichment speech about Martin Luther King Jr.'s civil rights rhetoric. By examining the topic through each of these lenses of arrangement, a speaker can experiment with different ways of presenting the speech.

1. *Chronological:* How King's oratory changed over time?
2. *Geographical:* Speeches given in the rural South versus the urban North.
3. *Cause–effect:* What inspired him to speak or what influence his speeches had?
4. *Pro–con:* The benefits and detriments of using nonviolent resistance methods.
5. *Topical:* Racism, poverty, and war as three dominant themes in his speeches.
6. *Problem–solution:* How nonviolent resistance was to overcome segregation?
7. *Comparative advantage:* The comparison between nonviolence and violence.

Testing out these different perspectives can be very useful in generating new ideas on a topic that may not have been obvious to a speaker at first. They force us to look at a familiar object in different ways and therefore make us ask new questions to arouse new interests.

Finally, like a play or a house tour, the audience should also know when this part of the work is coming to an end and what they will then be seeing subsequently. In a speech, this means using transitions, previews, summaries, and signposts help to create a smooth continuity to the speech as one progresses from point to point.

1. *Transitions:* Once you have sufficiently articulated a main point and concluded a section, it is necessary to provide a "bridge" to move your audience from one idea to another. A transition provides this bridge by showing the connection between the two ideas and the need to proceed from one to the other. For example, a transition between points 1 and 2 in the preceding parkland example could be accomplished by the following transition: "This space can be used not only by animals, however, but by humans who wish to 'get away from it all.'" This passage shifts our attention from one object (wildlife) to another (park visitors) that are nonetheless connected by the idea of how the park can be "used" in a practical sense.

2. *Internal previews:* An internal preview is a sentence within the speech that lets an audience know what they are about to hear—for example, "I shall show through a series of testimonials how experience with natural parks changes

the way that individuals see themselves as connected with nature." Previews of this kind are helpful with a long speech that contains complex details. For shorter, less complex speeches, internal previews are often unnecessary.

3. *Internal summaries:* A summary is the opposite of a preview. Instead of telling people what to expect, a summary reminds them what they have heard so as to reaffirm some important point. For example, at the end of the first section you could write, "All of these animal species I have described would find it hard to survive without continuous land preserved for their habitat." A summary should restate the idea of the main point but do so in a way that refers to the specific forms of evidence presented in the section.

4. *Signposts:* A signpost is a way of saying to your audience "You are here." It marks a path along the way and lets them know your location. In the earlier articulation of the main points, these took the form of "First," "Second," and "Third." Other signposts include "To begin," "In conclusion," "Next," and so forth. These very simple tools make a big difference in the way an audience follows along.

Conclusions

1. *Function:* Whereas the purpose of the introduction is to get attention and interest, the purpose of the **conclusion** is to satisfy an audience's desires and make them feel as if the speech has come together as a whole and therefore achieved qualitative unity in form. Specifically, the functions are as follows:

   a. *Summarize main points.* Although not usually effective as a rhetorical style of presentation, if done explicitly (as in, "To summarize, I have argued X, Y, and Z."), a conclusion should usually reaffirm the basic claims and arguments of a speech. The important thing is to embody these claims and arguments in a new way that makes them more interesting and poetic.

   b. *Help the audience remember the speech.* Sometimes this can be achieved by calling attention to the physical environment so that your speech is linked to some memorable object or event that is present. Other times you recall something important or imaginative in the earlier part of the speech and emphasize it again so as to leave the audience with a lasting "impression." Remember that complex memories are almost always recalled by simple associations.

   c. *Leave with a call to action.* Oftentimes, persuasion requires a lengthy detour through factual accounts, narratives, reasons, and explanations. A conclusion should show how all of these things lead to a specific action that is within reach of the audience. The phrase "think globally, act locally" in many ways summarizes the form of a rhetorical speech. One spends the large part of it thinking big only to end on a simple action, such as recycling, giving to charity, or boycotting a business.

   d. *Clearly end your speech.* Let people know when you are nearing the end of your speech. A conclusion should help the audience "wind down." It allows them time to think about what the speech meant to them. Letting an audience know that you are about to end gives them a sense of "closure" that makes a big difference in the quality of the lasting impression.

e. *End on a positive note.* Even with speeches that articulate the most graphic and devastating conditions, audiences want to know that there is some hope in making the world a better place. It is important to give audiences this hope at the end of a speech so that they leave believing they can make some small difference. This does not mean being naively idealistic. It simply means making the effort to overcome apathy by indicating that some kind of change is possible through action.

2. *Strategies:* Here are the basic strategies for leaving a good impression.

   a. *Startle your audience.* After a long speech, sometimes audiences get too relaxed or even bored. A conclusion that makes some startling claim or demonstration can "wake them up" and make them pay closer attention to your concluding arguments.

   b. *Challenge your audience.* Similar to startling the audience, a speaker can also take the risky move to challenge them. This usually involves a combination of critique and imagination. To challenge an audience means to suggest that they are not living up to their potential, and that a better future may be ahead of them if they rise to new heights.

   c. *Come full circle.* A very effective way of concluding a speech is to refer back to the introduction and pick up where it left off. If it asked a question, then answer it. If it began a story, give the ending. If it quoted a famous philosopher, quote that philosopher again. This does not mean simply repeating what is already said, but continuing a line of thought and bringing it to a proper conclusion.

   d. *Visualize a positive future.* One way of ending on a positive note is to dramatize the great future that will come about through the committed actions of the audience. This is the basic strategy of much advertising that features before-and-after sequences. Thus, you not only want to tell people that their future is going to be better; you want to visualize that future for them in order to develop an emotional attachment.

   e. *Visualize a negative future.* The opposite strategy is to visualize the negative future that would come about from inaction or choosing a different action. In the advertising analogy, this would be the future of choosing the competitor's product. Instead of a popular person wearing a colorful line of new clothes, for example, one would show a sad and lonely person wearing his or her old wardrobe.

   f. *Ask a question.* Unlike the introduction, which poses a question that will then be answered, this question should leave the audience with something to ponder.

   g. *Use a humorous anecdote.* An anecdote should sum up a major point already made in a funny way that encourages the audience to talk about it after the speech is over.

   h. *Employ quotations.* This strategy is similar to using an anecdote, except that it relies on the words of someone famous who has the weight of authority.

   i. *Tell a story.* Often used effectively to give "moral lessons," a story at the conclusion of a speech sums up in narrative what was already explained using logic.

Outlining   The outline is one of the primarily tools for helping to arrange all of your ideas into a concrete form. **Outlining** allows you to organize the "highlights" of a speech into sections and put them into a linear progression of beginning, middle, and end. A **working outline** is a tentative plan for the speech that allows a speaker to experiment with different arrangements before exerting the time and energy required to finalize the speech. In a classroom setting, a working outline also provides a medium of communication between instructor and student during the composition process. As a collaborative medium, outlines are often more valuable when they are incomplete, because they help identify the gaps that need to be filled. In the *creative stage*, a working outline should function as both a rough draft and a brainstorming session. The rough draft aspect records the basic arguments, facts, quotes, and strategies that the writer confidently feels are useful. The brainstorming aspect puts them together with ideas and possibilities that may not yet have any clear structure or backing. Both students and instructors should thus use outlines *as a tool for collaborative communication* during the process of invention and development. The **final outline** then represents the last stage of your speech preparations that precede the actual writing or delivery of a speech and is useful both for evaluation purposes (for the instructor) and to allow the speech to be performed again (for the speaker). The author should be careful to accurately record all quotations in full, as well as dutifully record all facts as faithfully as possible.

To be effective as a tool for creative composition, an outline should identify not only the content of what is going to be said but also the composition methods being used to organize the material. This includes not only methods outlined in this chapter but also the more specific strategies in subsequent chapters. As students become more familiar with the specific techniques, working outlines should become more complex. Each specific entry should therefore include not only examples, arguments, and proofs, but also labels (in parentheses) attached to those examples, arguments, and proofs that tell both the student and the speaker what persuasive strategy is being employed. The outline should also include a bibliography with sources cited according to MLA style (or the instructor's preferred style) discussed in the previous section on invention.

A helpful guideline for producing a finalized version of the outline can be found at the Purdue University website (http://owl.english.purdue.edu/owl/resource/544/02/).

Here is an example of a full manuscript speech written to support state funding of the arts in the 2010 Louisiana budget. In an old Louisiana tradition, it is intended to be spoken at a "jazz funeral" for the arts, in which a fake coffin would be carried in front of the state capital accompanied by a jazz band:

> Thank you all for joining together in our solemn remembrance for the loss of a dear friend. It is fitting that jazz accompanies our gathering here today, and not just because we lie upriver from the birthplace of America's classical music. Louis Armstrong said of jazz that: "The memory of things gone is important to a jazz musician. Things like old folks singing in the moonlight in the back yard on a hot night or something said long ago" (Collier, 32). So when we hear jazz, we think both of what was and what might be again, even as we face up to the reality of what is before us in the moment. We think of the sacrifice and

courage of those who struggled not only to forge a life along this sultry stretch of land, but who put their blood in the soil to bring forth something called beauty. We think of the lives stretching ahead of our children, who may, too, discover that a difficult life of creation is more rewarding than an easy life of consumption. And we think of the friend who lies prostrate before us in the knowledge that someone we cared about has passed into memory.

But we are also here for a specific reason. Today we hold a jazz funeral for the arts in order to accomplish a political task as well. We wish to protest the dramatic cuts in arts funding in Louisiana that will not only harm the state's vibrant cultural life but also diminish its economic growth, and by protesting these cuts we hope to give the arts a second life despite the financial challenges ahead.

But first, let us be clear about whom we eulogize. We do not mourn the passing of art itself. Art, like all great human inventions, is born out of struggle. There is no accident that jazz was invented in New Orleans. Art becomes great in proportion to the obstacles it must overcome. Violence cannot kill it. Poverty cannot starve it. Waves cannot drown it. And government irresponsibility cannot suffocate it. Indeed, though the small-minded and the thin-willed may occasionally place their bony thumb upon the pulse of invention as a display of power, they have more to fear from art than art from them.

Neither do we mourn the passing of artists. Those joining us today already prove them to be alive among us. But that is hardly a surprise. The artistic spirit has proven time and again that it does not give way easily, even to force. If it could survive in the harshest of times, who would expect it to acquiesce before a combination of stupidity and neglect? No, we do not mourn the death of artists. In fact, artists have joined us today in this funeral to honor what is lost.

But although art and artists will always endure, the Louisiana Decentralized Arts Fund will not. The estimated 83 percent cut in its relatively small $3-million-dollar budget effectively dismembers an organization that is not only a national model for local arts funding, but that economically produces a major return on every dollar invested. Gerd Wuestemann, the executive director of the Acadiana Center for the Arts, a regional grant-distribution agency, says he anticipates two things as a result of the cuts: "Some of the smaller organizations that do good work, especially in the more rural areas, may have to close doors," he says. "And I think it will result in fewer projects and less income to the communities and less vibrancy in our lifestyle, and I think that's a shame" (Pierce). But such reasoning runs too far ahead for those who have their heads screwed on backwards. As our governor remarked recently to Larry King about federal investment in the arts: "Fundamentally, I don't think ... $50 million for the National Endowment for the Arts is going to get the economy moving again as quickly as allowing the private sector to create jobs" (Knight). With the nonprofit arts sector bringing in millions of visitors each year to this state and creating jobs, one might have reason to object to the logic that kills the jobs in the village to save them. But we are not here for an argument, but a eulogy. And the death of the arts fund is more properly reserved for the memorial for the impending massacre of public agencies not only across the state but nationwide. The body of the arts fund will thus be thrown on the pyre with those of health care, education, environmental protection, and all the other extensions of the social body that have been sacrificed on the altar of rampant greed and high-sounding idiocy.

But there is yet another body to mourn as well in a larger sense. For without support of the arts, we eventually will mourn the passing of the community. Without democratic organizations that enable local communities to integrate the arts into their cultural fabric, the effects of art are broken into a thousand isolated threads that one encounters only sporadically and accidentally. Without collective investments in the arts, a community spirit withers and citizens retreat into their private spheres. Like we see here today, the arts bring people together into the open to share in their *common* world and to make it a *better* world.

There is, of course, no physical body here to mourn over. The community is not something one can witness. The community exists between us, and art not only forges those bonds that produce a sense of belonging and happiness, but also provides a vehicle for creative invention that is always produced when democratic citizens invest their collective energies in improving their common world. A great American philosopher, John Dewey, once wrote that "Creation, not acquisition, is the measure of a nation's rank; it is the only road to an enduring place in the admiring memory of mankind" (Dewey).

In summary, Louisiana, despite its natural wealth, has never been ranked high on the measure of acquisition. But it has achieved a standing in the memory of humankind as one of the greatest sources of creation ever seen. Jazz has been one of its grandest achievements, but we miss its power if we use it only to reflect on the greatness of what was. Its potential comes from memory but is power comes from its Second Line. So although the body of the community may lie prostrate before us at the moment, once that Second Line starts, you watch it get up and dance. Strike it up!

WORKS CITED

Collier, James Lincoln. *Louis Armstrong: An American Genius.* Oxford: Oxford University Press, 1985. Print.

Dewey, John. "Art as Our Heritage." *John Dewey: The Later Works,* vol. 14. Ed. Jo Ann Boydston. Carbondale: Southern Illinois UP, 1988. 255–257. Print.

Knight, Christopher. "Gov. Jindal Exorcizes Arts Funds from Louisiana Budget." *Los Angeles Times.* 30 March, 2009. Web.

Pierce, Walter. "Short-Sighted Solons Gut Arts Funding." *TheInd.com.* 4 June 2012. Web.

Now here is the same speech written in a highly condensed outline form that not only identifies strategies but also uses an abridged language capable of easy translation into notecards.

Title: Eulogy for the Jazz Funeral for the Arts

Topic: Budget cuts to arts funding in Louisiana

Specific Purpose: To advocate that funding to the Louisiana decentralized arts fund should be restored.

Thesis: We wish to protest the dramatic cuts in arts funding in Louisiana that will not only harm the state's vibrant cultural life but also diminish its economic growth, and by protesting these cuts we hope to give the arts a second life despite the financial challenges ahead.

INTRODUCTION

(Material to arouse interest—*Tell a Story/Use Quote/Utopia/Virtue*): Thank you all for coming. Fitting to be in birthplace of America's classical music. Louis Armstrong said of jazz that: "The memory of things gone is important to a jazz musician. Things like old folks singing in the moonlight in the back yard on a hot night or something said long ago" (Collier, 32). Jazz reminds of sacrifice/courage/beauty of people long past. Think of children choosing creation over consumption. And we think of the friend prostrate before us.

Thesis: But here for political task as well. We wish to protest the dramatic cuts in arts funding in Louisiana that will not only harm the state's vibrant cultural life but also diminish its economic growth, and by protesting these cuts we hope to give the arts a second life despite the financial challenges ahead.

BODY (*TOPICAL ORDER*)

I. (First main point—*Identification*): People in Louisiana love the arts and the arts will endure despite budget cuts.
  A. (Subpoint 1—*Idol*): New Orleans jazz is a symbol of art that arises out of suffering and challenge.
     1. (Sub-Subpoint 1—*Example*): Violence/racism of past.
     2. (Sub-Subpoint 2—*Example*): Poverty.
     3. (Sub-Subpoint 3—*Example*): Hurricanes Katrina and Rita.
  B. (Subpoint 2): Artists will continue to work in Louisiana as well.
(**Transition**: But although art and artists will always endure, the Louisiana Decentralized Arts Fund will not.)
II. (Second main point—*Causal Argument*): The budget cuts are unwise because they will result in the destruction of the agency and damage Louisiana culture and economy.
  A. (Subpoint 1): The 83 percent cut in $3-million-dollar budget effectively dismembers an organization that is a national model.
     1. (Sub-Subpoint 1—*Quotation/Wasteland*): Gerd Wuestemann, the executive director of the Acadiana Center for the Arts, a regional grant-distribution agency, says he anticipates two things as a result of the cuts: "Some of the smaller organizations that do good work, especially in the more rural areas, may have to close doors," he says. "And I think it will result in fewer projects and less income to the communities and less vibrancy in our lifestyle, and I think that's a shame" (Pierce).
     2. (Sub-Subpoint 2—*Quotation /Sinner*): Governor of Louisiana on Larry King speaking of arts in general: "Fundamentally, I don't think ... $50 million for the National Endowment for the Arts is going to get the economy moving again as quickly as allowing the private sector to create jobs" (Knight).
     3. (Sub-Subpoint 3): Tourism is important to Louisiana economy.
  B. (Subpoint 2): The reduction of support for the arts damages the community of Louisiana and destroys its cultural richness.
     1. (Sub-Subpoint 1—*Causal*): Without state support art and artists are not able to bring a community together.
     2. (Sub-Subpoint 2—*Wasteland*): Louisiana's culture thrives in nonprofit festivals and without them it will lose what makes it great.

3. (**Sub-Subpoint 3**— *Quotation /Virtue*): A great American philosopher, John Dewey, once wrote that "Creation, not acquisition, is the measure of a nation's rank; it is the only road to an enduring place in the admiring memory of mankind" (Dewey).

(**Transition:** "In summary, Louisiana, despite its natural wealth, has never been ranked high on the measure of acquisition.")

CONCLUSION

Concluding Remarks: (*Visualize a Positive Future*): But it has achieved a standing in the memory of humankind as a source of creation. Jazz is its grandest achievement. But we miss its power if only thought of as a past accomplishment. Its potential comes from Second Line. So although the body of the community may lie prostrate before us at the moment, once that Second Line starts, you watch it get up and dance. Strike it up!

WORKS CITED

Collier, James Lincoln. *Louis Armstrong: An American Genius*. Oxford: Oxford University Press, 1985. Print.

Dewey, John. "Art as Our Heritage." *John Dewey: The Later Works*, vol. 14. Ed. Jo Ann Boydston. Carbondale: Southern Illinois UP, 1988. 255–257. Print.

Knight, Christopher. "Gov. Jindal Exorcizes Arts Funds from Louisiana Budget." *Los Angeles Times*. 30 March, 2009. Web.

Pierce, Walter. "Short-Sighted Solons Gut Arts Funding." *TheInd.com*. 4 June 2012. Web.

Notecards   Notecards are used for extemporaneous speaking as a means of reminding the speaker of the order and content of material to be presented. Although based on the substance of the outline, they should not simply consist of the entire outline cut into small pieces of paper. Notecards act primarily as reminders rather than a manuscript. Only quotes, transitions, theses, and introductory and concluding remarks can be written out, although speakers should strive to reduce even this material to a minimum. Although it is tempting to add more "just in case," the fact is that the more one writes on a notecard, the more a speaker is tempted simply to read out loud, thereby ruining the purpose of extemporaneous speaking. Notecards should not be too "packed" with information, but should be written in clear, bold letters with a lot of "white space" so that one can easily see what comes next without having to hunt within a clutter of words.

Discussion: We often think of arrangement simply as putting things in order so that they do not appear as a chaotic mess. We organize our food cabinets, for instance, so that we know where things are and can access them. But arrangement also conveys its own meaning. For instance, in the movie *High Fidelity*, John Cusack's character decides to arrange his record collection not alphabetically but autobiographically. This form of arrangement then brings new meaning to the whole collection and forms the basis of the film. What other things do you arrange in your living space whose meaning depends on arrangement?

The Third Canon: Style

Style is the complement of invention; whereas invention provides the "content," style provides and fills out the "form." Although style is often thought of simply as "ornamentation," the Latin term *ornare* is substantive and means "to equip, fit out, or supply." A soldier was thus "ornamented" with the weapons of war, meaning that a soldier without style was not, in fact, prepared to fight as a soldier. Similarly, rhetorical **style** is not the frivolous decoration of ideas; it is the filling out and forming of ideas in order to allow them to stand on their own and organize themselves as a coherent whole. Just as the military is made up both of individual soldiers and whole platoons, style includes both particular parts of the speech ("figurative style") as well as the tone of the speech in its entirety ("formal style"). It is important to keep this distinction in mind, for often speakers focus too much on the style of the parts at the expense of the whole.

With respect to the notion of form as the arousing and satisfying of the appetites of the audience, style represents the unique manner in which a speaker guides an audience through a speech and makes transitions between different items gathered through invention and then structured through arrangement. One can think of style as a way of linking or threading different things together so that they all feel like parts of the same thing. For instance, one might think of a speech through the metaphor of a museum. Invention acquires the artworks and arrangement places them in certain categories and in certain rooms. However, arrangement itself does not guarantee a worthwhile experience for the museumgoer. Sometimes even the most masterfully arranged material seems to just hang there on the wall as people move methodically from room to room, looking at each individual picture but not feeling like it all adds up to anything. Yet a tour guide can add "style" to the experience simply by the manner in which he or she introduces a particular artwork and then transitions the audience to the next room or the next work with little more than his or her personality. A poor tour guide simply relies on the "psychology of information" to keep the attention of the audience by deluging them in surprising facts; a masterful tour guide will emphasize the "psychology of form" and rely more on creating a certain lively atmosphere that makes the experience intrinsically enjoyable. The feeling of "style" is thus akin to the overall feeling of movement produced by the tour guide—whether it was slow and deliberate or lively and entertaining or grandfatherly and contemplative, for example.

There are two kinds of style, with each serving an important function. **Formal style** is effectively synonymous with what I have called "form," which is the overall tone and feel of a speech in its totality. Formal style is connected with the notion of genre, such that we might think of a speech as fitting a certain type that carries with it a certain feeling, like a "somber eulogy" or an "impassioned defense" or a "soapbox oration" or an "old-time revival." It is the complete impression left upon us by a speech that allows us to reflect upon it as a whole experience and gives it its unique "character." **Figurative style** represents specific elements of the speech designed to capture the attention and seduce the ear of the audience, thereby making them engaged with what is being said and creating more of a feeling of continuity and unity. Figurative style focuses on providing short, refined, effective parts of a speech that give clarity and power to specific ideas or images.

The Meanings of Signs   Understanding the basis not only of style, but also of substance, requires a brief excursion into **semiotics**, or the study of signs. Whenever we ask why a word (a "sign") means what it does, we are discussing semiotics. This discussion is important for rhetoric for the simple fact that the success of speeches often is contingent on the very careful choice of words. Oftentimes, speakers will simply use words that are familiar to them without realizing that words can have multiple meanings for multiple audiences, and that often what we think is a very clear expression of a concrete idea becomes, when expressed in a speech, a vague expression of a muddled thought that results in misunderstanding. Correcting this state of affairs is what led the logician, scientist, and philosopher Charles Peirce to study the logic of signs. For him, "to know what we think, to be masters of our own meaning, will make a solid foundation for great and weighty thought."[15] Similarly, to know how to speak well and to be masters of our own meaning will make a solid foundation for great and weighty rhetoric.

For the goal of making our ideas and language clear, Peirce designed a triadic theory of the meaning of a sign that consist of a *sign*, an *object*, and its *interpretant*. A **sign** is that which addresses somebody, in some respect or capacity, for something else (for instance, when a child exclaims "doggy!" to her mother when she sees the neighbor's dog being walked on a leash). The **object** is what is represented by the sign (in this case, the thing which the child perceives to "be" the doggy out in the world). The **interpretant** is a more developed sign that mediates between the sign and its object that explains why they should go together (for instance, that "doggy" highlights the cute, furry, and friendly qualities of a domestic canine which makes the object more meaningful to a child). If one uses the metaphor of dictionary, the sign is the word, the interpretant is the definition, and the object is the picture which is the side the word and the definition. This relationship would be represented graphically in this way:

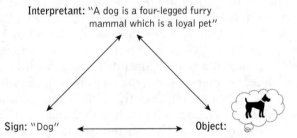

The arrows go in both directions because the relationship can begin with anyone of the three elements. For instance, a toddler might see a picture (the *object*) of a

---

[15]Charles Peirce, "How to Make Our Ideas Clear," in *The Philosophy of Peirce*, ed. Justus Buchler, 23-41(New York: Harcourt, Brace, and Co., 1950), 25.

dog and ask "what is it?" The response is the *sign*: "A dog." The child then asks: "But what is a dog?" The answer is the *interpretant*: "A cute, furry, friendly animal that people like to have as a pet." Or one might know both the *object* and the *interpretant* but forget the sign. For instance, an adult might ask "what is that brown and black dog with pointed ears that police usually use?" The answer is a *sign*, "German Shepherd." Or one might know the *sign* and *interpretant* but actively seek its "real" object. For instance, a parent wishes to find a "pet" (sign) which will be a gentle and affectionate friend for small children (interpretant). Although there existed an image of the object in the parent's imagination, only after seeing many dogs does she point to one and say "that one!" The sign has now found its "real" object which corresponds to the "idea" of the object previously in the parent's mind.

From this example, one can see that it is important to keep in mind that the "object" of the sign is not necessarily an actual, concrete thing; it is merely the "thing" that is called forth in the mind by the sign. Peirce writes that we should think of an object "in that sense in which we say that one man catches another man's idea, in which we say that when a man recalls what he was thinking of at some previous time, he recalls the same idea, and in which when a man continues to think anything, save for a tenth of a second, insofar as the thought continues to agree with itself during that time...it is the same idea."[16] An "idea" thus need not be real, only coherent and identifiable. This is what allows purely fictional entities such as centaurs or ghosts to still be "objects" despite the fact that they do not exist. "Real" objects are only rarely the content of signs, indicated by indexical terms like "this" or "that" that accompany an act of pointing. Most often, the objects of signs are ideas in the mind (as when we talk about somebody present "as if" they weren't there). However, the more our signs accurately represent "real" objects, the more they help us predict and control our environment when we do interact with them in the "real world." For instance, imagine that you have a friend under a great deal of stress at work who never seems to be able to relax. You might suggest: "Why don't you get a dog so you can take it for walks?" This calls forth the idea of walking a dog, which through imagined interaction, produces confidence in your friend that he or she would actually feel better if they bought a dog that could take his or her mind off of work. Obviously, then, there existed no "real" dog which was the object of the sign; it was only the idea of a hypothetical dog called forth by the sign which functioned as an object for that sign. But the usefulness of the advice is nonetheless dependent on the person having a relatively clear and realistic notion of the pragmatic effects of owning a dog as a pet. It is the function of interpretants to give us this greater understanding. The function of interpretants, then, is to tell us why certain signs are more appropriate to use over others when describing objects in certain situations. It makes a big difference, for instance, whether one uses the sign "dog," "canine," or "doggy" when speaking to a child, even if all three technically "refer" to the same object. This is because the interpretants

---

[16]Charles Peirce, "Logic as Semiotic: The Theory of Signs," in *The Philosophy of Peirce*, ed. Justus Buchler, 98–119 (New York: Harcourt, Brace, and Co., 1950), 99.

differ both in content and form. Peirce points out that interpretants come in three forms, emotional, energetic, and logical. The **logical interpretant** is analogous to the dictionary definition and corresponds to what is conventionally called the **denotative meaning** of a word, or what "thing" it objectively refers to. For instance, the term "dog" used in a veterinary classroom will mostly have a logical interpretant that emphasizes its biological characteristics as a type of mammal with certain health and nutritional needs. The **emotional interpretant** represents the feeling produced by the sign and comes closest to what is conventionally called the **connotative meaning,** or what qualities we associate with the object. The term "doggy" thus evokes feelings of affection and playfulness, whereas "carnivorous mammal" the same term would likely produce fear and anxiety for a person who has in the past been bitten by a dobrings about opposite affective responses. Finally, the **energetic interpretant** is the appropriate action or effect produced by the sign and corresponds to what we might call the **pragmatic meaning** of a word, or how if effects our behavior. The term "dog!" shouted by a burglar to his partner will literally "mean" that this object is something to flee from as soon as possible. In each case, the interpretant performs the function of telling the **interpreter** (the actual person interpreting the sign) what he or she should think, do, or feel about the object called forth by the sign.

Rhetorically, semiotics is important in encouraging us to take a close look at the words that we use in order to avoid misunderstanding and maximize our persuasive power. A rhetorical speaker must therefore be highly attuned to the unique circumstances of the speech act and the idiosyncratic qualities and attitudes of the audience and be prepared to modify a speech on the spot when it becomes apparent that words that were intended to do one thing start doing another. Here is a brief list of things to consider when trying to choose the right sign (or "word") for the right occasion:

1. *For certain audiences, some signs may not refer to any objects:* This simple fact is readily apparent any time we visit a foreign country in which we do not know the language and the signs simply do not call forth any object whatsoever. We also have this experience when we encounter unfamiliar slang or technical jargon. Simply because a sign may be meaningful to certain audiences does not mean it is meaningful to any audience. It is the responsibility of the speaker to speak in meaningful signs.

2. *Simply labeling an object with a sign does not produce an interpretant:* Oftentimes, people are content simply with pointing at something and giving it a name and thinking that is sufficient for the production of meaning. For instance, one might walk into a garden and find lots of Latin names stuck in front of plants. But this does not convey much in the way of meaning to those unfamiliar with botanical terminology. It does not tell us what characteristics the plant has, what emotions we should attach to the plant, or what we should do when encountering the plant. When introducing new signs for objects, the burden falls on the speaker to suggest to the audience the proper interpretants, as when the Latin name suggests a species of poison ivy that we should avoid direct contact with and then tear up from the root using gloves.

3. *A single sign may refer to multiple objects:* For instance, the sign "table" can be both a noun and a verb. As a noun, it can call forth the image of or of . As a verb, its object is the act of putting off an item of business until a later time. Only the context of its use determines which object is called forth by the sign.

4. *Members of an audience may each have different interpretants for the same object:* For instance, the sign "the American dream" for most people may call forth the same basic image of a person aspiring to a better life. However, for some people, the logical interpretant will be "the guiding principle of American political economy" (with its corresponding emotional interpretant of pride), whereas for others it will be "a myth propagated to mask economic inequality" (with its corresponding emotional interpretant of disgust). Still others will call forth an energetic interpretant to take out a loan and start a business.

5. *Some signs have only emotional interpretants:* For instance, Peirce writes that "the performance of a piece of concerted music is a sign" whose meaning "usually consist merely in a series of feelings."[17] Consequently, often when we talk about music, our reactions usually deal with our emotional responses of like and dislike. Most of our interactions with the signs of art or nature call forth objects that primarily have emotional interpretants.

6. *Some signs have only energetic interpretants:* For instance, imperative signs such as "Go!" or "Fire!" or "Hey!" are primarily intended to bring about immediate actions rather than any particular "idea" that can be stated as a proposition.

7. *Some signs have only logical interpretants:* Many technical terms bring forth neither emotional nor energetic reactions because they refer to objects that are not connected with our everyday lives. Few people feel passion or the need to act when they encounter the signs "hexide" and "blastocyst." However, it is not infrequent that signs normally confined to technical jargon become terms loaded with emotional and energetic interpretants when they cause potential health concerns, as with the signs "asbestos" and "dioxin."

8. *Referring to the same object with different signs produces different interpretants:* The interpretant is not tied to the object. It is produced by the interaction between the sign and the object. For instance, the signs "water" and "H_2O" technically both refer to the same object. However, the sign "water" produces stronger emotional and energetic interpretants than H_2O because water is something we drink and swim in, whereas H_2O refers simply to the atomic composition of a molecule. Similarly, the words "dog," "doggie," "mutt," "pooch," and "canine" all arguably refer to pretty much the same object; however, each one has very different potential logical, emotional, and energetic interpretants. A master rhetorician will select the precise sign for each audience that produces the desired interpretants of specific objects.

---

[17]Charles Peirce, "Pragmatism in Retrospect: A Last Formulation," in *The Philosophy of Peirce*, ed. Justus Buchler, 269–290 (New York: Harcourt, Brace, and Co., 1950), 277.

Concrete Words   We begin to see the practical utility of semiotics when we begin applying it to matters of style. For instance, most public speaking textbooks advise speakers to use concrete words in their speeches. A **concrete word** has a meaningful reference to specific and readily identifiable qualities or actions in order to give an audience a more vivid experience of some thing or an event. From a semiotic perspective, a concrete word is a familiar sign that immediately calls forth clear and distinct objects that have explicit logical interpretants and powerful emotional interpretants. Peirce defines something that is "clear" as being "so apprehended that it will be recognized where ever it is met with, and so that no other will be mistaken for it. If it fails of this clearness, it is said to be obscure."[18] Too often, we use relatively obscure words like "good" and "people" and "virtuous" because they come to mind easily, usually avoid risk, and are vague enough not to be wrong. When we are not sure what we are talking about and do not want to offend anyone, speaking obscurely is a way of playing it safe. However, obscure language never persuaded anyone of anything. Only language that calls forth vivid images in the mind that carry with them strong emotional and energetic responses can carry the day with rhetoric.

The advice to use concrete words therefore is simply to use clear and powerful words whenever possible. Usually when people think of concrete words, they think of nouns. For instance, the noun *the red table* is preferable to the pronoun *it*, the word *Brazil* is preferable to *country* , or the word *fire ants* is more concrete than *insects*. However, it is important to point out that a concrete word does not refer only to nouns. Concrete words also apply to verbs and adjectives. In terms of verbs, the weakest way of writing is the use of the "passive voice," which makes the subject a target of an action rather than the initiator of one. Consider, for example, "The book <u>was read</u> today" or "He <u>is being</u> punished." Notice how much more "concrete" it sounds to write, instead, "Janet <u>read</u> the book" or "His father <u>punished</u> him." Also, overuse of the verb *to be* tends to make a speech repetitive. A sentence like "I am mad" can be turned into "My blood boils," and "Rain is good" can be turned into "Rain gives life." Finally, adjectives can also be made more concrete. Rather than sticking to generic adjectives such as *good, bad, happy, sad, helpful, harmful*, and the like, try to pick out the specific aspects of a thing that makes it those things. For example, "That's a pretty car" can be made into "The red color on the hood made a striking contrast with the bright white roof." In other words, the more specifically you can describe something, the more vivid the image will be in the mind of the audience and the more they will enjoy your speech.

Figures and Tropes   Whereas concrete words attempt to use clear language that conveys ideas that cannot be mistaken for any others, figures and tropes exploit the capacity for signs to take on multiple meanings and to convey multiple feelings. A **figure** is a series of signs designed to produce emotional interpretants based on an appeal to the ear (e.g., alliteration: "The day dawned with delight"). A figure uses language that departs from its conventional structure for the purpose of integrating

---

[18]Charles Peirce, "How to Make Our Ideas Clear," in *The Philosophy of Peirce*, ed. Justus Buchler, 5–22 (New York: Harcourt, Brace, and Co., 195), 23.

poetic style and a musical sense of rhythm, which usually produces feelings of pleasure and harmony that we associate with beautiful works of art. By contrast, a **trope** is a series of signs designed to produce complex logical interpretants based on appeal to the mind (e.g., metaphor: "The year began with a sigh"). Whereas a figure seduces and calms the ear, a trope stimulates and challenges the mind to discern the logical meaning behind on ironic play of signs. In this case, the mind knows that a year cannot literally begin by exhaling a great deal of air once; it therefore uses the emotional interpretant of "sigh" (being a state of sadness, exhaustion, and resignation) and uses that as the proper sign to interpret the beginning of the year.

Figures are valuable to speeches because they provide a sort of "musical accompaniment" to the speech, thereby setting the tone for the occasion as well as placing the audience in a certain frame of mind to receive the message. It is a commonly known fact that messages tend to be recalled with greater clarity and emotional weight when they have a sense of rhythm and rhyme. The fact that complex song lyrics are easier to remember than clear but abstract definitions indicates the power of figures to leave a lasting impression. The same message conveyed without figures has a far greater chance of being forgotten than the one that was composed by a speaker who took the time to listen carefully to the sound of language with a musical ear. Following are listed some of the most important figures that appear in rhetoric:

1. *Parallelism:* Placing similar rhythmic structures, words, phrases, or clauses into repetitive sequence ("Rich and poor, young and old, they came here to live, and we embraced them with love.").
2. *Antithesis:* The juxtaposition of contrasting ideas, often in parallel structure ("Do not weep for my death, but smile for my having lived.").
3. *Alliteration:* The repetition of words that begin with the same consonant sound ("The soft, slow, surge of the sea.").
4. *Epistrophe:* The repetition of the same word or group of words at the ends of successive clauses ("When we came, they were here. When we left, they were here.").
5. *Repetition:* The repetition of the same word or groups of words at the beginnings of successive clauses ("We shall fight in the land, we shall fight in the sea, we shall fight in the air.").

Tropes are useful because they stimulate the rational imagination to discern the meaning behind signs, thus generating a pleasure in participation very similar to the effects of a good puzzle or a riddle. The basis behind tropes can be understood through the previous discussion of semiotics. As described previously, not only can a single sign refer to multiple objects, but multiple signs can refer to the same object and therefore produce multiple interpretants. For instance, the statement "the man is a lion" is meaningful to us even though we know that the man is not literally a lion. The mind realizes that the two objects cannot be synonymous, so it starts sifting through other possible interpretants of those objects that then can be translated into appropriate meanings. The harder and more difficult the trope, the harder the mind has to work to discern its meaning. This can increase the pleasure and level of participation in an audience when it reaches the correct level of difficulty, but beyond that it becomes too much labor and thereby acts as a repellent to the audience members, who will turn their attention to other things.

Writing tropes that convey the correct meaning and challenge the audience at the ideal level is a most difficult art.[19] Following is a list of the most important tropes:

1. *Metaphor:* A description of one thing directly in terms of something of unlike nature to emphasize a particular quality that they share ("My love is a beautiful rose.").
2. *Synecdoche:* The use of a part of something to stand in for the whole of it ("After the World Trade Center bombings, we were all New Yorkers.").
3. *Metonymy:* A description of something personal and abstract in terms of a concrete object associated with it ("The other baseball team has its two big bats coming up.").
4. *Irony:* The use of a word or phrase in such a way that it conveys the opposite meaning ("Lucky for us, World War I was the war to end all wars.").
5. *Simile:* Explicit comparison between two things of unlike nature (generally using "like" or "as" to make it explicit: "She runs like a deer.").
6. *Personification:* A description of abstract or nonhuman objects as if they possessed human qualities ("The waves leapt forward and pulled me back into the ocean.").
7. *Hyperbole:* The use of extreme exaggeration to highlight a specific quality or idea ("When my boss started yelling at me, I could feel the whole office building shaking.").
8. *Oxymoron:* The placement of two terms together that seem contradictory ("There is no such thing as a smart bomb. They are all equally mindless.").
9. *Paradox:* The statement of an apparent contradiction that nevertheless contains a measure of truth ("How strange it is that getting cancer saved my life. Only now have I come to value what is important in the world.").

Visual Aids A visual aid supplements the verbal component of a speech with graphic displays intended to effectively condense complex material or to convey meanings that cannot be captured with language itself. Visual aids are different from visual rhetoric. In visual rhetoric, the image is the form of persuasion itself—as in a billboard, a political cartoon, or an iconic photograph. This textbook, focusing on the act of speaking, will not address the complexities of visual rhetoric. A **visual aid**, by contrast, is a part of figurative style, using an image to more effectively convey a specific idea or emotion. Such aids include the bar graphs and tables of speech of administration, the personal objects often used in introductory speeches, the graphic images and statistics used in speeches of advocacy to dramatize problems, and the photographs or symbols useful in commemorative speeches in stimulating memory and emotion. Visual aids perform two major functions:

1. They simplify complex information that otherwise could not effectively be explained.
2. They graphically visualize an event, object, person, or process whose details are necessary for understanding a speech.

---

[19]See I. A. Richards, *The Philosophy of Rhetoric* (Oxford, UK: Oxford University Press, 1936).

To be effective, visual aids should be large enough to see and colorful and interesting enough to capture an audience's attention. However, more is not necessarily better. We are often so inundated with visual images that we often assume that we should always try to use as many visual aids as possible. But as a general rule, visual aids should be kept to a minimum and should never be forced into a speech simply to "dress it up" if there is no reason for them to be there. If a good description can describe something with eloquence, then a picture of that event does not "add" to the speech. It replaces or competes with it. Visual aids should never be in competition with the speaker or the speech. Whenever a visual aid takes attention away from the speech itself, it has failed in its purpose as an *aid*. In other words, a visual aid should be used to supplement a speech by performing a task that only a visual aid can perform. For example,

1. A *bar graph* will easily compare the gross national products of twenty nations at a glance.
2. A *line graph* will show the growth and decline of a nation's economy over a decade.
3. A *pie chart* will demonstrate the economic wealth of ten different social classes.
4. A *map* will show where the highest concentrations of population are in a nation.
5. A *representation* will reveal the process of offshore oil drilling.
6. An *object* will best show the amount of butter people were allowed during World War II.
7. A *flowchart* will show the steps that it takes for grain to get to market.
8. A *photograph* will show how far glaciers have retreated in twenty years.
9. A *chalkboard* drawing will spell out what NAFTA stands for.
10. A *handout* will provide an audience with the specific language of a proposed law.
11. A *posterboard* will show different types of fabric manufactured in the 1900s.

The U.S. Occupational Safety and Health Administration website has a useful summary of strategies for visual aids (http://www.osha.gov/doc/outreachtraining/html-files/traintec.html).

Spoken Citation Style   Finally, style deals with the proper way of relating information. Especially for informative speeches, it is vital not only to acquire but to cite and quote accurate sources to give yourself credibility. Here are some guidelines for how to smoothly incorporate citations into your speech.

1. *Well-known and uncontroversial facts:* There is no citation needed for the obvious. Do not clutter a speech by citing things an audience takes for granted.
   a. GOOD. "Over 2,000,000 people were killed in the Civil War."
   b. BAD. "According to *Encyclopedia Online. . . .*"
2. *Unknown or controversial facts released by people and institutions in press releases:* When your information comes directly from the source and you have access to that source, just cite that original source by name. Do not cite any subsequent news publication that may have repeated this information.

    a. GOOD. "The Economy Institute released a report in June that claimed environmental restrictions hurt economic growth."

    b. BAD. "*The Times* reported in July that a report by the Brookings Institute in June said. . . ."

3. *Unknown or controversial facts published secondhand by news publications:* When a newspaper has cited some startling fact, make sure to cite *both* the source and the news publication that first reported it. The fact is that sometimes news reports will "spin" facts in certain ways, so it is important to acknowledge that you are getting it secondhand.

    a. GOOD. "Hodgedale Industries recently was reported in the *New York Times* as saying that its medical screening technologies have saved over 2,000 women's lives in the year 2001."

    b. BAD. "*The New York Times* claims that Hodgedale Industries has saved. . . ."

    c. BAD. "Hodgedale Industries has saved. . . ."

    d. BAD. "Hodgedale Industries claims to have saved. . . ."

4. *Quoting famous people:* Generally, important quotes by famous people only need a citation by the name of the person, not the time, place, or manner in which the passage was written or spoken.

    a. GOOD. "Socrates once said that "the unexamined life is not worth living."

    b. BAD. "In 430 B.C., Socrates was once quoted in Plato's *Critias* that. . . ."

5. *Quoting professionals or experts:* For all other quotes, cite the name, status or position, and the forum in which the quote appeared.

    a. GOOD. "In the *New York Times*, of Sept. 3, Gail Hansen, an epidemiologist who works for Pew Charitable Trusts, said 'at some point the available science can be used in making policy decisions.'"

    b. GOOD. "In today's *New York Times*, a notable epidemiologist said…"

    c. BAD. "Gail Hansen said. . . ."

    d. BAD. "The *New York Times* reported that 'at some point. . . .'"

6. *Citing bare, uncontroversial facts reported in newspapers:* For isolated facts that do not merit a lot of attention, just cite the publication in which that fact appeared.

    a. GOOD. "The *New York Times* reported in 2010 that 34 percent of the population is obese."

    b. BAD. "Thirty-four percent of the population is obese."

    c. BAD. "A study based on national surveys that record heights and weights of a representative sample of Americans, in which people are considered obese if their body mass index—a ratio of height to weight—is thirty or greater, noted that 34 percent of the population is obese."

7. *Using stories or anecdotes found in magazines or websites:* When you use examples, it is important to make them sound like stories. The temptation is to ignore the need for citation. However, it is very important to cite the source and its author to give examples credibility. You simply need to find a discrete way to fit it in without ruining the flow of the narrative.

    a. GOOD. "Anna had just arrived from Russia when she was arrested by police, who accused her of spying. She was put in a cell for two months and was not able to see anyone. Her story, finally told last August in *The New Republic*, raises serious questions about our civil liberties."

    b. BAD. "Anna had just arrived from Russia when she was arrested by police, who accused her of spying. She was put in a cell for two months and was not able to see anyone. Can we let this happen in the United States?"

    c. BAD. "In a recent issue of *The New Republic*, a story appeared about a girl. . . ."

Discussion: We are constantly challenged to judge when a style has "substance" and when it is just "superficial." In terms of our judgments of self, the former is associated with reflections of "character" (like the unique habits of a superstar athlete) and the latter is indicative of mere "fashion" (like that athlete's name-brand merchandise). How do you distinguish between substantial and superficial style? When do you think our style choices not just show something significant about ourselves and our character, but actually form our character?

The Fourth Canon: Memory

The art of memory naturally followed style because once a speech was written, an orator in the Classical age had to memorize it before delivery. **Memory** as the fourth canon refers to the ability to memorize a text and to reproduce it in a manner that seems natural rather than artificial. The canon of memory, in short, is the act of absorbing the content and form of the speech so fully into oneself that the speech feels like an unforced expression of one's thoughts and feelings. Often neglected, the canon of memory remains one of the most important facets of an effective speech for two reasons. For the speaker, memorizing and therefore internalizing a speech provides the level of confidence we normally feel in our casual conversations with others. One of the reasons we do not feel nervous speaking to people during most of the day is the fact that we know what we are going to say and have a reason to say it. When we fail to memorize a speech adequately, we often feel like we are speaking someone else's words and therefore feel awkward and self-conscious. For the audience, hearing a speech that feels like it comes "from the heart" and not from a manuscript or a teleprompter makes the message more powerful and more sincere and therefore creates a much greater feeling of community and participation.

    Unfortunately, memorizing a speech has never become a science. After several thousand years of human beings giving orations and performing dramas, there remain as many techniques for memorizing speeches and lines as there ever have been. However, certain general principles have largely been established that can be useful in developing one's own preferred technique for memorization. It is important to try out various combinations and strategies in order to find the one that best suits you:

1. *Read the speech out loud:* When we read to ourselves silently our minds and bodies are not preparing themselves to perform the text out loud. We read silently to absorb information and to process it, not to memorize it and reproduce it. An absolutely essential component of memorization is reading this speech out loud and in a strong voice that fills the room. Whispering to oneself on the bus will not produce a confident speech. One must find a private place in which one can hear one's own voice.

2. *Practice with your whole body:* Do not practice a speech by sitting in a chair. Use your entire body. Walk around the room (ideally the room where you will be speaking) and use gestures as you speak to an imaginary audience. The more your body becomes engaged in the speech act, the more your mind becomes engaged as well. Treat your body as a partner in the speech and it will help you.

3. *Record and listen to yourself:* Listening to your own voice not only helps you improve delivery by hearing your own voice as an audience would hear it; it also improves memory by externalizing your voice and making you encounter it as you might encounter popular song lyrics.

4. *Break the speech into parts:* Think of a speech as you might think of rooms in a house. Each part of the speech should be a room with its own unique feel and purpose. Practice each part of the speech separately. Spend time in each room getting to know what it is like, including where you walk in and where you leave. Only after you know the atmosphere of each room should you put together the entire house tour.

5. *Use graphic conceptualization:* Diagram your speech on a piece of paper using creative images and drawings that represent your main points and forms of evidence. Feel free to be as ridiculous as possible, just so long as you remember the meanings of your icons. We may forget the specific words of a written manuscript; but we will not forget that we drew a picture of a person sunbathing next to an unhappy polar bear to remind us of the fact that global warming will melt the ice caps.

6. *Identify key points:* Try to summarize your speech out loud to yourself in as condensed a manner as possible, as if you were simply describing to somebody what your speech is "generally about" in casual conversation. This provides a general cognitive roadmap that allows you to always get back to the speech should you ever stumble or get lost.

7. *Take breaks:* Relying on one extended practice session is generally not sufficient to good memorization. Memory needs time to filter out what is important and then to solidify long-term memory by continually returning to the same thing. Taking breaks for a couple of hours, during which time you do nothing that is related to the speech, is often very helpful in retention. Memorization is a process and not a one-time event.

Discussion: In professional life, the importance of memory is made clear in both interview settings and formal business presentations. In both cases, using notecards or scripts often shows a person to lack knowledge and confidence, whereas the ability to answer questions about oneself or one's sphere of expertise simply from memory holds an audience's attention and commands their respect. What are some common techniques you have used in preparation for these situations? How successful were they?

The Fifth Canon: Delivery

The final requirement of rhetorical "form" is delivery. **Delivery** deals with the manner in which a speaker physically performs the speech through crafted use of the voice and gesture. Whereas the canon of style addresses the manner in which a speech is composed through words, the canon of delivery addresses the manner in which a speech is actually performed with the body. Although conceptually the simplest of the canons, it perhaps is the most difficult to master and requires a great deal of training and experience. It also is one of the most important. Emerson provides the following encomium to deliver in his essay "Eloquence," focusing specifically on the importance of voice:

> A good voice has a charm in speech as in song; sometimes of itself enchains attention, and indicates a rare sensibility, especially when trained to wield all its powers. The voice, like the face, betrays the nature and disposition, and soon indicates what is the range of the speaker's mind...Every one of us has at some time been the victim of a well-toned and cunning voice, and perhaps been repelled once for all by a harsh, mechanical speaker. The voice, indeed, is a delicate index of the state of mind. I have heard an eminent preacher say that he learns from the first tones of his voice on a Sunday morning whether he is to have a successful day. A singer cares little for the words of the song; he will make any words glorious.[20]

For Emerson, not only can for delivery to undermine even the most carefully crafted composition, but it can also turn ordinary ideas into a glorious oration. Delivery has this power because of the unique capacity of the human voice to portray what Emerson refers to as the "nature and disposition" of the speaker. We are naturally drawn to people who speak with confidence and grace and power, trusting that the ideas contained within the language match the character in virtue conveyed through voice and stature.

Considered in its specific parts, the components of delivery are as follows:

1. *Appearance:* How a speaker dresses and physically presents him- or herself in terms of grooming and posture? The function of **appearance** is not only to please the eye but also to identify oneself to an audience as a certain type of person who will deliver the message in a certain type of way.
2. *Gesture:* How one uses one's arms, legs, and face to convey nonverbal meanings. The function of gesture is to condense complex meanings into simple and elegant movements. Oftentimes we can say with a look what requires several sentences in words.
3. *Position:* How a speaker orients his or her body with respect to the audience, including the choice of whether to stand behind a podium, walk around, or sit down. The function of position is to develop a certain relationship to an audience and to the environment in which one is speaking.
4. *Eye contact:* The degree to which a speaker actually looks at members of the audience while speaking. Merely glancing at the audience during moments of silence does not constitute eye contact. Ideally, one must "look" as if one is having a conversation with somebody. The function of eye contact is to create a relationship with the audience.

---

[20]http://rwe.org/complete-works/viii-letters-and-social-aims/eloquence.html.

5. *Articulation:* How distinctly words are pronounced so that each stands out. The opposite of articulation is mumbling. The function of articulation is to convey the impression that each word is meaningful and deserves attention.

6. *Pronunciation:* Being able to accurately pronounce words. The function of pronunciation is not only to accurately convey meaning but to show one's own credibility.

7. *Dialect:* Local phrasings common in a particular group but not used universally. The function of dialect is to either emphasize the unique characteristic of one's heritage to an audience that does not speak in it or to create a sense of identification with an audience that does.

8. *Pitch:* A musical term that refers to the ability to speak each word as if it was a separate note in a melody, moving up and down the scale. (Function: See Rate.)

9. *Volume:* The dynamic between softly and stridently spoken parts of the speech. (Function: See Rate.)

10. *Pauses:* The intentional silences that punctuate a speech. (Function: See Rate.)

11. *Rate:* The dynamic between rapidly and slowly spoken parts of the speech. Collectively, the function of pitch, volume, pauses, and rate is to convey emotional and connotative meaning as well as create tensions and resolutions. These are the most "musical" qualities of a speech and consequently have the most emotional and aesthetic effects on an audience.

Although it is important to consider each of these elements of delivery individually, when actually performing the speech one should think of delivery as a coherent whole. An effective way to think of the overall strategy of delivery is simply to consider how different acting styles dramatically alter the way that an audience interprets the language of a character. Just as different actors bring different elements to the same character, different delivery styles alter the way the same speech text is received. Consequently, one should think of an oratorical rostrum as a kind of stage in which one steps into a certain "role" or "character." Rather than isolating each of the elements of delivery and building them up into a unity, one should simply think of certain familiar performance styles and imitate them as best one can. Not only does this method provide a coherent delivery style to imitate, but it also puts speakers into a performative frame of mind that relieves the anxiety of feeling as if they have to "be themselves." The fact is that when people are delivering public speeches, the last thing they should do is act like they always act in everyday life. A speech is a performance and should be treated as such. Indeed, it is not infrequent that people who are quiet or reserved in everyday conversation turn out to be the best public speakers. As Emerson says, "The most hard-fisted, disagreeably restless, thought-paralyzing companion sometimes turns out in a public assembly to be a fluent, various and effective orator."[21] The rostrum can be liberating for those who know it is a performance.

---

[21]http://rwe.org/complete-works/viii-letters-and-social-aims/eloquence.html.

Here are some general tips for preparing for delivery:

1. *Put the speech to memory:* All of the advice included in the canon of delivery will assist in producing a competent and persuasive delivery. Even the most charismatic individuals find it hard to look confident and composed when they forget their lines and must continually look down at their notecards. If the core elements of the speech are not adequately memorized, attempts at delivery often appear mechanical and forced.

2. *Know your audience:* Although this does not appear directly related to delivery, it is actually one of the most important elements. It is the difference between how we engage in conversations with our friends and how we speak to strangers. When we know our audience, we instinctively adapt our manner of speaking to their personalities and expectations, most notably in our level of formality but also in many other subtle aspects, including our rate of speaking, our volume, our level of animation, our use of humor, and our incorporation of slang terms or jargon. Knowing something about the audience ahead of time allows us to develop a presentation style adapted to their attitudes.

3. *Know yourself:* Not only is good delivery contingent on knowing the audience, it is also contingent on knowing how one stands in relationship to that audience. In our everyday interactions with other people, we play many roles adapted to those situations—for example, father, sister, friend, boss, employee, classmate, customer, entertainer, and so on. "Knowing yourself" with respect to public speaking does not refer to a deep philosophical inquiry into the soul; it simply means know who you are for the people you are speaking to at that moment. Oftentimes, awkward speaking situations arise because speakers try to play a role that they are not suited for, most comically when older professionals try to speak to younger students as if they are "classmates" and adopt the students' mannerisms and ways of speaking. Adapting to an audience does not mean mimicking it; it simply means understanding the audience's needs and expectations and trying to fulfill them using the best of one's own resources.

4. *Know the speaking environment:* Whenever possible, a speaker should become familiar with the environment in which the speech is to occur, regardless of whether it is in a room, a park, a stadium, or an auditorium. The serves several purposes: (a) knowing the environment simply makes one feel more comfortable, much as walking into a gym familiarizes a visiting basketball team; (b) if the speech is to be amplified, testing equipment makes the speaker accustomed to the sound of his or her own voice; and (c) standing at the rostrum (or equivalent) allows a speaker to know where the audience will be sitting, where he or she can move while speaking, and what physical elements of the environment might be useful to incorporate into a speech in passing reference (e.g., the giant moose head hanging on the wall behind the podium as a resource for an opening joke).

5. *Have something to say:* It is very difficult to give an inspired delivery if the speech itself is boring and uninteresting for the speaker. Delivery is a natural outgrowth of enthusiasm, and enthusiasm is difficult to fake. Many

people who are charismatic and charming in their everyday interactions are surprised to find themselves speaking awkwardly and timidly when they step up to the rostrum because of the mistaken impression that their charisma and charm will make lemonade out of lemons. The only thing that a speech made out of lemons will produce is a sour taste and considerable disappointment.

6. *Break the speech into dramatic acts:* Think of a speech as a play. Determine the "feel" of each act and develop a performance style that makes the most of the material. Ideally, each act should demand a slightly different type of delivery. For instance, the introduction may require a storytelling delivery in which the speaker steps away from the rostrum and speaks directly to the audience in a lively and animated style. But the story may serve to introduce a serious thesis that demands a more formal delivery that sticks closer to the text that is read from the podium. And this action, in turn, might be followed by a commentary on a video presentation and then conclude with an informal question-and-answer session.

7. *Rehearse nonverbal gestures in front of a mirror:* Identify key moments in the speech that create opportunities for specific facial gestures or hand movements that can reinforce the points or themes in the speech. The importance of mastering these sorts of gestures can be seen in the act of standup comedians in particular, when the success or failure of jokes often is dependent on very subtle bodily movements and expressions. Rehearse these in front of a mirror until they become natural.

8. *Vary rate, pitch, volume, and pauses:* Public speaking requires us to speak in a manner that is much more animated and musical than our everyday speech. Experiment with different speech patterns as you would think of trying to create different ways of singing song lyrics. Record yourself saying the same sentence multiple ways to hear the difference. Avoid the mundane speech pattern of simply speaking each word with the same volume and rate and then simply dropping the pitch at the end of the sentence.

9. *Rehearse for time:* Do not time yourself by reading silently. Speaking out loud always takes more time than silent reading. Practice the speech from beginning to end and time yourself to ensure that you stay within set limits. Failing to rehearse for time creates enormous speaking anxiety once a speaker realizes he or she is approaching or over the allotted time.

Speaking Anxiety   A speaker may say brilliant things, but if delivery is lacking, nobody is going to pay attention to what is said. Not surprisingly, then, the pressure that accompanies delivery leads many people to have intense speaking anxiety that is difficult to overcome. It is thus appropriate that our discussion of delivery continues with this challenge. Fear of public speaking traditionally ranks among the top three fears that people have. Being nervous, scared, and worried before making a public speech is completely normal. Michael Beatty identified eight factors of a speech situation that tend to increase **speaking anxiety**: the novelty of the experience, the formality of the occasion, the subordinate status of the speaker, the degree of conspicuousness felt by the speaker, an unfamiliar environment, the dissimilarity and degree of attention from others, the degree to which one is being evaluated, and prior history.[22] Added to these situational factors is also the degree to which speaking anxiety, for many people, is akin to an inborn, genetic predisposition.[23]

Dealing with speaking anxiety is thus a complex challenge, as each speaker's anxiety will be unique and derived from different sources. The following are some basic strategies for dealing with speaking anxiety that can be employed by any speaker in preparation for a speech:[24]

1. *Nervousness is natural:* Being nervous is a biological manifestation of the "fight-or-flight" mechanism. It shows that your body is preparing you to deal with a challenging situation. The goal is not to get rid of nervousness but to harness that energy and use it to your advantage.
2. *Everyone experiences it:* Speaking anxiety is universal. Even the greatest speakers get anxious because so much is riding on their words. But the feelings they experience are the same as those of a beginning student. The difference is that they have more tools to deal with that anxiety.
3. *You appear more relaxed than you feel:* Anxiety rarely manifests itself in overt signs of stress that can be seen by an audience. The most common expressions of stress are shaking hands and flushed faces, but usually they bother the speaker more than the audience.
4. *Have something important to say:* Nothing rattles a speaker more than standing up only to find that one's speech is boring even to oneself. Hastily written speeches made simply to "get it over with" are, more often than not, the causes of speaking anxiety because one starts judging one's own speech as a failure. Taking the time to say something you want to say makes speaking a much more pleasurable experience.
5. *Visualize success:* Like almost any coach in competitive sports will tell you, if you focus on the little things, you will get so caught up in minutiae that you lose sight of the "big picture." As simplistic as it sounds, sometimes success comes from visualizing oneself succeeding.
6. *Release tension before speaking:* Purely on a physical note, clenching and then releasing muscles or exerting energy in some way loosens you up and often gets rid of nervousness that has been built up in your muscles.
7. *The audience is usually on your side:* With rare political exceptions, people do not attend speeches to watch people fail. They attend speeches to listen to people they find interesting. Hence, the audience will almost always wish for a speaker to do well. Despite the fact that they are ultimately "judging" your speech, they are a jury that hopes you succeed.

---

[22]M. J. Beatty, "Situational and Predispositional Correlates of Public Speaking Anxiety," *Communication Education* 37 (1988c), 28–39.

[23]M. J. Beatty et al., "Communication Apprehension as Temperamental Expression: A Communibiological Paradigm," *Communication Monographs* 65 (1998), 197–219.

[24]For more on speaking anxiety, see Virginia P. Richmond and James C. McCroskey, *Communication: Apprehension, Avoidance, and Effectiveness,* 5th ed. (Boston: Allyn & Bacon, 1998); Peter Desberg, *No More Butterflies: Overcoming Stagefright, Shyness, Interview Anxiety, and Fear of Public Speaking* (Oakland, CA: New Harbinger, 1996).

8. *Practice:* Nothing replaces simple practice. Simply knowing the words of a speech is not sufficient for a good performance. You need to feel "at one" with the speech so that your words and actions occur naturally together. Practice until you have memorized the speech and then practice again until you have completely internalized it. Usually, shoot for reading a speech out loud to yourself three times before delivering it to your audience. Reading it "in your head" *is not* the same as reading out loud. Actually verbalizing the words helps your mouth get used to saying the words and your ears get used to hearing them.

9. *Experience makes you more confident:* The more you speak in public, the easier it will become. We learn by habit, and public speaking can become a habit once you break through the initial fear. By the end of a public speaking class, one may even begin to find pleasure in this habit.

This series of "tips" addresses the basics of putting oneself in the right frame of mind for public speaking. However, not all speaking anxiety can be dealt with by such simple attitude adjustments. A more systematic and clinical list of treatments includes the following:[25]

1. *Systemic desensitization:* This procedure attempts to change unconscious negative associations with speaking situations. First, it introduces students to methods of relaxation (e.g., meditation), and once relaxed, a trainer has them visualize a series of speech situations, beginning with the least stressful and progressively increasing in perceived anxiety. Through repetition, individuals become more familiar with public speaking situations, thus normalizing them.

2. *Cognitive modification:* This treatment deals with negative and irrational cognitions of public speaking that take the form of beliefs, such as "I can't do this" or "It's too frightening." With a trained therapist, individuals discuss specific fears about public speaking, including their self-evaluations, after which the therapist shows the irrationality of such self-evaluations and provides a coping statement (e.g., "I can handle this") that can be used while speaking.

3. *COM therapy:* Another method of treatment is to change an individual's orientation toward the function of public speaking. For those who hold a "performance-oriented" view, public speaking is like a trial by jury in which one is to perform and be judged. COM therapy attempts to change this orientation into a "communication-oriented" view in which public speaking is more like conversation in which each party is simply taking longer turns.

4. *Visualization:* Similar to systemic desensitization, visualization also begins with relaxation techniques, but instead of focusing simply on familiarizing oneself with the public speaking context, it focuses on visualizing success within that context. Visualization is thus a natural extension of cognitive modification.

---

[25]The following list is a paraphrased summary of the conclusions presented in Graham D. Bodie, "A Racing Heart, Rattling Knees, and Ruminative Thoughts: Defining, Explaining, and Treating Public Speaking Anxiety." *Communication Education* 59, no. 1 (Jan. 2010), 70–105.

5. *Skills training:* Skills training is another way of saying that practice, experience, and mastery will improve the confidence of public speakers.

6. *Performance feedback:* Another term for *constructive criticism*, performance feedback involves using nonverbal, oral, or written responses to a speaker's performance directed toward improving that performance. Notably, research shows that negative comments (when given in a constructive and honest spirit) are more helpful than positive ones, as they give speakers a sense that they know the problem and have the means to address it.

After years of research, studies have shown that no one method tends to work for all individuals. Each person faces his or her own particular type of anxiety and must develop a method tailored to individual needs. However, employing a variety of methods at different times, each overlapping the other, tends to have more benefit than adopting only one.

Delivery Form   One of the most basic elements of any speaking genre involves the expectations for how the speech is going to be delivered. The choice of how you will deliver your speech has important consequences for how it will be received by an audience. The choice also opens up and limits certain possibilities for how a speech will be written, how much information it will contain, and how long it will be. The following are considerations in delivery form:

1. *Manuscript:* Reading from a manuscript means writing out every word of a speech and delivering it as written. Except in cases with a teleprompter, the manuscript should be on a podium and the speaker should have practiced the speech to the extent that much of it has been partially memorized. This allows a speaker to look down briefly to keep his or her place but still maintain eye contact with an audience. In this regard, it is helpful to write marks on the speech for when to breathe (~), when to look up (↑), and when to look back down (↓) so that you can memorize particular sections that you think warrant a more significant delivery. Manuscript reading allows for a careful sculpting of stylistic language (in the cases of commemorative speaking) or complex arguments (in deliberative speaking) that would otherwise be difficult to convey. Manuscripts are most proper for formal occasions in which the audience expects and demands this kind of complexity and subtlety. However, manuscript may provide a "crutch" that speakers rely on too much, which causes them to effectively ignore the audience and deliver the speech as if they were simply reading out loud.[26]

2. *Memory:* Delivering from memory is to write a manuscript first and then rehearse it until one knows it by heart. At its best, it has all the advantages of manuscript style without the disadvantages, for it allows a speaker to engage an audience directly and to walk around a "stage" without being tied to a podium. However, speeches from memory also put one at great risk. If one forgets even the smallest part of a speech, there is the danger that one's mind

---

[26]See James C. Humes, *Talk Your Way to the Top* (New York: McGraw-Hill, 1980).

might go blank like that of an actor in a play, at which point there is nothing to help the speaker find his or her place. In addition, relying on memory makes it almost impossible to adapt to an audience during the speech, such as when external interference occurs or when a speaker simply realizes that something isn't working. Speeches from memory are thus best when they are short and have only a few simple points, such as a wedding toast or an argument in a public meeting. They also are excellent for storytelling exercises, as stories are easier to remember and audiences enjoy hearing stories from people as if they simply sprung naturally from memory.

3. *Impromptu:* Delivering impromptu speeches means to speak without preparation on a subject given to you at the moment. This form is the most natural and spontaneous and thus often the most interesting to hear. However, it also limits one's ability to sculpt a careful argument and also provides no safety net should one run out of ideas. The classic case of impromptu speaking is parliamentary debate, in which a subject is announced and debaters have just a few minutes to come up with opposing arguments. Exercises of this kind, also helpful in public speaking classes, allows you the freedom to be creative and to gain experience speaking before audiences without having anything "at stake." In public, impromptu speaking may be required during deliberative meetings, such as in the boardroom, the town hall, or the family kitchen, and also during celebratory occasions in which people are called upon to make a speech about themselves or others. And sometimes impromptu speaking is simply a way to entertain friends.

4. *Extemporaneous:* The essential feature of this speech is the notecard, which includes key points, quotes, and transitions drawn from a larger outline but leaves the speaker to fill in the gaps during the actual delivery of the speech. This form provides structure but allows for adaptation in such a way that, ideally, the speaker will be able to connect with the audience on a personal level while still making a formal argument or presentation. A good notecard will thus be easy to read, will not be cluttered with information, and will support the speech by providing both information and delivery instructions, such as when to look up, when to make a gesture, when to speak loudly, and when to slow down. Extemporaneous speeches are ideal for people making "official" presentations in front audience members who feel free to break in and ask questions at any time. The speaker is able to deal with such interruptions because he or she still has all the important information directly at hand, and he or she can flip backward and forward without completely disrupting the flow of the speech.

Discussion: Although attention to delivery in public speaking often feels forced, we in fact modify our delivery all the time to suit different occasions. The words, pace, volume, and articulation of our language varies depending on whether we are speaking to parents, friends, employers, teachers, or strangers. Think of a time when you had to "break bad news" to multiple people at different times. How did you adapt your delivery for each audience in order to maximize positive effects and minimize negative ones based on your understanding of the situation?

KEY WORDS

SUMMARY

Delivering a rhetorical speech is the consummation of a long process that begins not with an "idea" but with a response to a situation. Rhetoric draws its energy from its surroundings and puts it into a form capable of mobilizing public audiences to act in such a way that corrects that situation, in either the long or the short term. By "form," then, we do not simply mean a pre-given shape, like a template or shell. Form means the ability to rouse the interests, energies, and appetites of an audience, to carry them through a logical and narrative structure from one place to another, and to bring together elements in such a way that satisfies these interests and leaves a lasting impression on the mind, imagination, and emotions. A good rhetorical speech therefore constructs a message that produces "form" in the psychology of the audience by giving form to a previously unformed situation, an act that produces both pleasure and learning.

The canons of rhetoric provide a method for building a speech that produces such form. Invention reveals to us where to find material for persuasion by showing us where and how to look. Most of the time, we cannot find things because we are not looking in the right place or with the right perspective. *Invention* provides categories that are helpful in focusing our attention on specific aspects of our environment to see what we can find, much like one would use a flashlight in a dark room. *Arrangement* then provides conventional templates or frameworks we can use to organize the things that we have found. It helps us rearrange material in new patterns to find the most appropriate and effective way to bring order out of a chaos of resources, much as the way a certain type of case influences the way we display a loose collection of items. *Style* then brings all of these elements together into a fluid whole by crafting language that embeds specific facts and examples within more pleasing and comprehensible images and feelings. Style is often the jagged edges of specific parts of the speech as well as the arrangement of these parts in such a way that the whole thing is attractive to an audience because it seems like all of the parts fit together smoothly, much as a meal is given style not by adding a superficial garnish but by actually uniting all the flavors and textures into a single elegant dish. *Memory* provides the techniques for making a speech feel like a natural expression of one's self rather than a written text. Committing a speech to memory is very much like an actor learning his or her lines so that the words feel as if they are one's own. Last, *delivery* ensures that the brilliance of the composition is effectively transmitted to the audience through the actions and words of the speaker. Delivery is the medium by which speaker and audience communicate and the means by which they are able to cooperate in producing form.

Perhaps the most important lesson the canons teach us is that producing a speech is not something that happens all at once. A good speaker does not simply sit down and produce a speech text in one sitting. The best speeches are those that grow in stages, with each part of the canon potentially influencing other parts, and in no particular order. Although there is certainly a sequential logic implied in how the canons are organized, in actual practice there is a more back-and-forth movement. Sometimes a good speech simply begins with a metaphor. Other times one is given an arrangement and has to find content to fill it. Frequently when a speaker rehearses the speech out loud, he or she hears something that is incorrect or needs elaboration, thus returning the speaker to invention. And finally there are moments when memory subtly alters the speech we had written and when we make impromptu changes in arrangement during delivery because of the demands of adaptation. The point is simply that by looking at a speech as a product of multiple methods, we are given multiple ways of improving a speech over time.

CHAPTER 1 EXERCISES

1. Select a speech on americanrhetoric.com that you will explore throughout the semester. This will be called your "rhetorical artifact." No two students should have the same speech. Now outline the speech according to the basic outlining structure that was previously discussed, such as breaking the speech into its main points, identifying its thesis, and documenting its evidence and sources.

2. Break yourselves into four groups. Each group should concentrate on making a speech that argues the same point. (This argument should not require research and should be simple and creative, e.g., "Everyone should get a dog" or "Chickens should not cross roads."). Each group should select a different strategy of introduction, conclusion, and way of structuring main points. Each group should then present its argument, and the class should judge which was the most persuasive.

3. Have the instructor provide every student the same short editorial or opinion piece. Each student is then responsible for making an impromptu speech of a few short sentences that argues some point (it does not matter what) and explicitly quotes the article for support. The intention here is to develop the skills of verbal citation style.

4. Bring in one of your favorite poems that employs many of the tools of style. Memorize it and deliver it in front of the class.

5. Choose an editorial from a national newspaper. Translate that editorial into two notecards (written by hand). Deliver a speech from the notecards that conveys the argument of the editorial as if you were the author (i.e., without actually quoting the article or citing it as an authority).

6. Select a famous passage by an American president that is part of public memory. Have everyone in class memorize it and deliver it differently. Discuss how delivery style altered the meaning of the speech and what it reminded you of.

7. As a class, select a particular topic of controversy. Everyone should do a search for sources from (a) a website, (b) a book, and (c) an academic journal article. Compare these sources as a class, and determine which sources are most appropriate for the topic and which methods were most productive in finding them.

Genres of Public Speaking

This chapter defines the appropriate contexts for public speaking and identifies the genres that are appropriate for distinct occasions. The notion of rhetorical "genre" refers to different arrangements of elements in a composition or discourse that are appropriate to certain occasions. Identifying what kind of genre is appropriate within a situation is perhaps the most important consideration any public speaker can make, for it provides the proper "form" in which claims can be made and ideas structured and expressed. Although the number of speech genres is, literally, countless, they generally can be divided into speeches of introduction, identification, deliberation, solicitation, commemoration, enrichment, administration, and advocacy. The goal of this chapter is to provide a general method of organization and invention that enables a public speaker to achieve a level of decorum.

All **public speeches** are interpreted by members of an audience as fitting a certain "genre." A rhetorical speech **genre** represents a coherent and recognized arrangement of elements in a composition or discourse that is appropriate to certain occasions and that creates audience expectations that constrain and guide a speech's content, style, and delivery. In rhetoric, genres are not properties of the speeches themselves in the way we think of, for example, color as a property of flowers; genres exist primarily in the mind. A genre is a method of interpreting a particular type of object, much in the way that a painting of flowers by Monet would be interpreted by the genre "Impressionism," whereas a painting of flowers by Picasso might be interpreted by the genre "Cubism." Genres are therefore practical tools that speakers can use to anticipate and control the reactions of an audience. Related to notions of appropriateness and occasion, speaking genres refer to what people *actually expect* (and prepare themselves to hear) when they attend a speech, much in the way that rooms in museums are given "generic" labels so that visitors will know what to expect on entering.[1]

---

[1]The importance of expectation is emphasized by Karlyn Kohrs Campbell and Kathleen Hall Jamieson, who write that: "A genre is a group of acts unified by a constellation of forms that recurs in each of its members. . . . External factors, including human needs and exposure to antecedent rhetorical forms, create expectations which constrain rhetorical responses. By the internal dynamic of fused elements also creates expectations which testify to its constraining force. Generic exemplars have an internal consistency." Karlyn Kohrs Campbell and Kathleen Hall Jamieson, "Form and Genre in Rhetorical Criticism: An Introduction," in *Readings in Rhetorical Criticism*, ed. Carl R. Burgchardt (State College, PA: Strata Publishing Co., 1995), 403.

The function of a genre is therefore to provide an audience with a framework of interpretation that situates any novelty within a stable and predictable structure that the audience can readily understand. Audiences attend and listen to public speeches at certain occasions with certain expectations of what they will hear and how they will hear it. Attendees of celebrity roasts, for example, *expect* that good friends of the "roastee" will all stand up to offer witty but biting remarks at his or her expense. To hear someone praise the host would be to violate the norms of appropriateness for the occasion—it would be to ignore the constraints of the speaking genre. The political stump speech also represents a certain genre, as does the religious sermon, the graduation speech, the parental lecture, the soapbox diatribe, the tearful public apology, the sales pitch, the friendly advice, the boss's reprimand, and the coach's inspirational rant. When we encounter these types of speeches, we can expect to hear certain things while knowing that other parts will be left out.

As with most things rhetorical, it was Aristotle who provided the first articulate categorization of the speech genres. When Aristotle defined the three dominant rhetorical genres, he based his definitions on what he saw in actual life. As the foremost scholar of Greek civilization, Aristotle could not ignore rhetoric precisely because it was so ingrained in almost every aspect of the Greek world. For a Greek philosopher to ignore rhetoric was to ignore what it meant to be a Greek in the Classical age. In his time, most public affairs were dealt with through the medium of face-to-face **public speaking**. Speeches in the courts (law), in the assembly (politics), and at ceremonial events (culture) structured and guided the collective life of the city-state. Aristotle's genres thus corresponded to these circumstances: **Forensic speech** occurred in law courts, dealt with the past, and addressed matters of the just and unjust, **Deliberative speech** occurred in the assembly, dealt with the future, and addressed matters of the expedient and the inexpedient, and **epideictic speech** occurred at ceremonial events, dealt with the present (or eternal), and addressed matters of praise and blame (including the playful praise and blame of animals and things).

Aristotle's crucial insight is his definition of a genre not by the qualities of the speech itself but by the expectations of the audience under the circumstances of the occasion. As he writes: "rhetoric falls into three divisions, determined by the three classes of listeners to speeches. For of the three elements in speechmaking—speaker, subject, and person addressed—it is the last one, the hearer, that determines the speech's end and object."[2] The rhetorical speech genres of deliberative, forensic, and epideictic should therefore be considered *ways of listening* before they should be considered *ways of speaking*. That is to say, we identify a speech as a certain type of genre less because of the inherent qualities in the speech itself and more because we interpret those qualities as being designed to satisfy certain expectations in an audience. When we visit a parliamentary body we expect to hear deliberative debates about what to do about pending problems; when we enter a courtroom we expect to hear forensic debates about the nature and quality of past actions; and when we gather for national holidays we expect to hear epideictic

---

[2]1358b1.

addresses giving praise to the objects, events, and people we value as a nation. To fail to satisfy these expectations as a speaker is not to deliver one genre instead of another; it is simply not to deliver the goods at all.

The important lesson to be taken away from this discussion is that any successful speech must begin with a detailed consideration of the expectations of an audience before developing persuasive strategies to meet those expectations. Too often, speakers begin composing speeches by asking the question: "What do I want to say?" The actual question to begin with is: "What does my audience want to hear?" In other words, the outgoing act of listening by audience members always precedes successful expression by the speaker. After all, rhetorical public speaking as an oral performance is not delivered to a random group of people who simply happen to have found themselves at the same place at the same time. They have gathered there for a reason. They have a purpose for listening. For the speaker to take their interest for granted, and then to simply say whatever happens to be on his or her mind, reveals a speaker who is highly inconsiderate and overly self-involved. Thinking about your speech in terms of conforming to a genre is therefore an essential step in the act of composition, for it encourages thinking about the listener as an active agent rather than a passive target.

Although Aristotle's three categories remain useful in interpreting contemporary speeches, new speech genres are necessary to adapt to changing speech contexts. Unfortunately, the tradition of public speaking has long held to the rather unimaginative triad of informative, persuasive, and commemorative speaking, usually understood to mean speeches that convey accurate and relevant information, speeches that take a position pro or con on an issue, and speeches that praise something the speaker thinks is valuable. The problem with these categories is that they do not begin with the listener and the occasion, but instead imply that the nature of the speech is rooted in the intentions of the speaker and in the structure of the speech. Anyone who has taught public speaking for any length of time using such categories has encountered situations in which "The life of our Savior Jesus Christ" is submitted as an informative speech, in which "Why I think smoking is bad for you" is submitted as a persuasive speech, and in which "My loyal dog Max" is submitted as a commemorative speech. From the perspective of the speaker, these may seem to be valid speech topics. But from the perspective of the audience (in this case being a diverse group of two dozen university students), they are not. Clearly the "informative" speech will be interpreted by most people as being persuasive, the "persuasive" speech will be interpreted by most people as being redundant, and the "commemorative" speech will be largely frivolous. But these topics are difficult to reject using criteria that do not bring the audience into account.

Compounding this problem is the fact that the distinction between "informative" and "persuasive" speaking is largely erroneous. As Aristotle and every other Greek well understood, rhetoric is the art of **persuasion**. Consequently, there is no such thing as a rhetorical public speech that does not persuade in some way. The only question is what it is persuasive *about*. But that question cannot be understood apart from the perspective of the audience. On the one hand, the most dry and technical "informative" speech may be interpreted very persuasively by specific audiences. To use a very simple example, a speech about the history and origin of the myth of Santa Claus would be considered by most adults to be an informative speech. But for a three-year-old child, it would be a highly persuasive speech intended to challenge one of his or her most core beliefs. On the other hand, the most passionately delivered "persuasive" speech may be completely boring to audience member who already believe everything that the speaker is trying to advocate. No child, after all, wastes her time trying to persuade her brothers and sisters that Santa Claus should bring them all as many gifts as possible. The child instead tries to persuade her siblings that Santa Claus favors her the most and hence will give her the most gifts—a most difficult, if not impossible, task.

This chapter will therefore replace the conventional categories with speeches of introduction, identification, deliberation, solicitation, commemoration, enrichment, administration, and advocacy. The goal of these new categorizations is to focus attention on the occasion of the speech and the expectations of the listeners during those occasions in such a way that provides a general roadmap for how to structure a speech so as to satisfy those expectations. However, it is important to keep in mind that each term only points out the dominant *tendency* of certain speeches delivered at certain occasions. For just as all speeches persuade, most speeches, in some way, also *introduce, identify, deliberate, solicit, commemorate, enrich, administer,* and *advocate.* Yet each individual speech will emphasize certain tendencies over others and may ignore some tendencies completely. One should think of each tendency of a speech as being one column on a music equalizer, therefore giving each speech its own unique equalization. Selecting a speech genre is therefore much like selecting a preset equalization on a stereo as a starting point before making more detailed modifications based on the unique circumstance.

Discussion: Consider Aristotle's three speech genres of forensic, deliberative, and epideictic and their respective emphasis on the past and justice/injustice, the future and expediency/inexpediency, and the present and praise/blame. Now consider the perspective of a parent in a household. In what context does a parent make these three types of speeches in a family context? In which room do they occur most of the time? What is the purpose of each type of speech, and what kinds of situations does each respond to?

SPEECHES OF INTRODUCTION

Speeches of **introduction** seek to establish the ground for a productive and positive future relationship with an audience of strangers by using narratives to disclose central aspects of one's character that the speaker believes he or she shares with others. In many ways, an introductory speech fulfills the same function as a conversation or interview. However, the context is different. Whereas conversations or interviews happen among a few people, speeches of introduction are given before a larger group. Introductory speeches thus emphasize perhaps the first dominant quality of public speaking: generally, the establishing of a relationship between speaker and audience that is meant to endure beyond the meaning of the message itself. In introductory speaking, the important facts are not so much the words coming out of one's mouth, but the very fact that one has made the effort to be present before others.

There are two typical occasions for such speeches. First, introductory speeches are given by candidates for official positions vying for support or by those who have newly been assigned some official position and who wish to introduce themselves to a group. In these cases, speeches of introduction are meant to solicit support and establish credibility. Second, introductory speeches are given by members of a group who wish to establish friendly and trustworthy relationships with one another. The speeches are either delivered by select individuals who have recently been assigned a role in a pre-established group (such as a new boss at work) or are delivered by each member of an impromptu group of strangers (such as a newly formed neighborhood book club) who have come together to pursue a shared goal. The overall goal of introductory speeches in this context is to create trust and a feeling of cooperation.

The *listeners* for introductory speeches are people who expect to have some future interaction with the speaker in a cooperative environment, such as the workplace, the dormitory, the church, the classroom, the athletic team, or the community association. Consequently, they will want to gauge the overall attitudes and interests of the speaker in order to know what to expect of the speaker and to determine whether there are any qualities or experiences that they share that can form the basis of future conversations. The *speaker* in such occasions should usually present him- or herself as "one of the group" by speaking with good humor but also with humility, thereby avoiding the sense that one is simply putting on a show for the sake of applause. This does not mean having to dress and speak like everyone else, of course. One should preserve one's own unique personality in an introductory speech. The point is rather that one should not amplify such unique traits as a way of "impressing" an audience with one's charm and intellect, which usually simply serves to alienate one from the group. The *speaker* should strive to preserve individuality while at the same time putting him- or herself on the same level with others. The content of the *message* should largely be stories and anecdotes that are intrinsically interesting and that demonstrate some quality of the speaker's personality rather than those that are designed to prove a point. The message should be delivered casually and should strive to feel more like a conversation then a lecture delivered from the podium, which carries with it hierarchical connotations.

Discussion: Almost all of us, at some point in our lives, have had to give an introductory speech (in school, at camp, at church, at work, etc.) in which we select some "interesting fact" about ourselves to tell a group. Thinking back on that experience, what did you select? Was it effective in actually forming future relationships, or did it backfire?

SPEECHES OF IDENTIFICATION

Speeches of **identification** invite diverse members of an audience to share a common identity that makes it possible for them to act as a unified group with common interests and values. These speeches are also called "constitutive rhetoric" because of their ability to constitute, or form, a coherent group or movement through symbolic representations.[3] This kind of speech is frequently used in athletic contexts for rallying "team spirit," in business contexts for generating employee loyalty, in interpersonal contexts for creating group unity, or in political contexts for forming political parties or movements, as when American revolutionaries such as Sam Adams formed the "Sons of Liberty" or civil rights activists such as Huey Newton formed the "Black Panthers." Thus, the core function of the speech of identification is to create a sense of group participation and solidarity. Whereas introductory speeches deal with the relationship between speaker and audience, speeches of identification deal primarily with the relationships among audience members, with the speaker being secondary.

The occasion for such a speech is generally one in which a group of people, either strangers or a loosely knit group, feel it necessary to create a tighter bond in order to accomplish some task. The paradigmatic speech of identification is thus the coach's rallying oratory before the beginning of the game, consummated by the unified cheer, "Go, team!" These speeches gain even more power by being given in a particularly meaningful place that signifies this bonding. A football game speech made in a parking lot is different than one given in a locker room; a family reunion speech is more powerful when made at the family farm than a rented hall; and patriotic speeches intended to bind people together into a political whole are often more effective when made before memorials, near landmarks, or near significant battlefields. Of course, the function of identification holds for almost all speeches. But some speeches are clearly focused on *creating* that sense of common bond, whereas others *reinforce* one already in existence.

The *listeners* of a speech of identification wish to feel part of something that is larger than themselves and that provides a meaning and value for their actions that could not be accomplished their own. Whereas listeners of introductory speeches are interested in getting to know individuals so that they can cooperate on some future task, listeners of speeches of identification are more interested in the value of simply being part of the group itself. Consequently, they are not interested in the unique characteristics or experiences of the speaker, but only those characteristics and experiences that are representative of group membership. The *speaker* must therefore portray him- or herself as a kind of representative of the group who speaks for the whole rather than from a particular perspective. In many groups this means dressing in a kind of "uniform" (whether literal, as in athletics or the military, or figurative, as in business or social groups) as well as speaking in the common vernacular of the group, often employing slang terms or technical jargon that would not be understood by those outside the group. Finally, the *message* should typically rely on highly emotional narratives loaded with value judgments and appeals to shared symbols and beliefs. In this way, speeches of identification are very similar to commemorative speeches, but differ in emphasizing the construction of an explicit "we" identity that carries with it explicit commitments to action and responsibilities to other members of the group. Consequently, any act of

---

[3]See Maurice Charland, "Constitutive Rhetoric: The Case of the Peuple Québécois," *Quarterly Journal of Speech* 73 (1987), 133–150.

commemoration in a speech of identification usually ends on an explicit imperative to act in a specific manner that often requires sacrifice on the part of the individual for the sake of the group.

Discussion: What was an "identification" you tried to make with your childhood friends growing up? Did you give yourselves a group name? What were the qualities you attributed to your group identity? Did you develop any practices or rituals to express those qualities in public? Is this process fundamentally different than what occurs in a workplace?

SPEECHES OF DELIBERATION

Speeches of **deliberation** occur when an audience wishes to hear a diverse group of speakers give different perspectives on how to address a common topic in order to come to an informed judgment about a matter of common concern. Deliberative speeches are similar to group introductory speeches insofar as they often require "turn taking." A deliberative speech cannot occur if only one speaker is allowed to express a single uncontested viewpoint, for that would be either a speech of solicitation or of advocacy. The essence of the deliberative speech, such as those that occur in town halls, boardrooms, courtrooms, and parliamentary bodies, as well as at kitchen tables, is that it is delivered in support or in criticism of opposing views that are given a chance to present a case or respond to other speeches. A parliamentary session, for instance, would be much different if representatives of opposing parties did not present their speeches alongside each other. This feature is important because it puts an audience in a deliberative frame of mind in which words, phrases, and arguments are always in a state of contestation with opposing words, phrases, and arguments. A deliberative speech thus requires a structured competitive environment that allows speakers to overcome objections and present defensible claims.

Contexts that call for deliberative speaking tend to occur when there exist clear divisions of opinion within a group or institution that cannot be resolved by further inquiry or polite conversation. The deliberative speaker often comes not with a mere "opinion" but with a specific point of view that is developed in relationship to competing arguments. However, the deliberative speaker differs from someone who is merely argumentative. Deliberation requires not only competition but also respect for rules of the deliberative forum and the institution or group that regulates it. In parliamentary bodies, arguments are directed not at the opposition so much as the uncommitted center, whose vote will determine the course of actual policy. Likewise, lawyers do not persuade one another; they address their arguments to the jury. Two opposing lawyers simply arguing with each other are not deliberating about anything. Therefore, deliberative speaking, to be successful, must not only provide a chance for the airing of different perspectives; it also must guarantee procedures of judgment based on a consideration of those arguments by an audience with respected authority, which may include the family, Congress, the jury, the board of directors, the stockholders, or the spectators. Deliberative speaking provides a method of coming to resolution such that all parties feel they have had a chance to be heard and considered before a decision is reached by a respected authority.

The *listener* for a deliberative speech is someone who is responsible for making a decision and wishes to hear two or more sides of an issue in order to consider every angle and alternative before coming to a judgment. Often, deliberative speaking is called for when no consensus has yet been reached, when intractable divisions remain within a group, and when legitimate judgment must be made without appearing biased or unfair. Genuine deliberative listeners are therefore neither partisans nor merely disinterested observers; they are individuals whose primary concern is what to do about a specific issue. The *speaker* therefore presents him- or herself as someone with experience or knowledge who is worth listening to, who is equally concerned about the problem, who expresses goodwill toward the audience, and who tries to save the audience's time by getting to the point as quickly as possible. To accomplish this task, the *message* tends to advance by very clearly defined logical propositions that are well defended while also satisfying our emotional need for a happy ending. Furthermore, because the deliberative speaker is always up against counterarguments, a deliberative speech must also refute opposing positions while seeking to make an "airtight case." Consequently, deliberative speeches tend to be highly compressed, logical affairs that have no room for extraneous detours or lengthy personal narratives; they get to the point quickly and defend their positions articulately.

Discussion: Although deliberation occurs from different perspectives, the context of deliberation requires some basic shared values and procedures so that deliberations do not degenerate into a shouting match or a fist fight. For instance, "arbitration" is a formal procedure by which competing parties invite a third party to help them make a deliberative decision. Have you ever been a party to such arbitration? What were the ground rules?

SPEECHES OF SOLICITATION

Speeches of **solicitation** persuade an audience to adopt some policy, object, process, or attitude based on the perceived rightness or utility of the subject matter. In other words, speeches of solicitation are same as deliberative speeches insofar as they present a case before an audience that has the authority to accept or reject what is being offered. However, whereas deliberative speeches always face counterargumentation, speeches of solicitation are typically made by a single speaker before an audience that may simply accept or reject the speaker's proposition rather than compare and contrast it with other points of view. In addition, deliberative speakers often present themselves as objective and unbiased parties who simply want to give the best advice about a current problem. In contradistinction, speakers who make solicitation speeches are often directly benefited by the audience's adoption of their judgment, as when a salesperson gets a commission, a fundraiser gets money for a cause, or a religious evangelist gains another faithful member. Thus, the challenge for most speeches of solicitation is to prove that the speaker is not simply being greedy or self-interested, and that the adoption of the speaker's judgment also benefits the audience in specific ways as well. This is another way of saying that the best salesperson is one who believes in the worth of the product.

The explicit goal of speeches of solicitation is to thus argue before a reluctant and skeptical audience for the mutual benefit in buying some product, adopting some policy, or changing some behavior favored by the speaker. There are two contexts for speeches of solicitation. The first context is the proverbial "door-to-door" sales pitch (which today happens via the phone or the Internet) in which the speaker simply makes the same speech to whoever will listen. The audience here is almost always an individual or small group that may simply have time to spare and may be curious about what is being offered. Such solicitations are almost always failures, but if one has the capability to solicit a million people, a 1 percent success rate is still very substantial. Furthermore, such blanket solicitation, particularly in politics, may be the only method for many people with few resources or little established credibility to gain a foothold of support. The second context is a more formal presentation in which an organized group invites a speaker to make a case for something that group members believe may actually benefit them. The latter is frequent in economic conditions in which businesses must adopt the most efficient products in order to compete in a changing marketplace. In both settings, however, the key aspects of speeches of solicitation are that the audience acts as the sole authority and judge and that the decision is usually one of "yes" or "no" rather than a more nuanced opinion.

The *listeners* for speeches of solicitation usually have almost no prior interest in establishing any sort of relationship with the speaker and are usually only interested in hearing how a speaker's proposal or product can benefit their own interests. Of all the listeners for speeches, those for speeches of solicitation tend to be the most impatient and the most willing to interrupt or put an end to a speech at any moment if they feel that their time is being wasted. In other words, speeches of solicitation are guided by the ethic of self-interest on the part of both speaker and audience. The *speaker* is almost always a self-conscious performer who knows he or she is on stage and acts accordingly. The worst types of salespeople are those who deny that they are selling something. Accordingly, the most appropriate way to present a speech of solicitation is to acknowledge what is to be gained by both parties and to make the interaction as pleasurable (and usually entertaining) as possible. The *message* therefore tends to be dominated by *if/then* causal arguments that show how *if* the audience chooses to adopt the advice of the speaker *then* good consequences will be produced, with the desirability of consequences emphasized by entertaining narratives that dramatize ideal results. And because of the impatience of the audience, these arguments are usually presented with a fairly rapid pace that maintains a lively and enthusiastic atmosphere often punctuated with jokes and good-natured hyperbole but always ending on a serious note that reinforces the importance of making the right decision.

Discussion: Although we often poke fun at the "hot-sell" salesperson who is somewhat pushy, talks fast, is full of jokes, and is ready to take the money and run, anyone who has actually worked in sales knows that this only works for people selling trinkets on the street corner. In your experience selling anything, what qualities make a successful salesperson? And how are those qualities dependent on what one is selling? A child selling lemonade uses a different solicitation strategy then a real estate agent selling a house. What characteristics do they have in common, and what aspects are different?

SPEECHES OF COMMEMORATION

Speeches of **commemoration** establish or reinforce bonds between audience members by praising something or someone that the speaker believes reflects their shared values. Specifically, commemorative speeches make moral judgments about, and attribute values to, particular people, objects, or events important to the audience in a way that alters or reinforces their long-term attitudes toward those things. In other words, commemorative speaking is often directed toward things that have historical value. We commemorate something when we want to remember and preserve it. Most often in our lives, commemoration happens when we wish to remember loved ones who have died and to preserve in our memories the celebrations and triumphs of our lives. Cultures, too, memorialize certain people, events, or objects that have played an important role in their historical development. The purpose of the commemorative speech is thus to create a shared sense of reverence and memory for things of common value, thus reinforcing the close bonds of members of a group by celebrating that group's best qualities.

Contexts for commemorative speeches are either ritualistic, as with annual national holidays, or situational, as with weddings or graduations. Both, however, serve the same basic function. A commemorative speech brings people together to honor the values that unite them as a group and that are embodied in their members and their actions. Consequently, any group or institution that relies on the motivation of its members makes frequent use of commemorative speeches both to inspire excellence and to create a shared sense of commitment. Even commemorating loved ones at a funeral binds people together in a uniquely powerful way by using their stories to create a sense of reverence and legacy. Thus, although speeches of commemoration often do not usually argue specific points, they create and reinforce the values on which people often rely when called to make concrete judgments in practice. In speaking to the past and future, they endeavor to create a lasting impression in historical time.

The two central components of a commemorative speech are the *value,* which is an abstract and universal concept, and the *subject matter,* which is a specific and concrete thing. Either the value or the subject matter may be the starting point for a commemorative speech. A speaker before an audience such as the Veterans of Foreign Wars, for instance, may start with the values of honor and sacrifice and then seek to commemorate those soldiers who uphold those values. Or that speaker might begin with a particular person who has recently passed away and then seek to find appropriate values with which to praise that individual based on his or her own unique personality and contribution. One starts with a value and then finds subject matter to praise; the other starts with subject matter and finds values with which to praise it.

The *listener* for speeches of commemoration genuinely wishes to be inspired by something that represents the very best of life and that the listener believes should be valued and respected by all those present. Like audiences for speeches of identification, listeners for speeches of commemoration usually find pleasure in feeling common bonds with other audience members; however, they are different because the bond is established by common values rather than by explicit signs of group membership. Consequently, listeners for commemorative speeches are often very diverse, sometimes even bringing together people who otherwise may be competitive or antagonistic toward one another. This means that the *speaker* for speeches of commemoration is often very different than those for speeches of identification. A speaker seeking identification will often be very animated, charismatic, and vigorous in order to rally an audience around a common set of symbols, beliefs, or attitudes; a speaker seeking to commemorate is usually controlled, deferential, and eloquent, making sure that it is the object, event, or person being commemorated that is the focus of the audience rather than the cleverness of the speaker. The *message* for commemorative speeches relies heavily on *pathos* arguments that use highly stylistic narratives to generate emotional attachments and to show how the object commemorated possesses certain qualities worthy of praise. Commemorative speeches are not cluttered with facts and details; they select a few essential narratives and spend a great deal of time investing them with rich emotional nuance and power.

Discussion: How do popular advertisements work as commemorative speeches? Think of competing brand names that make the same basic product. Do they praise the same values as their competitors, or do they praise different ones in order to distinguish their product?

SPEECHES OF ENRICHMENT

Speeches of **enrichment** satisfy an audience's desire to successfully pursue preexisting interests by giving entertaining instruction about objects, events, processes, or concepts that promise to benefit the audience members' lives in some way. The term *enrichment* is meant to bridge the supposed division between information and entertainment. As noted earlier, there is no such thing as an "informative" speech; and even if there was one, written forms of communication are better suited to disseminating detailed information anyway. Oral speech simply cannot even hope to mimic the logical complexity and efficiency of writing. Moreover, oral forms of communication, by their very nature, must satisfy more demands than simply the conveyance of data or else an audience will get restless. *Enrichment* thus closer approximates the *actual* function of so-called informative speaking, insofar as it does not seek so much to deliver "the facts" as it does to motivate an audience and to generate enthusiasm for things that the audience may have heard about but never took the time to investigate.

Speeches of enrichment are generally given in situations in which an audience has already acknowledged its lack of awareness about some problem or issue and has voluntarily attended an occasion to gain this knowledge in order to resolve a situation (such as learning how to get a job in a bad economy), to satisfy curiosity (such as learning about the latest discoveries of planets outside our solar system), or to enrich one's life (such as learning how to appreciate good wine). A good speaker in this genre will base whatever is said on the audience's **interests**, which are things that people enjoy doing, want to know about, or desire to attain. The speaker will present information in an entertaining but *noncontroversial* manner such that he or she is not advocating a particular position. Once audience members feel that they are not being informed, but being manipulated or pushed, they will no longer receive the information as a gift for enrichment, but as an active solicitation.

The most common speeches of enrichment (outside of the formal classroom) occur either as public lectures (usually by academics, celebrities, or authors) or paid seminars concerning methods of self-help or self-advancement. But why seek enrichment from a speech rather than a book or video? First, with respect to written instruction, a speech promises to condense the main points of a subject and present them in a smooth, understandable, narrative form that speaks directly to an audience's everyday experience. Although it clearly leaves out a great deal of detail, a speech nonetheless makes a subject more immediately interesting and relevant to one's life. Second, with respect to multimedia or **online communication**, a speech of enrichment makes it a *community experience* of sharing knowledge rather than an isolated or detached event. Attending a speech of enrichment is itself an experience, and often it includes the discussion after the fact with other interested members of the audience. Not surprisingly, then, public lectures often serve an important community-building function, which is what makes their frequent setting in public libraries or public universities so appropriate.

The *listener* for speeches of enrichment has a clear and expressed interest to hear the subject matter presented as well as a desire to gather together with other like-minded people. Of these two motives, the second is often the most important. The reason people go to conventions, for instance, is usually to meet other people who share the same interests and to talk about the various enrichment speeches they have heard at those conventions (regardless of whether those speeches are about classic cars, Russian literature, chemical engineering, or Star Trek). Audiences listen not only to acquire information but also to establish camaraderie. Naturally, then, the dominant quality of the speaker of enrichment is goodwill toward the audience, displayed usually through interaction with audience members and constant attention to how the subject matter of the speech relates to the audience's everyday experiences. Demonstrating that one possesses sufficient knowledge to speak on the topic is important, but should be done in an understated way and usually just in passing. An overemphasis on the "credentials" of the speaker as a means of establishing credibility often comes off as arrogant, which is why this task always falls to the one who introduces the speaker. The *message* should strike a balance between argument and anecdote, with clear claims and evidence supplemented by lively stories and examples. The message should challenge the intellect of the audience so that they feel they are learning, but not so much that it starts to sound like a written text; in fact, the result of a successful speech of enrichment will often be the purchase of a book.

Discussion: It is characteristic of public speaking that one person's enrichment is another person's solicitation, particularly when it comes to politics and religion. Can you recall an experience in which a speech was interpreted in two different ways by different members of an audience? What was the reason for this difference in interpretation in which one person felt enriched and the other manipulated?

SPEECHES OF ADMINISTRATION

Speeches of **administration** are delivered by officials of a group or institution to an audience whose presence is usually mandatory in order to justify policy decision and improve the procedures and communication structures of an organization. Although often presented as speeches of enrichment, introduction, or identification, administrative speeches are different because the audience was compelled to be present, and therefore such speeches do not have the power and influence characteristics that these other speeches hold. In other words, the same exact content delivered to a voluntary audience and interpreted as an enrichment speech (for instance, one on "how to be successful in business" delivered at the public library) is interpreted as a speech of administration when delivered to newly hired employees at a sales firm. Whereas a self-help speaker may be received with a lively and energetic response by an audience that pays to attend, that same speaker might receive only polite applause from an audience of employees who have had to take time out of the day to learn the power of networking. It is the difference between a politician giving an introductory speech to prospective voters and a new manager of the office introducing him- or herself as the boss, as well the difference between the speeches of identification given at pep rallies and the speeches by managers at early morning gatherings of employees at retail stores to get them enthusiastic about serving the customers. The difference between the speeches is that the latter are not designed to appeal to the preexisting, voluntary interests of the audience, but rather to implement decisions made by administrative authorities. The result is that speeches of administration tend to be experienced more as a duty than a pleasure.

The situations that call for an administrative speech, as opposed to a memo, a manual, or a video, are those in which changes must be implemented or announced to everyone simultaneously in order to generate a certain level of shared enthusiasm and to maximize efficiency by reducing the possibility for misunderstanding. Because everyone attending an administrative speech receives the same information at the same time, any problems, objections, or questions can be aired by the audience at once, and listeners can receive the same answer from the administrative officials. Administrative speeches often have the side effect of making "ignorance" an insufficient excuse for not implementing new policies. This function is particularly important when the information is bad news rather than good news. Finally, speeches of administration simply create an opportunity for members of the same organization to get together in one place and talk to each other before and after (and sometimes during) the speech. Unlike speeches of enrichment, however, the conversations may not actually be about the subject matter of the speech (except ironically) but simply about casual topics. In other words, the sheer fact that everyone has been mandated to attend the speech is often the most significant aspect of administrative speeches well beyond anything that is actually said.

The *listener* for speeches of administration represents the most challenging audience for any speech, precisely because he or she may not want to be there but has been compelled to be present. This does not mean that the listener is not aware of the intended function of the speech and its relevance to his or her professional interests; it simply means that such interests are not what may be forefront in the listener's mind or that he or she does not feel the need to know or hear anything more about it. Resistance only increases when punitive measures are threatened for absences, which compels people to be physically present but allows them to be mentally absent. The *speaker* for such speeches therefore has a considerable challenge. On the one hand, the speaker must present him- or herself as a credible and respected authority who is in charge of the situation and has a perspective of proven and recognized value. On the other hand, the speaker must also strive to adapt to the needs of the audience, not the least of which is the desire to be entertained and even, at times, flattered. This means that the ideal speaker for administrative speeches has something of a "parental" quality that strikes a balance between disciplinary authority and good-natured affection. The *message*, to be successful, should not consist of simply going over material that is better given in a pamphlet or handout. The message should go over the "high points" as quickly and articulately as possible and should intersperse "thou shalts" and "thou shalt nots" with amusing stories and lighthearted banter. It should also strive to be as short as possible and conclude on a positive note, which leaves people in good spirit and with a short time to talk to each other casually (often over coffee and doughnuts) before they return to their responsibilities.

Discussion: Of all public speaking genres, speeches of administration are probably lowest on the bar of eloquence. What is the worst speech of administration you ever experienced? And was it even necessary? By contrast, have you ever experienced a good speech of administration? What do you think is the essential quality of making a good administrative speech as a "boss"?

SPEECHES OF ADVOCACY

Speeches of **advocacy** persuade an uncommitted audience to place certain beliefs and attitudes at the top of a hierarchy of needs (and others at the bottom) by showing how they are necessary to achieving ideal ends. The term "advocacy" is used in the sense that the speaker is an "advocate," which is literally defined as one who speaks on behalf of something or someone else, as when we might "advocate" for a friend by using our influence with others to help that friend. This means that speeches of advocacy always speak "on behalf" of some higher cause or ideal that transcends the self-interest of the speaker or even of the audience, thereby marking it, in many ways, as the very opposite of a speech of solicitation. Despite the fact that they use explicit persuasive appeals, solicitation speeches do not challenge an audience's basic beliefs or attitudes in any way; in fact, they usually flatter an audience and then show how something in possession of the speaker can benefit them. A speech of advocacy, by contrast, often explicitly criticizes members of an audience for being too concerned with their own immediate problems and not willing to sacrifice time and effort to strive for something greater than their own self-advancement. It therefore "advocates for" an idea by showing how it should hold a greater place in people's lives and thoughts than it currently does.

One of the puzzling things about speeches of advocacy is why people would voluntarily go to hear speech that challenges them in this way. In almost every other speech genre, the audience has a clear reason for being there—to get to know someone (introduction), to feel part of a group (identification), to make an informed decision (deliberation), to pursue self-interest (solicitation), to pay homage to something important (commemoration), to make one's life more enjoyable (enrichment), or to fulfill one's professional responsibilities (administration). Why would an audience choose to attend a speech in which their beliefs and attitudes would be challenged and would demand of them a great deal of sacrifice? There is no easy answer to this question, but most attempts to answer it come down to one basic fact of human nature—the desire to overcome our immediate obstacles in search of becoming something higher than what we currently are. Richard Weaver says that rhetoric at its truest seeks to perfect men and women "by showing them better versions of themselves, links in that chain extending up toward the ideal, which only the intellect can apprehend and only the soul have affection for."[4] A lofty definition, to be sure! Yet it is an undeniable fact that when people are discontented with their current situation, they will willingly cast aside all conventional comforts and remake themselves according to a new ideal. Speeches of advocacy therefore rely on a basic level of discontent to make these transformations possible; and when discontent is not present, sometimes it must be manufactured first. That is why the basic model of all such speeches is a combination of two sentiments, "this is intolerable" and "this is what must be done."

Making speeches of advocacy even more complicated is the fact that, very often, they speak to two audiences simultaneously. The first audience consists of *listeners* in attendance who usually already share some degree of the same discontent and aspirations, but who have attended the speech in order to solidify their commitment and more fully understand what is to be asked of them. With the exception of hecklers who attend primarily to disrupt the event, in speeches of advocacy, the people gather in attendance to hear the speech because they already are in support of the speaker's overall position, as with protest rallies, religious revivals, or political campaign events. And even those who attend and who are uncommitted are nonetheless curious enough to listen attentively. The second audience consists of *spectators* who witness the spectacle of the gathering through the mass media, whether it is disseminated through conventional news sites or is reproduced through social networking sites or the blogosphere. This audience may have very little connection at all with the speaker or the issue, but may simply be interested to know what is going on that would attract so many people. In effect, then, speeches of advocacy gather like-minded people together to reinforce their beliefs and identify themselves as a group, and by doing so hope to produce a show of constituent support that justifies bringing their viewpoints to the attention and consideration of a larger public.

The context for speeches of advocacy thus occurs when a smaller public wishes to make its position heard by a larger public through the power of spectacle. Whereas speeches of identification and commemoration may help that smaller public form close bonds and establish long-term working relationships and attitudes, speeches of advocacy bring their perspective and arguments into the light of the public sphere. To contribute to a larger public discussion or advance a social movement, an effective speech of advocacy thus relies on having agencies of mass media to distribute news of the speech, which generates public attention and discussion about what was said and argued at the event. Thus, the effect of most public protest rallies is often determined by the level of press they generate after the fact. This is one reason why eloquent speaking that is quotable, and that generates

---

[4]Weaver, *The Ethics of Rhetoric*, 25.

a powerful but brief image, is crucial for producing the kind of media spectacle for which a speech of advocacy is intended. Speeches that may have actually been heard by but a few people have such power that they become reproduced and talked about in written or online communications, only to finally be discussed in oral speech between friends and within communities.

The ideal *listeners* for speeches of advocacy are people ready to commit themselves to a cause. This does not mean that listeners must be willing to throw themselves completely into a social movement. Sometimes it simply means that they must change their daily habits as a way of contributing to a long-term goal, such as when people start recycling, start voting in a certain way, or choose not to purchase certain products. Regardless of how much time and effort listeners are willing to expend, they nonetheless desire *some* kind of commitment in order to feel as if they are "doing their part" to help improve some aspect of the world and to be a part of something that expands their vision and horizon beyond the everyday. The *speaker* is somebody who has not only demonstrated his or her own level of commitment by having sacrificed for a higher ideal, but who also is something of a role model, and whose actions are capable of being successfully imitated by an audience. Unlike deliberative speakers, who may be called to speak because they possess a specific element of expertise that is beyond that of the ordinary person, successful advocacy speakers usually present themselves as "one of us" and tend to themselves be a part of the community they are addressing. The message is therefore delivered in a colloquial, vernacular style that typically mirrors the way that the audience members themselves speak. Whereas commemorative speeches tend to be highly poetic, deliberative speeches tend to be very logical, and solicitation speeches tend to be aggressively performative, advocacy speeches are written as if they are "speaking what is already on everyone's mind." The message should therefore be received with the expression "That's exactly what I have been thinking!" In other words, the function of speeches of advocacy is to rally an audience around a common cause and give them a language with which they can speak to each other about that cause that is consistent with their own perspectives.

Discussion: Have you ever attended a rally or protest of any kind in which someone gave a speech of advocacy to the crowd that was covered by the media? After seeing the reporting of the event, what was different about your experience in attendance and the way it was portrayed in the news? If the speech itself was quoted, why do you think the media selected that particular passage? And do you think that the media coverage conveyed the spirit of the speech itself, or did it cover something that had very little to do with the speech?

KEY WORDS

SUMMARY

A speech genre represents a familiar, conventional, and appropriate way of responding to a particular and recognizable type of speech situation. As indicated by Aristotle's initial distinctions among forensic, deliberative, and ceremonial speaking, which were based on the Greek experience in law courts, the assembly, and funeral orations, speech genres do not simply exist "on paper"; they exist in the habits and expectations of a particular culture whose members experience recurrent types of situations that demand predictable forms of rhetorical response. We can, of course, violate these expectations at any time if we so choose, either for the sake of humor or surprise or confrontation, but doing so always comes with a risk that must be calculated ahead of time. It is bad taste, for instance, to give a speech of solicitation when one is supposed to be commemorating the accomplishments of someone else, just as it makes you appear ridiculous to give a speech of administration to an audience with absolutely no obligation to listen to you. The easiest way to invite rhetorical failure is to misunderstand or to simply ignore which speech genre is appropriate to one's audience at a particular time and place.

Although each speech genre therefore performs a specific function in a specific type of situation, we can generally categorize speech genres into two distinct types, those whose primary function is to form the character of an audience and those whose primary function is to encourage an audience to come to a particular type of judgment. The first type of speech is what is represented by introduction, identification, enrichment, and commemoration speeches. We give speeches of *introduction* whenever we have to establish relationships with strangers in a situation that usually calls for some sort of cooperative activity. This type of activity might be practical, such as being part of a research team or a court jury, or social, such as having to live together in a dormitory or be a part of a new neighborhood. Most often our speeches of introduction are not formal "stage" speeches but informal narratives that we deliver in the context of conversation. Speeches of *identification* thus follow naturally from those of introduction, for after we introduce ourselves to each other there comes a demand to "identify" the nature of the group to which each of us belongs. Usually, such speeches are accompanied by symbols, such as team mascots, flags, squad colors, and the like, that embody some set of qualities and virtues that the group can rally around. Once a group is formed around common characteristics and goals, speeches of *enrichment* then provide more resources to educate an audience about the things that it finds interesting and holds valuable. A platoon of soldiers will thus be enriched about famous battle strategies, just as members of a political party will learn about the justification for their economic policies. Finally, *commemorative* speeches will praise exemplary people, objects, and actions that embody the values held dear by that particular group, thereby solidifying group identity by showing how representatives of that group are accomplishing great and worthwhile things.

By contrast, speech genres of deliberation, solicitation, and advocacy focus more on specific matters of judgment than on questions of group identity. Speeches of deliberation, for instance, occur far more often *within* an identified group than between two contentious groups. This is because speeches of deliberation require shared commitment to certain procedures that allow deliberation to occur without breaking down into overly contentious polemics or even violence. Therefore, speeches of deliberation are about debates over issues that members of a group have not come to common decision about and therefore require the consideration of pro and con positions. That is why, perhaps, the ordinary large family is one of the most frequent sites for deliberative speeches. Speeches of solicitation, on the other hand, usually occur when representatives of outside interests approach a specific group to market an idea or product that purports to serve their mutual interests. Whereas members of the family trying to decide where to take a vacation use deliberative speeches, travel agencies offering available trip packages to that family use solicitation speeches. Finally, speeches of advocacy manage to cross all boundaries between audiences, speaking both to the committed and the noncommitted that it is in the interest of all to pursue a certain idea for the sake of some value higher than self-interest. That is why speeches of advocacy often are heard in the street, where anyone can come, and broadcast through the media so that everyone can hear. Speeches of advocacy are the only type of speeches that break the conventional boundaries of group identifications in the name of some higher good or more prudent action.

CHAPTER 2 EXERCISES

1. Examine the speaking context of your rhetorical artifact selected in Chapter 1. What made oral speech a preferable method of communication in that situation? Also, examine its genre. When this speech was given, under which genre was it interpreted? Was there any difference in interpretation from critics or audience members?

2. Compose and deliver an introductory speech to the class in the form of a haiku (three metrical phrases with 5, 7, and 5 syllables). How did the condensed phrasing alter your content? Now do the same exercise with a speech of enrichment.

3. Choose a very ordinary object. Now commemorate this object by attributing to it a very grand value that playfully exaggerates its importance. Students should present their commemorative speeches to the class. Did any of the speeches make you value these objects any differently?

4. To simulate the dual audience of speeches of advocacy, divide yourselves into four groups, one in each corner of the classroom. Come up with a fictional "identification" for yourselves; then write a brief speech of advocacy that is intended to further your cause. Then, taking turns, have each group arrange itself so that all members of the group are seated in the corner with their chairs facing the very center of the classroom. Choose a speaker from each group and have the speaker deliver the speech directly to his or her identified audience (such that speakers face their own group but have their backs to the rest of the class). Each speaker must deliver the speech with vigor and elicit a forceful response from his or her particular group. However, while one group is speaking, the other three groups should watch silently behind that group while the identified audience should be cheering madly and looking only at the speaker. How does this experience change the feeling of the speech from both perspectives?

5. Divide yourselves into three groups: a pro group, a con group, and a jury. Select a topic of deliberation. Have the pro and con groups take affirmative and negative positions on this topic and present their cases before the members of the jury, who may interrupt and ask questions at any time. After arguments are completed, have the jury make an honest verdict based purely on the cases presented to it. What were some of the factors in the jury's decision?

The Rhetorical Situation

This chapter introduces rhetoric as a situated discursive act within a larger public context of deliberation about controversial and pressing issues. It expands the notion of "public speaking" beyond the walls of the classroom to encompass one's larger social and historical environment. The rhetorical situation is divided into rhetorical background, which provides the broader historical and social context of the speech and its audience, and rhetorical foreground, which represents those aspects that stand out significantly to specific audiences in the immediate present. The rhetorical background includes components such as the public, public opinion, public memory, social knowledge, counterpublics, and the state; while the rhetorical foreground includes the components of exigence, audience, constraints, motive, practical judgment, and occasion. The most important of these concepts for rhetorical public speaking is attention to exigence, which focuses rhetorical public speaking on the shared problems that an audience wishes will be addressed in a timely manner.

In much of our daily lives, we take most of the aspects of our environment for granted. Like fish in water, we are rarely aware of the medium through which we are moving—and rightly so. If a fish was always dwelling on the water, it would undoubtedly have little energy left for eating and finding shelter. Our "critical" spirit usually arises whenever some **contingency**—some unexpected obstacle, perplexity, or problem—arises out of that environment, stands out concretely before us, and threatens to disrupt our lives in some way. The appearance of contingency makes us look critically at our previous choices in the assumption that the path we had earlier chosen may not, in fact, be the best way forward. According to John Dewey, this process of reflection, judgment, and valuation "takes place only when there is something the matter; when there is some trouble to be done away with, some need, lack, or privation to be made good, some conflict of tendencies to be resolved by means of changing conditions."[1]

Rhetoric is the creature of shared contingency. Thus, a **rhetorical situation** is one that occurs when public contingencies generate concern and uncertainty within a public audience and give force and effectiveness to persuasive discourse that encourages collective

---

[1]John Dewey, "Theory of Valuation," in *John Dewey: The Later Works*, vol. 13, ed. Jo Ann Boydston (Carbondale: Southern Illinois UP, 1988), 34.

action.[2] In rhetorical situations, contingencies are problematic aspects of a situation shared by a group of people who must collectively deliberate about which actions to take to resolve their common problem. Contingencies are experienced this way whenever people encounter shared obstacles without knowing for sure the nature of the problem or the way to proceed effectively. Aristotle summed this up best:

> The duty of rhetoric is to deal with such matters as we deliberate upon without arts or systems to guide us. . . . The subjects of our deliberation are such as seem to present us with alternative possibilities: about things that could not have been, and cannot now or in the future be, other than they are, nobody who takes them to be of this nature wastes his time in deliberation.[3]

Of course, not all contingencies require rhetorical resolution. Many contingencies already have pre-established means of resolution that are generally accepted as effective. In such cases, we have a **technical situation**, which exists when we confront problems with a proven discourse and method to guide us. A technical situation does not guarantee a positive result, but it does resolve the uncertainty about how to proceed. For example, a person diagnosed with cancer faces a contingency—his or her health might go this way or that way. But most people treat cancer by following the advice of established medical authorities and pursue some combination of chemotherapy or radiation treatment. Although they do not know their fate, they know the course to pursue. Yet the same applies for one who might choose alternative methods of healing, such as prayer or herbal medicine. What makes a situation "technical" is not the prudence of the response, but the assurance that one knows the way forward. A situation only becomes "rhetorical" when the way forward is in doubt and multiple parties engage in symbolic persuasion to motivate cooperative action.

There are two major components to the rhetorical situation. The first is the **rhetorical background**, which represents the larger environment that defines the historical and social context for any particular rhetorical event.

Knowing the rhetorical background provides a speaker with a broader perspective to more efficiently identify resources from which to draw when creating the speech and to better anticipate the possible long-term consequences after speaking. In chapter 1, we have already encountered certain aspects of the rhetorical background in the discussion of **public memory, social knowledge,** and **maxims**. These are the basic building blocks of what holds any public together. This

---

[2]The literature on the rhetorical situation includes Lloyd Bitzer, "The Rhetorical Situation," *Philosophy and Rhetoric* 1 (1969), 13–14; Richard E. Vatz, "The Myth of the Rhetorical Situation," *Philosophy and Rhetoric* 6 (1973), 154–161; Barbara A. Biesecker, "Rethinking the Rhetorical Situation from Within the Thematic of Difference," *Philosophy and Rhetoric* 22 (1989), 110–130; Alan Brinton, "Situation in the Theory of Rhetoric," *Philosophy and Rhetoric* 14 (1981), 234–248; Scott Consigny, "Rhetoric and Its Situations," *Philosophy and Rhetoric* 7 (1974), 175–186; Kathleen Hall Jamieson, "Generic Constraints and the Rhetorical Situation," *Philosophy and Rhetoric* 6 (1968), 162–170; John H. Patton, "Causation and Creativity in Rhetorical Situations: Distinctions and Implications," *Quarterly Journal of Speech* 65 (1979), 36–55.
[3]Aristotle, *Rhetoric*, 1357a.

"public," then, forms the rhetorical background for any rhetorical speech act. In common interpretation, the public is thought to represent the total population of any national culture. However, a "public" is more than just a "mass." A **public** is a complex interaction of individuals that constitutes a political culture. Defined in a functional way, a public is a group of citizens who recognize each other's interests and have developed habits of settling disputes, coordinating actions, and addressing shared concerns through common communication media. Therefore, what ultimately characterizes the American public in general is common participation within a political process. A public, then, comes about when a group of strangers comes together for a common purpose that affects them all directly or indirectly. The **state** is thus distinct from the public insofar as it represents the instrument that the public uses to address consequences that it deems important enough to manage. In this sense, democracy is defined in terms of a state developed as a means for the public to regulate itself.[4]

However, if a state (in the name of one clearly defined public) formally excludes other publics, then **counterpublics** develop outside of and counter to the established mechanisms of the state. As Michael Warner writes, the discourse that constitutes a counterpublic "is not merely a different or alternative idiom, but one that in other contexts would be regarded with hostility, or with a sense of indecorousness."[5] Consequently, their rhetoric tends to be directed internally, toward group cohesion, rather than externally, at social persuasion. Yet the goal of a counterpublic is usually to form a genuine public able to express its will through legitimate public institutions and governing bodies. They exist as counterpublics only when this access is denied and they are forced to organize through alternative channels of communication. Once democratic reforms are initiated, they reclaim their status as one public among many.

The idea of the public influences rhetorical invention in three ways. First, rhetorical persuasion can produce visible and concrete changes in reality only if there is an audience capable of acting on its beliefs through organized channels. Speaking to people who had opted out of collective social life may produce persuasion, but those persuaded people will have few means of acting upon that new belief in collaboration with others—unless they have been persuaded to participate in the public. Second, a functional definition of the public encourages a speaker to think of people as something other than a stereotyped group of generic individuals who all think and feel the same thing. A functional definition of the public helps us realize that what binds people together is common interests in regulating social affairs and resolving common problems for the benefit of everyone *despite* their obvious differences. Third, it reminds a speaker that there is almost always a plurality of "publics" that exists within any more generic "public." It is a relatively straightforward matter to adapt to the specific group of people who might be arranged in a room. It is quite another to interpret that specific group as an amalgam of overlapping publics joined together in a common space.

---

[4]This notion of the public comes from John Dewey, *The Public and Its Problems* (Athens: Ohio University Press, 1927).
[5]Michael Warner, "Publics and Counterpublics," *Public Culture* 14, no. 1 (2002), 49–90 (86).

What is most important in constructing a speech with respect to knowledge of the public is the current state of public opinion. **Public opinion** thus represents the percentage of people who hold certain views to be true. Often we see this portrayed in "opinion polls" that represent public opinion with a series of bar graphs and pie charts. Although there are many flaws to such polls, not the least of which is the assumption that opinions are discrete entities that can be discerned by narrow questioning, they are nonetheless valuable to the extent that they show general trends of opinion.[6] Walter Lippmann defines public opinion this way:

> Those features of the world outside which have to do with the behavior of other human beings, insofar as that behavior crosses ours, is dependent upon us, or is interesting to us, we call roughly *public affairs*. The pictures inside the heads of these human beings, the pictures of themselves, of others, of their needs, purposes, and relationship, are their public opinions. Those pictures which are acted upon by groups of people, or by individuals acting in the name of groups, are Public Opinion with capital letters.[7]

The important thing about public opinion from a rhetorical perspective is the fact that it represents the collective *opinions* of a public audience. An **opinion** is a conscious personal belief expressed as a commitment to a certain matter of fact or value. We might have opinions that television is a wasteland, that our neighbor's yard is a mess, that America's foreign policy is too isolationist, or that gay marriage is a sin. Public opinion is thus valuable for rhetoric in that it provides a starting point to approach an audience. It lets rhetors know what truths they can take for granted, which ones they need to challenge, and which ones they need to promote.

The rhetorical background, as represented by the current state of the public and of public opinion, is important to consider, in order to provide a broader perspective on how to understand a specific speech act. One encounters extensive explanations of a speaker's rhetorical background in any biographical account of famous orators. Here, for instance, is biographer Douglas L. Wilson providing a bit of the rhetorical background to Abraham Lincoln's Gettysburg address:

> Lincoln had a theory about public opinion. He told a meeting of his fellow Republicans in 1856 that public opinion "always has a *'central idea'* from which all its minor thoughts radiate. That central idea in our political public opinion, at the beginning was, and until very recently has continued to be, 'the equality of all men.' And although it has always submitted patiently to whatever of inequality there seem to be as a matter of actual necessity, its constant working has been a steady progress toward the practical equality of all men." What had changed by 1856 was that the defenders of slavery had begun either to deny that this assertion from the Declaration of Independence was meant to apply to blacks, as Stephen A. Douglas would do in his debates with Lincoln, or to disparage it as a "self-evident lie." Lincoln had discovered in his campaigning

---

[6]For an exploration of public opinion, see Carroll J. Glynn, Susan Herbst, Garrett O'Keefe, and Robert Shapiro, *Public Opinion* (Boulder, CO: Westview Press, 1999).
[7]Walter Lippmann, *Public Opinion* (New York: Simon & Schuster, 1922), 18.

in the 1850s, if not previously, that the declarations theme of the equality of all men had an especially powerful effect on ordinary citizens, appealing, it would seem, to something deeper than parties or policies, something, perhaps, having to do with ordinary people's sense of themselves.[8]

As this account demonstrates, considering the rhetorical background of any particular rhetorical situation provides a speaker added resources from which to draw upon, namely, the general values, maxims, conventions, memories, attitudes, and aspirations that hold together publics over time and provide good reasons for particular judgments, in this case embodied in the language of the Declaration of Independence. Without acknowledging the rhetorical background, a speaker will have tunnel vision that risks either ignoring or even offending the core beliefs of an audience, thereby making even the most well-defended position fall flat.

By contrast, the **rhetorical foreground** represents the specific and salient aspects of a common situation as it affects or interests some audience at a particular moment in time, including the motives of the audience itself. The rhetorical foreground represents those aspects of a situation that "stand out" from the background. These aspects include not only the problem or contingency at hand, but also the components of the specific speech situation in its relative immediacy. Expanding on the model initially posed by Lloyd Bitzer, these include exigence, audience, constraints, motive, practical judgment, and occasion. Although each of these aspects emerges out of the rhetorical background, the nature of the contingency gives each a distinct individuality that demands our focused attention. Importantly, every rhetorical speech begins with an understanding of the rhetorical situation; it does not begin with the desires or ideas of the speaker. What the speaker initially wants to say is merely a stimulus to learn about a specific rhetorical situation. But it is knowledge and acquaintance with the situation that is the ground on which any worthwhile speech is constructed.

Discussion: Consider the relationships between publics, public opinion, and the state in a democracy. In theory, the actions of a democratic state are guided by the dominant public opinion expressed by various publics about matters of public concern. In this system, rhetoric becomes the way that public opinion is formed during large-scale rhetorical situations. In your experience, do you feel that the democratic governance actually works this way? If so, when have you actually felt that your opinion (outside of the act of voting) has actually influenced the actions of a state?

EXIGENCE

What dominates the foreground of any rhetorical situation is the presence of an exigence that requires an act of persuasion to resolve. An **exigence**, in a general sense, is any outstanding aspect of our environment that makes us feel a combination of *concern*, *uncertainty*, and *urgency*. Not all exigencies are rhetorical. During our everyday lives, we encounter numerous exigencies, both large and small, that

---

[8]Douglas L. Wilson, *Lincoln's Sword: The Presidency and the Power of Words* (New York: Alfred A. Knopf, 2007), 202.

require on exertion of energy to deal with and possibly overcome but that may not call out for any particular rhetorical response. For instance, you may have woken up too late to get to work on time, you might have forgotten your spouse's anniversary, you may be at risk of losing your home to foreclosure, or you may be anxious about an oncoming hurricane. In each of these situations, you are concerned because they each have the possibility of impacting your life negatively or positively, you are uncertain because you are not sure what to do about it, and you feel a sense of urgency because you must act soon if you are to change the outcome. But you may be able to deal with these situations by non-rhetorical action, such as not taking a shower and running red lights to get work on time, buying an extra-special gift for your spouse and pretending it is a surprise, taking out a loan to cover a mortgage payment to avoid foreclosure, or packing things in a car and driving north, out of the hurricane's path.

A specifically *rhetorical* exigence is more than just the existence of a pressing problem; a **rhetorical exigence** must be an issue that generates concern and uncertainty for some organized or semi-organized group that can be resolved, in whole or in part, by persuading an audience to act in a way that is actually capable of addressing the situation. For instance, each of the four examples just given can become rhetorical under certain circumstances. If you discover that lateness to work is a constant problem in the office due to more structural problems such as pervasive road construction or cuts to public transportation, you can make a case to management of the need for flex time. If you decide that you forgot the anniversary because both you and your spouse have been working too many hours and not seeing each other enough, you can persuade your spouse that you should both quit your jobs and hitchhike around Europe for year. If your home foreclosure is a result of what you think to be a systematic policy of unethical loan practices, you can form a network with other homeowners to petition Congress to alter financial policy. And if you have no resources with which to use to escape the hurricane, you can make public demands that the state provide adequate shelter for you and your family. In each of these cases, what makes the situation rhetorical is a practical problem, or contingency, experienced by a large number of people, a shared desire to address that problem, and a realization that certain significant parties need to be persuaded to act in a certain way in order to solve it.

The concept of a rhetorical exigence can be difficult to grasp because there is often no agreement about the nature or even the existence of a particular problem. Indeed, convincing people that there *is* an exigence is often one of the most significant challenges to any speaker. Consequently, it is helpful to distinguish between two kinds of rhetorical exigence relative to the different nature of consensus and uncertainty. With a **contested exigence**, not everyone agrees that a problem exists. Sometimes people disagree whether certain things exist or not, such as whether or not Saddam Hussein of Iraq actually possessed weapons of mass destruction that threatened the United States. Others acknowledge the existence of things but question whether we should consider them a problem, such as those who might argue that even if Hussein did possess such weapons, he would never use them. In these cases, speakers have to work to persuade people of the nature of the exigence itself before ever getting to proposing a solution. By contrast, an **uncontested exigence** is one that everyone acknowledges to be a pressing problem that demands to be addressed; the issue is not to acknowledge the problem but to come up with an adequate solution. In such cases, a speaker concentrates on advocating some solutions over others, such as the preference for sanctions over war or for war instead of appeasement.

Patrick Henry: "Suffer not yourselves to be betrayed with a kiss."

Following the Boston Tea Party of December 16, 1773, the British Parliament passed a series of acts intended to suppress the rebellion in Massachusetts. In May of 1774, General Thomas Gage arrived in Boston with four regiments of British troops. For the next two years, uncertainty spread as to whether Britain was preparing for a full-scale war on the colonies or whether tensions could be resolved through political petition and deliberation. When the Virginia Convention met in 1775, many delegates clung to the hope that the British government would rely on sensible reasoning instead of force and therefore remained skeptical that a pending war was a genuine exigence that required urgent action.

However, Patrick Henry firmly believed that war was imminent, and in his famous speech "Liberty or Death," he set out to resolve any doubt about the reality of the contested exigence even while acknowledging the limits of his own knowledge. For Henry, one had to act on the best available knowledge to avoid disastrous consequences, and his knowledge led him to the conclusion that the British were about to attack. To convince more skeptical "gentlemen," he attempted to undermine the feeling of "solace" that many American diplomats felt when their petition of grievances to the British Crown was given a friendly reception. But Henry then points to the contrary evidence that shows how, despite conciliatory remarks by the British, they were, in fact, preparing for war. He continues:

> Is it that insidious smile with which our petition has been lately received? Trust it not, sir; it will prove a snare to your feet. Suffer not yourselves to be betrayed with a kiss. Ask yourselves how this gracious reception of our petition comports with these warlike preparations which cover our waters and darken our land. Are fleets and armies necessary to a work of love and reconciliation? Have we shown ourselves so unwilling to be reconciled that force must be called in to win back our love? Let us not deceive ourselves, sir. These are the implements of war and subjugation—the last arguments to which kings resort. I ask gentlemen, sir, what means this martial array, if its purpose be not to force us to submission? Can gentlemen assign any other possible motives for it? Has Great Britain any enemy, in this quarter of the world, to call for all this accumulation of navies and armies? No, sir, she has none. They are meant for us; they can be meant for no other. They are sent over to bind and rivet upon us those chains which the British ministry has been so long forging.[9]

Henry's powerful oral performance combined attention to factual detail with passionate argumentation that accused those not willing to recognize the "reality" of

---

[9]Patrick Henry, available from <http://www.bartleby.com/268/8/13.html> (accessed 6 September 2012).

being dupes, cowards, and ultimately slaves. With Thomas Jefferson and George Washington both in attendance, the result of his speech was said to be a unified cheer, "Give me liberty or give me death!" The contested exigence was contested no more and the audience had become a unified public body prepared to act in the face of uncertainty. [10]

Discussion: One way of thinking about a rhetorical situation is to consider situations in which you simply have a problem that forces you to call upon reluctant others for help. Oftentimes, then, one of the obstacles to effective rhetorical action is the stubbornness that comes from the reluctance to ask for that help. Do you think that this fear of appearing "weak" is one of the obstacles to effective rhetorical action in a problematic situation?

AUDIENCE

In its most general sense, an audience represents any person, or group of people, who hears, reads, or witnesses any communicative event. However, there are always multiple audiences to consider in any speech act, some existing in other places, some existing at other times. In an age of reality television, for instance, navigating multiple audiences simultaneously has become something of an art form. One contestant, for instance, might conspire with a second with the pretense of knocking a third out of the game. Yet the first one does this with the knowledge that the second contestant will tell a fourth contestant (at a later time) about their conversation, and therefore influence the actions of the fourth contestant from a distance. Meanwhile, all of the contestants are well aware of the television audience, with individuals watching simultaneously (in different places) all across the country. And many of them hope that their performance will be so engaging that it will persuade other television producers (in a different place at a later time) to cast them for exciting roles once their current show has ended. Only those unfamiliar with the genre interpret the on-screen characters to be the "real" audience; similarly, only those unfamiliar with rhetoric believe that an audience consists only of those immediately listening to a speech at a particular place and time.

We can break down audience into three categories: the primary audience, secondary audience, and the target audience. The **primary audience** for rhetorical public speaking consists of those people actually assembled together to hear the speech as it is delivered in person by the speaker—for instance, the delegates at the Virginia convention for Patrick Henry. **Secondary audiences** represent all those people who encounter the speech either through some another media or second-hand through the spoken word of another person; in the case of Henry's speech, this would include not only the King of England and the American colonists but also readers of this textbook. Finally, **target audiences** are those individuals or groups in either the primary or secondary audiences who are able to be persuaded and are capable of acting in such a way to help resolve the exigence. For Henry, the

---

[10]For more on Henry's speech, see Judy Hample, "The Textual and Cultural Authenticity of Patrick Henry's 'Liberty or Death' Speech," *Quarterly Journal of Speech* 63, no. 3 (1977), 298–310.

target audiences included not only the Virginia delegates but also the opinion leaders throughout the colonies who would read his words as they were reprinted and distributed through the printing press. For he understood that even if the Virginia delegation voted to support a war policy, actually raising an army would require the full support of the majority of the property-owning class, those who held all of the resources necessary for an extended campaign.

As indicated by the discussion on speeches of advocacy, the relationship between the primary and secondary audiences is actually very significant. Even though secondary audiences may only receive transcripts of the speech (as we do with Henry), knowing that his actual speech brought the entire delegation to its feet chanting "give me liberty or give me death!" has a direct impact on how we receive and interpret his words. We are naturally drawn to read speeches that we know had a very powerful effect on the primary audience, for we interpret their reaction as we do the reviews of a movie critic. Their excitement is a sign to us that the speech contains something significant, particularly when the crowd in attendance is of a significant size. Bringing thousands of people to their feet, as Martin Luther King Jr. did on the Washington Mall with his "I have a dream" speech, draws the attention of the news media and these days becomes a candidate for a viral video or an e-mail distribution campaign. Consequently, even if the primary audience has only minimal significance as a target audience (as many audiences do during presidential campaigns in which candidates deliver major policy addresses in front of select organizations), they cannot be ignored. With only rare exceptions (and those usually for unflattering reasons), nobody wants to read a speech that was a complete dud during its actual delivery. Almost any successful public speech must therefore satisfy the expectations and desires of the primary audience even if the target audience is a secondary audience watching from a distance.

Maria Stewart: "Let us make a mighty effort and arise!"

Shockingly, before September 1832, no African-American woman had ever delivered a "public" lecture in the sense of being authorized by the state. They were a **marginalized** group, denied access to the **public sphere** by the norms of convention and the **social knowledge** concerning matters of race and gender. So it must have been a surprise to her diverse audience, including men and women, both black and white, when Maria Stewart stood up in Boston's Franklin Hall to give a speech (despite the fact that the meeting was being sponsored by the women of the African-American Female Intelligence Society!). What made her speech even more provocative is that she spoke directly to the black women in her audience, targeting them (rather than men) as the primary agents of social change because of their power as mothers to influence and educate their children. Her strategy of speaking directly to women, in their roles as mothers, is announced early on in the speech. Challenging their sense of despair and resignation, she appeals to them:

> Oh, do not say you cannot make anything of your children; but say, with the help and assistance of God, we will try. Perhaps you will say that you cannot send them to high schools and academies. You can have them taught in the first rudiments of useful knowledge, and then you can have private teachers,

who will instruct them in the higher branches. It is of no use for us to sit with our hands folded, hanging our heads like bulrushes lamenting our wretched condition; but let us make a mighty effort and arise...Did the pilgrims, when they first landed on these shores, quietly compose themselves, and say, "The Britons have all the money and all the power, and we must continue their servants forever?" Did they sigh and say, "Our lot is hard; the Indians own the soil, and we cannot cultivate it?" No, they first made powerful efforts to raise themselves. And, my brethren have you made a powerful effort? Have you prayed the legislature for mercy's sake to grant you all the rights and privileges of free citizens, that your daughters may rise to that degree of respectability which true merit deserves, and your sons above the servile situations which most of them fill?[11]

The combination of criticism, challenge, and plea is indicative of Stewart's belief that her audience had the capability to change and the power to alter the situation for the better.[12] The fact of her speaking at all at this event, and with such eloquence and passion, probably had a significant impact on her primary audience, including both men and women. Yet her message remained powerful to secondary audiences who heard of it in print or by word of mouth, particularly because of her use of historical analogy that made the motive of former slaves identical with the motive of the pilgrims and the founders of the nation. In her speech, she addresses her target audience of African-American women and tells them, in effect, that they are the new founders of a new nation based in equality rather than in servitude.

Discussion: The easiest way to understand the importance of identifying the right target audience is to consider moments of failure. Oftentimes in comedy, part of the humor comes from cases of mistaken identity in which one person targets another for persuasion or manipulation only to find out that it is the wrong person. Can you think of any movie plots that failed in identifying target audiences for part of the narrative? And have you ever experienced similar failures in your own professional life?

CONSTRAINTS

Almost nothing that we do in life happens without resistance. Only in the realm of fantasy or dream does a wish become a reality by a word and a snap of the fingers. And even our most simple tasks often require an exertion of physical and mental effort, as we have all experienced on mornings when we simply cannot get out of bed for one reason or another. Every single reason why we cannot accomplish a task is a **constraint**, which represents any counterforce that stands between us and the attainment of our interests. Sometimes these constraints are physical things,

---

[11]Maria Stewart, "Speech at Boston's Franklin Hall." Available at <http://sankofareadinggroup .blogspot.com/2011/02/maria-stewart.html> (accessed 15 July 2012).
[12]For more on Maria Stewart's role in abolitionism, see Jacquiline Bacon, "'God and a Woman': Women Abolitionists, Biblical Authority, and Social Activism," *Journal of Communication & Religion* 22, no. 1 (1999), 1–39.

such as when the car doesn't start or when we hit traffic on the road. Sometimes they are emotional things, such as when we dislike our job so much that it is hard to perform up to our potential. And sometimes they are other people, such as when our co-workers resist our suggestions about how to streamline an office's business practices. Anything that restrains or inhibits movement toward a desired end functions as a constraint.

In rhetoric, constraints are defined in relationship to interests or ends that require rhetorical persuasion to achieve. **Rhetorical constraints** are those obstacles that must be overcome in order to facilitate both the persuasive and practical effects desired by the speaker. By "persuasive" effects, we mean those effects that make people think and act differently than they did before the speech. Constraints relating to persuasive effects are thus called **internal constraints**, referring to the beliefs, attitudes, and values of an audience that must be changed if persuasion is to occur. For example, convincing a population to support a tax on junk foods to cut down on child obesity may require challenging the **belief** that obesity is not a social problem, changing the pervading attitude of resisting higher taxes, and dissociating the eating of junk food from the value of personal choice and freedom. Unless these internal constraints can be modified, they will lead to the rejection of the proposal. However, a public speaker who actually desires to make a lasting change in actual conditions must also consider **external constraints**, which are the people, objects, processes, and events that may physically obstruct any productive action even if persuasion of an audience has occurred. A *person* acting as a constraint is someone who cannot be persuaded and who possesses the power to obstruct your goal, such as the governor who threatens a veto of your bill. An *object* is defined here as any tangible and enduring thing that tends to resist change while having constant influence on an environment, such as the presence of vending machines in schools (a "physical" object) or the laws that give schools financial incentives to place them in schools (a "legal" object). An *event* that is a constraint is a tangible but ephemeral thing that occurs at a specific point and time and has a distinct beginning and end, such as a sudden downturn in the economy that makes new taxes unpopular. Last, a *process* represents a sequence of events that must be followed in order to bring something to conclusion. As a constraint, such a process might be a lengthy and burdensome petition process by which any changes in tax laws require years of persistent effort.

Any of these external constraints may impede successful social action even *after* an audience has been persuaded to act. Consequently, public speakers who fail to account for external constraints may recommend a course of action, only to find it to be impossible to implement later, thereby wasting everyone's time and energy. Successful speakers should always consider all possible constraints before creating and delivering rhetorical discourse. Ignoring constraints often ruins any possibility of instigating effective social action. On the one hand, if external constraints are ignored, a speaker risks appearing ignorant about the "realities" of the situation. On the other hand, ignoring internal constraints is the common flaw of all "technical" discourse believing that the only things needed for persuasion are accurate facts and reasonable solutions. The most effective speaker combines elements of both types of discourse by adapting his or her language to both types of constraints.

Gen. George S. Patton: "You are not all going to die."

If any one governmental institution understands the logic of constraints, external and internal, it is the military. In wartime, for instance, there is an obvious external constraint to attaining one's goal—the enemy. But there are also significant internal constraints that have to do with "morale," meaning the state of mind of the soldiers. Perhaps the most famous administrative speech ever given during World War II was by Gen. George S. Patton to the U.S. 3rd Army on June 5, 1944, the day before D-Day. On June 6, U.S. forces would storm the heavily defended beaches of Normandy and begin the ground assault against Germany. Knowing that many of the soldiers would be facing battle for the first time and had already heard stories about the ferocity of the battle-hardened German military, Patton knew he had to confront their fears head-on and provide them the courage and motivation to fight as a team despite the horrors around them. He said:

> Men, this stuff some sources sling around about America wanting to stay out of the war and not wanting to fight is a lot of baloney! Americans love to fight, traditionally. All real Americans love the sting and clash of battle. America loves a winner. America will not tolerate a loser. Americans despise a coward; Americans play to win. That's why America has never lost and never will lose a war.
>
> You are not all going to die. Only two percent of you, right here today, would be killed in a major battle. Death must not be feared. Death, in time, comes to all of us. And every man is scared in his first action. If he says he's not, he's a goddamn liar. Some men are cowards, yes, but they fight just the same, or get the hell slammed out of them. The real hero is the man who fights even though he's scared. Some get over their fright in a minute, under fire; others take an hour; for some it takes days; but a real man will never let the fear of death overpower his honour, his sense of duty, to his country and to his manhood.[13]

Given the fact that he was giving an administrative speech, Patton could have simply told the soldiers that they had no choice but to follow orders or else be court-martialed. However, administrative speaking is not simply about laying down the law; it is about justifying the law and motivating the audience to embrace it by helping them overcome their internal constraints. The soldiers had no choice but to fight, but Patton gives them the motive to fight as a team with honor and duty, and therefore hopefully survive, or to give in to the internal constraint of fear and be killed more easily by the external constraints resisting their invasion.

Discussion: Consider the notion of providing universal health care for all Americans. What are the external and internal constraints to instituting such a policy? And what is the relationship between these two types of constraints? How is it sometimes difficult to tell the difference between an internal and external constraint in such complicated matters of policy?

---

[13] <http://www.famousquotes.me.uk/speeches/General_George_Patton/index.htm.>

MOTIVE

As indicated by the discussion of internal constraints, the psychological state of the audience is a crucial component of a rhetorical situation. Following Burke, we can describe this psychological state as a structure of motives. A **motive** refers to any conscious psychological or physiological incitement to action within a particular situation.[14] A motive is not to be confused with a mere "wish," however. Wishes merely exist in the abstract realm of fantasy and need not relate to anything actual; a motive only exists within a situation in which successful attainment of a goal is possible. For instance, a child may wish to fly to Mars and take great pleasure in imagining a fantastic voyage; this wish only becomes a motive when it stimulates the child to earn a degree in astrophysics while training to be a pilot. In other words, the number of wishes we might have at any one time is nearly infinite, which of course means they are all equally powerless to alter our actual behavior at any one time. By contrast, motives only occur in particular situations when a single desire or goal moves us to action and judgment.

The study of rhetoric in many ways is equivalent to the study of how to influence human motivation through conscious symbolic appeals. For Aristotle, audiences were motivated by respect for the speaker (**ethos**), by emotional affection or dislike (**pathos**), and by the strength of reason and evidence (**logos**). This study of motivation then took a "scientific" leap during the Age of Enlightenment when the new study of psychology was used to explain the phenomenon of persuasion. Rhetorician George Campbell, for example, wrote that the function of rhetoric is "to enlighten the Understanding, to please the Imagination, to move the Passions, or to influence the Will." The novelty behind this definition was the application of the recently discovered mental "faculties" to the study of rhetoric. Much like different departments within a modern corporation, these faculties were explained as existing in our minds as discrete units, each with its own unique process and function. So when we wanted to think about ideas, we called on the Understanding (sometimes called Thought or Reason); when we felt like stimulating our bodies, we sought out the Passions (sometimes called Emotions or Feeling); when we pondered the unknown, we appealed to the Imagination; and when we wanted to act, we rallied the Will. The most successful rhetoric engaged all the faculties at once. We argued logic to the Understanding, aroused the Passions through visual examples, used fantastic possibilities to excite the Imagination, and moved the Will through imperatives to action.

Today, we tend not to think in terms of discrete "faculties" that exist as separate entities in our minds. We simply talk about having beliefs, feelings, emotions, habits, desires, and values. However, the basic model of crafting language that is imaginative, thoughtful, and passionate in order to redirect human motivation remains effectively the same. The specific concern for rhetoric is those motives that arise in the context of the exigence as a means of resolving the situation in accordance with the needs and desires of an audience. The following concepts are therefore useful in

---

[14]For an explanation of Burke's theory of motive, see Andrew King, "Motive," *American Communication Journal* 1, no. 3 (1998).

understanding the structure of motivation of an audience. Each of these components represent one of three things for the speaker: (a) *a preexisting resource* to draw upon in support of judgments, (b) *a constraint* to overcome because its presence in the audience obstructs a course of action, or (c) *a possibility* to create as a means to encourage people to think, feel, or act a certain way as a means to resolve a situation.

1. **Belief:** A belief is a statement of fact on which a person is prepared to act. Beliefs can be stated as propositions, such as "the earth goes around the sun" or "all men are created equal" or "cutting taxes increases economic growth" or "people shouldn't smoke." Each of these beliefs only acts *as* a belief for a person if he or she actually acts in accordance with its content. When someone says one thing but does another, we do not attribute belief but accuse that person of hypocrisy. Rhetorically, beliefs are the building blocks of judgments, for they provide a concrete place to stand so that we know we are acting on a firm basis of understanding of reality (e.g., "Clean water is an essential component of a healthy nation.")

2. **Value:** A value is an abstract ideal quality that guides our behavior across a variety of situations. Whereas beliefs are propositions, values are usually stated as single virtue terms, such as "love" or "justice" or "liberty" or "equality." A value is a "quality" because it is something that we feel to be present in certain situations and that we treasure and wish to preserve for as long as possible. Usually values are things that almost everybody agrees are valuable; contention arises only in the clash between two competing values and their relative importance. "Love" and "justice" are in competition when a parent must decide whether to turn in a child who has committed a crime, and "liberty" and "equality" are in competition in economic debates that weigh the balance between the unregulated pursuit of individual wealth and the regulated distribution of resources to all. Rhetorically, values guide the speaker by investing the speech with an overall quality that resonates with the treasured values of the audience (e.g., "Our rivers should be as free and pure as the day the *Mayflower* landed.")

3. **Feeling:** A feeling is a sensory response to some environmental stimulation or physical state. Feelings make up the substance of our perceptual world, and represent the basic elements that physically connect us with the world around us. However, each audience comes to a situation being acquainted with a unique set of feelings based on that audience's particular experiences in an environment. For instance, people who live in a busy metropolis know the feelings associated with traffic, crowds, skyscrapers, construction, and city parks, whereas those who live in a rural farming community know the feelings associated with quiet landscapes, isolation, farmhouses, animals, and swaying fields of grain. Rhetorically, the familiar feelings (both negative and positive) of an audience can be effectively re-activated through language by calling forth familiar senses and by incorporating them into metaphor (e.g., "Many of us here remember the first time we walked with our bare feet through the cool, rocky streams during a sultry August day.")

4. **Emotion:** An emotion is a dramatized feeling that attracts or repels us to certain objects because of their specific character and qualities. An emotion is a

kind of "feeling" because it is usually a reaction to sense perception and also is attached to feelings of pleasure or pain; but it is a "dramatized" feeling because emotions carry with them narrative elements in which we play out scenarios in our minds of what will happen. It is the difference between simply perceiving the color red (as in feeling) and seeing a blinking red warning light on a console (as in emotion). Our emotional response to the red light is based on our narrative sense of whether the light signifies a danger that brings about a state of fear and urgency. Consequently, emotions are always related in some form or another to the "things" that surround us and are never simply "in our heads." Rhetorically, emotions are powerful tools to direct people toward or away from certain actions or judgments by connecting them to the people, objects, and events that bring about powerful emotions (e.g., "The month after a chemical spill in a nearby town, a thousand dead, stinking fish washed ashore and the water was covered with a frothy yellow scum.")

Despite their incredible variety, all emotions can be characterized by two things—orientation and salience. An **orientation** represents how we stand in relationship to a thing, whether we are attracted to (+) or repulsed by (–) it. A *neutral* orientation in which we have no stance thus represents the absence of emotion. For instance, I might have a positive orientation toward my family, a negative orientation to the fire ants in my back yard, and a neutral orientation to my neighbor's mailbox. **Salience** represents how strongly this emotion is felt within a particular situation. When I go on a long business trip I might miss my family terribly (high salience), whereas I like to look at the picture of my family during my lunch break at work (low salience).[15] Chapter 6, on pathos, will explore how rhetoric attempts to encourage orientations and heighten or reduce salience in order to encourage certain beliefs or actions.

5. **Habit:** A habit is a learned sequence of behavior in which mental and physical energies work relatively effortlessly together to accomplish a familiar task. Habits are what Aristotle called "second nature" because once acquired they take almost the same form as instinct, guiding our thoughts and actions in familiar groups without the requirement of deliberative choice or reflective thought. Habits therefore include more than simply ordinary tasks such as tying shoes or waking up early or cleaning up after oneself; they also include complex tasks such as writing depositions and painting landscapes and fly fishing. Any type of group, no matter how large or small, has common goals and common activities and shares a core group of habits. There are habits of being a carpenter, an engineer, a bachelor, or a U.S. citizen. Rhetorically, habits can be problems ("we are careless with our waterways"), resources ("let us apply the habits of housekeeping to our rivers"), or goals ("we need good habits of water conservation").

6. **Desire:** A desire is a concrete energetic ideal that propels people to action in pursuit of some value or pleasure. Desires are products of either *imagination*

---

[15]For an exploration of the situational characteristic of emotional response, see Phoebe C. Ellsworth, "Some Reasons to Expect Universal Antecedents of Emotion," *The Nature of Emotion: Fundamental Questions*, ed. Paul Ekman and Richard J. Davidson (Oxford, UK: Oxford University Press, 1994), 150–154.

or *memory*—imagination when they are products of novel creations of the mind and memory when they are recollections of the past that a person aspires to re-experience. Like a motive, a desire is not simply a "wish" that exists in an ideal and impossible realm of fantasy; it is something that we invest energy in seeking and that guides our decisions in actual situations of choice. Our desires are based on how clearly we can envision a future state of affairs and how powerful the subsequently produced emotions are. Rhetorically, similar to habits, desires can be problems ("We dream too much of big houses and fast cars"), resources ("Don't you all want to bring your kids to the same clean streams?"), or created products ("Let us imagine a whole nation of clean waterways where humans and nature care for one another.")

The motives of the audience are thus a product of how all of these components interact. An audience enters into a situation holding to a specific set of beliefs; treasuring certain values over others; being acquainted with a general sphere of feelings; associating specific emotions with types of events, objects, and people; having developed a nexus of habits that helps them deal with their environment; and harboring certain desires for which they will sacrifice time and energy to attain. A speaker must then decide which of these things to draw from in support of the position, which represent problems that prevent an audience from attaining their goals, and which need to be created in an audience in order for them to accomplish something new.

Lucy Stone: "I have been a disappointed woman."

Because speeches of advocacy have as one of their primary functions the capacity to mobilize a group around a common cause, many of the most influential of these types of speeches have occurred at conventions organized for this explicit purpose. One of these was the National Women's Rights Convention first held in 1850, initiated in part by American suffragist and abolitionist Lucy Stone. As the first woman from Massachusetts to earn a college degree in 1847, Stone dedicated her life to the cause of women's rights so that more women could challenge the often oppressive social norms that kept women in their "place"—the home. Organization of the convention was thus designed to unify the movement and give individual women a collective voice and purpose. At the convention in Cincinnati, Ohio, in 1855, she delivered one of her most famous speeches of advocacy that addressed the motives of her audience:

> The last speaker alluded to this movement as being that of a few disappointed women. From the first years to which my memory stretches, I have been a disappointed woman. When, with my brothers, I reached forth after the sources of knowledge, I was reproved with "It isn't fit for you; it doesn't belong to women." Then there was but one college in the world where women were admitted, and that was in Brazil. I would have found my way there, but by the time I was prepared to go, one was opened in the young state of Ohio—the first in the United States where women and Negroes could enjoy opportunities with white men. I was disappointed when I came to seek a profession worthy of an immortal being—every employment was close to me, except that of the

teacher, the seamstress, and the housekeeper. In education, in marriage, in religion, in everything, disappointment is the lot of woman. It shall be the business of my life to deepen this disappointment in every woman's heart until she bows down to it no longer. I wish that women, instead of being walking showcases, instead of begging of their fathers and brothers the latest and gayest new bonnet, would ask them of their rights.[16]

As Stone appeals to the motive of the audience, one can also see demonstrated here three common characteristics of speeches of advocacy. First, Stone clearly identifies her audience as fellow women who share her experience. Second, she attempts to motivate this audience by rousing emotions of dissatisfaction and frustration with their situation and also their own failure to act. Last, she points out exactly what she wants them to do—demand their rights rather than ask for a new bonnet. At each point, she touches on aspects of motive. Challenging belief: "It isn't fit for you; it doesn't belong to women." Praising values: courage, integrity, honesty. Arousing emotion: disappointment. Cultivating habits: assertiveness instead of passivity. And arousing desire: ask for your rights. Only by transforming the motives of the audience is change possible.

Discussion: Think of a situation of a master and slave relationship, in which two individuals with two competing motivations are nonetheless acting together despite their differences. How do we account for this apparent "cooperation" by understanding each person's motives in terms of belief, value, feeling, emotion, habit, and desire? What would have to change in the situation for cooperation to come to an end?

PRACTICAL JUDGMENT

Once an exigence becomes universally recognized, the immediate question becomes "What do we do?" The answer to this question always involves a **practical judgment**, which is the act of defining a particular person, object, or event for the purposes of making a practical decision. In other words, practical judgment tells us both *what things are* and *what we should do about them*. The mere giving of commands—such as "Go!" or "Halt!—is therefore *not* a practical judgment because it does not satisfy the first criterion of the definition. A practical judgment demands action but only after an act of cognition that explains to our minds the relationship among a *thing*, an *idea*, and an *action*. For example, I wake up at night and hear a tapping sound (thing). Fearful that it is a burglar (hypothetical idea), I get up and discover it is just the rattling of the air conditioner (conclusive idea). I then decide to go back to sleep (action). As indicated by this example, usually our practical judgments are absorbed into the habits and **conventions** (or shared, normative habits) of our everyday lives. We do not need to think consciously about whether we should respond to a stop sign (thing), by associating it with the command to stop

---

[16]Lucy Stone, "A Disappointed Woman." Available at <http://www.dupage88.net/aths/resources/ AT%20MCweb02/Pathfinders/AmSpeeches/stone.htm> (accessed 3 September 2012).

(idea), and then stopping (action). We just stop. But when we are learning to drive, all of these practical judgments must be consciously taught and enforced through instruction.

As indicated by the discussion of exigence, practical judgment takes on rhetorical qualities when we are unsure about what *to do* because we are unsure about what things *are*. Are British soldiers in Boston "peacekeepers" or "oppressors"? Should we view the violence in Darfur as "genocide" or "civil war"? In each case, rhetorical conflict involves the struggle to properly name things in such a way as to advance one judgment over another and thereby encourage forms of action on the basis of that judgment. The question of practical judgment thus centers around the matter of naming and therefore of meaning. We must be very careful of the words we use to describe our environment, because every word is loaded with particular denotations and connotations and associations that inevitably lead people to act in a certain ways instead of other ways. One of the central challenges of any rhetorical public speaker is to promote his or her version of practical judgment and thereby provide the correct "names" for any contingency that will make an audience prefer certain options over others.

Frederick Douglass: "Must I argue that a system thus marked with blood is wrong?"

It was not until the nineteenth century that a concerted movement to abolish slavery finally took hold in the United States. Previously, the majority of Americans made the practical judgment that slavery was a necessary (if at times grotesque) means to the advancement of the nation's economic growth and political power. Although Thomas Jefferson had originally included a long condemnation of the slave trade in the Declaration of Independence, it had been struck out by the representatives of the Southern colonies. It took several generations following the American Revolution for slavery to become the dominant question of practical judgment in the United States. What is interesting, then, about the speech given by Frederick Douglass, a former slave turned writer and abolitionist, to the Rochester Ladies' Anti-Slavery Society on July 4, 1852, is that Douglass addressed the matter of slavery as if the matter of practical judgment had already been decided, and that the only thing that remained was to act upon it:

> What, am I to argue that it is wrong to make men brutes, to rob them of their liberty, to work them without wages, to keep them ignorant of their relations to their fellow men, to beat them with sticks, to flay their flesh with the lash, to load their limbs with irons, to hunt them with dogs, to sell them at auction, to sunder their families, to knock out their teeth, to burn their flesh, to starve them into obedience and submission to their masters? Must I argue that a system thus marked with blood, and stained with pollution, is wrong? No! I will not. I have better employment for my time and strength than such arguments would imply.
>
> What, then, remains to be argued? Is it that slavery is not divine; that God did not establish it; that our doctors of divinity are mistaken? There is blasphemy in the thought. That which is inhuman, cannot be divine! Who can reason on such a proposition? They that can, may; I cannot. The time for such

argument is passed. At a time like this, scorching irony, not convincing argument, is needed. O! had I the ability, and could reach the nation's ear, I would, to-day, pour out a fiery stream of biting ridicule, blasting reproach, withering sarcasm, and stern rebuke. For it is not light that is needed, but fire; it is not the gentle shower, but thunder. We need the storm, the whirlwind, and the earthquake. The feeling of the nation must be quickened; the conscience of the nation must be roused; the propriety of the nation must be startled; the hypocrisy of the nation must be exposed; and its crimes against God and man must be proclaimed and denounced.[17]

According to Douglas, slavery by its very existence calls forth the practical judgment that it is an expression of barbarism rather than some divine order of things. What is required, rather, is a thunderous judgment upon the nation for its tolerance of this inhumane institution. Douglas therefore does not waste his time persuading us to make a radical judgment about slavery; rather, he directs the nation's attention to making a practical judgment upon itself.[18]

Discussion: Although we might not intuitively associate practical judgment with leisure, it is in our social relationships and choices of pleasure that we often make the most important practical judgments—whom we should associate with, where we should go, what we should consume, how we should act. What was the worst practical judgment you made while at a social gathering? Did it have lasting negative consequences? How did it affect your future judgments?

OCCASION

Rhetoric as a form of public speaking specifically refers to rhetoric that occurs at a specific time and place shared by both speaker and audience. In other words, occasion represents all of those elements that characterize a particular rhetorical act as a distinctly *oral* performance. The **occasion** is the specific setting shared by speaker and audience whose circumstances determine the genre, the purpose, and the standards of appropriateness of what is said. Examples of different types of occasions include a wedding ceremony, a political rally in front of City Hall, a Thanksgiving dinner, a graduation ceremony, or murder prosecution at a law court. The power of occasion is its tendency to focus attention and interest on a single subject, a tendency that on the one hand significantly constrains the freedom of a speaker but on the other hand allows him or her to more powerfully use language to unify the audience's emotional, intellectual, creative, and physical capacities around a single theme. Consequently, it is not unusual for speakers to provide two rhetorical responses to any rhetorical situation, one using the spoken word to address people at a specific occasion, and the other using writing or electronic media to communicate to secondary audiences without the constraints of occasion.

---

[17]<http://www.pbs.org/wgbh/aia/part4/4h2927t.html>.
[18]For more on Douglass, see Kevin McClure, "Frederick Douglass' Use of Comparison in His Fourth of July Oration: A Textual Criticism," *Western Journal of Communication* 64, no. 4 (2000), 425–444.

The most important function of occasion is to establish a common purpose for bringing speaker and audience together in the same place. The **purpose** for rhetorical public speech represents the reason for and circumstances under which an occasion occurs. To be clear, the purpose is not the purpose of the *speaker;* it is the purpose for the *event.* Purpose establishes common expectations among members of a diverse public that help direct their attention and focus. This is obvious for most conventional occasions. The occasion of the wedding establishes the purpose of the best man's speech, regardless of who is chosen for that role, just as the purpose of a defense attorney's speech is not up to the whim of the lawyer. In these cases, the occasion came first, and the speaker was selected based on his or her ability to fill its purpose. However, many times the speaker's intent and the occasion's purpose coincide. These are situations in which an individual creates an occasion explicitly for the purpose of speaking his or her mind and generates an audience on that basis alone. These types of speeches are usually given by well-known celebrities or political figures capable of attracting an audience based on the strength of their *ethos* alone, although one cannot rule out the proverbial "soapbox" oratory of the anonymous citizen standing up on a street corner. However, once these speeches begin, they nonetheless take on a purpose of their own that still constrains what can be said.

In addition to purpose, the occasion determines the genre and standards of appropriateness of the speech. A selection of genres has already been defined in Chapter 2, but these should not be taken as comprehensive. Speech genres are literally infinite. Speeches of commemoration alone can be broken down into endless subgenres, such as wedding speeches, graduation speeches, award ceremony speeches, Veteran's Day speeches, coronation speeches, and so on. The important thing is simply to keep in mind that any occasion creates generic expectations in an audience for what they will hear and how they will hear it based on tradition and on past experiences. Finally, occasion determines **appropriateness**, or how "fitting" the speech is to all of the particular elements and unique circumstances of the speech.[19] An appropriate speaker considers the audience's needs and desires before composing the speech, whereas an inappropriate speaker thinks first of his or her own self-interest and only afterward makes minor accommodations to the audience. For instance, the speech by a best man at a bachelor party has norms of appropriateness vastly different from a speech given in front of grandparents and grandchildren. More than one movie has used a best man's ignorance of standards of appropriateness as a source of comedy.

It is important to note, however, that the constraints of appropriateness are not fixed rules or absolute responsibilities. They are norms of behavior usually established through cultural tradition and social habit. In everyday life, following the dictates of appropriateness as determined by the purposes of the occasion is the easiest way to get our voices heard. Anyone preparing for a job interview quickly realizes the importance of saying the right thing in the right way in order to get what one wants. Yet sometimes norms of appropriateness are so narrow as

---

[19]For the Sophistical view of appropriateness, see John Poulakos, "Toward a Sophistic Definition of Rhetoric," in *Contemporary Rhetorical Theory: A Reader,* ed. John Louis Lucaites, Celeste Michelle Condit, and Sally Caudill (New York: The Guilford Press, 1999).

to be oppressive. What is considered appropriate might not equate with what we consider ethical or moral. It is simply what is expected. It is up to rhetors to judge whether their conformity to or violation of these constraints helps enable the productive resolution of some larger problem.

Susan B. Anthony: "Resistance to tyranny is obedience to God."

The power of occasion is demonstrated in the testimony of Susan B. Anthony before a court of law. Anthony still appears on the face of some dollar coins, but it is not as well known that she also was convicted of a crime—the crime of casting a ballot in the 1872 presidential election, which happened during a time when women could not vote. On June 19, 1873, after having been denied the opportunity to say a word in her defense, she stood before Judge Ward Hunt after her lawyer appealed the guilty verdict. This excerpt from her interaction with the judge demonstrates how occasion and appropriateness influence the performance of situated rhetorical discourse. The fact that her words were spoken in resistance to the formal requirements of a defendant and the direct commands of the judge make her words much more powerful. Imagine, for instance, the courage it must have taken to respond to the judge as she does in this exchange:

JUDGE HUNT	(Ordering the defendant to stand up) Has the prisoner anything to say why sentence shall not be pronounced?
MISS ANTHONY	Yes, your honor, I have many things to say; for in your ordered verdict of guilty, you have trampled under foot every vital principle of our government. My natural rights, my civil rights, my political rights, my judicial rights, are all alike ignored. Robbed of the fundamental privilege of citizenship, I am degraded from the status of a citizen to that of a subject; and not only myself individually, but all of my sex, are, by your honor's verdict, doomed to political subjection under this, so-called, form of government.
JUDGE HUNT	The Court cannot listen to a rehearsal of arguments the prisoner's counsel has already consumed three hours in presenting.
MISS ANTHONY	May it please your honor, I am not arguing the question, but simply stating the reasons why sentence cannot, in justice, be pronounced against me. Your denial of my citizen's right to vote, is the denial of my right of consent as one of the governed, the denial of my right of representation as one of the taxed, the denial of my right to a trial by a jury of my peers as an offender against law, therefore, the denial of my sacred rights to life, liberty, property and . . .
JUDGE HUNT	The Court cannot allow the prisoner to go on . . . . The Court must insist the prisoner has been tried according to the established forms of law.
MISS ANTHONY	Yes, your honor, but by forms of law all made by men, interpreted by men, administered by men, in favor of men, and against women; and hence, your honor's ordered verdict of guilty, against a United States citizen for the exercise of *"that citizen's*

right to vote," simply because that citizen was a woman and not a man. As then, the slaves who got their freedom must take it over, or under, or through the unjust forms of law, precisely so, now, must women, to get their right to a voice in this government, take it; and I have taken mine, and mean to take it at every possible opportunity.

JUDGE HUNT   The Court orders the prisoner to sit down. It will not allow another word. . . . (Here the prisoner sat down.)

JUDGE Hunt   The prisoner will stand up. (Here Miss Anthony arose again.) The sentence of the Court is that you pay a fine of one hundred dollars and the costs of the prosecution.

MISS Anthony   May it please your honor, I shall never pay a dollar of your unjust penalty. All the stock in trade I possess is a $10,000 debt, incurred by publishing my paper—The Revolution—four years ago, the sole object of which was to educate all women to do precisely as I have done, rebel against your man-made, unjust, unconstitutional forms of law, that tax, fine, imprison and hang women, while they deny them the right of representation in the government; and I shall work on with might and main to pay every dollar of that honest debt, but not a penny shall go to this unjust claim. And I shall earnestly and persistently continue to urge all women to the practical recognition of the old revolutionary maxim, that "Resistance to tyranny is obedience to God."[20]

The power of occasion, in this case, was to focus attention on Anthony's testimony, which was then recorded and distributed in subsequent newspapers and pamphlets. Without the trial, public attention would not have been focused on her protest or the courage it took to speak her mind in the context of education in which she was told to be silent. The fact that she was not allowed even to defend herself (it being considered inappropriate at that time for a woman to speak during the formal proceedings) made her act of speaking all the more powerful, an effect magnified by her appeal to the legacy of the American Revolution to justify her own resistance to American law. Because she consciously attends to the rhetorical background, she is able to speak beyond the immediate particulars of her exigence and occasion. She speaks to a broader public, including the public of today.[21]

Discussion: The spread of social media has altered the way we think of occasions. "Flash mobs," for instance, are spontaneous gatherings by strangers at a particular point in time to perform some random activity, such as having a pillow fight in a subway station or square dancing in a mall. Do you think that rhetoric can exploit this new type of occasion?

---

[20]Susan B. Anthony, available from <http://law2.umkc.edu/faculty/projects/ftrials/anthony/sbaaccount.html> (accessed 6 September 2012).

[21]For more on Anthony's significance as a public speaker, see Elaine E. McDavitt, "Susan B. Anthony, Reformer and Speaker," *Quarterly Journal of Speech* 30, no. 2 (1944), 173–180.

KEY WORDS

SUMMARY

Considering the rhetorical background that frames any rhetorical public speech provides a speaker with the broader perspective that is necessary for any sustained effort at persuasion. This perspective not only expands the spatial horizon beyond the immediate physical context, but it also extends the temporal horizon so that it speaks to the past and looks toward the future. For example, simply thinking in terms of a larger "public" makes even one's immediate audience representatives of a larger social group with a shared history. One must simply remember that the qualities of the rhetorical background should never be taken to represent anything more than convenient and pragmatic shorthand that ultimately proves the worth of those qualities within the successful act of rhetorical persuasion. In the end, all groups and individuals are unique and exceed the capacity for such broad generalizations. But these generalizations are necessary starting points nonetheless, for they help us look beyond the immediate moment and give us perspective. As Roman orator Cicero observed long ago, audience adaptation requires a great deal of labor beyond just adapting to what the members of an audience might be thinking, feeling, and saying in the present:

> We must also read the poets, acquaints ourselves with histories, study and peruse the masters and authors in every excellent art, and by way of practice praise, expound, emend, criticize, and confute them; we must argue every question on both sides, and bring out on every topic whatever points can be deemed plausible; besides this we must become learned in the common law and familiar with the statutes, and must contemplate all the olden time, and investigate the ways of the senate, political philosophy, the rights of allies, the treaties and conventions, and the policy of empire; and last we have to cull, from all the forms of pleasantry, a certain charm of humor, with which to give a sprinkle of salt, as it were, to all of our discourse.[22]

Although we are far from ancient Rome, the same principles apply. The best public speakers always think beyond the scope of their immediate situation and audience, thinking not only in terms of the past and the future but also the larger publics that might encounter their speeches in various mediated contexts. The more one knows about the complexities of history and culture, the richer and more durable one's speech becomes.

However, no speech is successful without first and foremost being able to address the *unique* and *pressing* character of the problem in the *present*.

---

[22]Cicero, 221.

The considerations of the rhetorical foreground thus link us to the concrete characteristics of our present surroundings that help balance the more universal characteristics of our larger social and historical environment. Attention to exigence, practical judgment, audience, constraints, speaker, and occasion gives a speech its energy and life. Whereas the rhetorical background helps to identify the general aspects of a somewhat generic American audience, the rhetorical foreground puts us in a specific place and time. It tells us what stands out from a background environment and strikes us as being something urgent and important.

Each of the concepts within the rhetorical foreground distinguishes different parts of a rhetorical situation to help focus attention on specific aspects before addressing the whole situation. The *exigence* defines the immediate problem at hand rather than some vague moral abstraction or political maxim. The *constraints* represent the known obstacles to resolving this problem, whether they be physical constraints in a situation or emotional and psychological constraints within an audience. The *audience*, in turn, identifies that particular group, often a subset of some public, whose members are capable of resolving that problem if they act in a specific way. The *motives* represent all of those characteristics of an audience (actual or potential) that influence their decision in that particular moment. *Practical judgment* represents the specific action they are called upon to make by the speaker, in this case a judgment upon a certain event, person, or object that affects the course of future events. Finally, the *occasion* stands for the actual context of the speech situation, including the place and time of the event, the purpose for the occasion, and the expectations of the audience in attendance.

CHAPTER 3 EXERCISES

1. Analyze your rhetorical artifact selected in Chapter 1 according to the table provided in the summary.
2. Identify a convention in your immediate environment that annoys you. Explain why it bothers you in terms of its consequences. Then violate this convention. Explain what happens and how you feel.
3. As a class, select a major historical event in the nation's history. Have everyone privately draw a historical lesson from this event and present it as a brief commemorative speech. How are these lessons the same or different?
4. Find an actual written text or speech created by someone whom you would consider as belonging to a "marginal" group. Read this text out loud in class and discuss how that group's marginalization may have affected certain aspects of the speech— for example, consider constraints and occasion. Can you think of any situations in which the marginalization of a group might be justified?
5. Bring in a common object that has no mysterious or controversial aspects (e.g., a fork, a rock, a hat). Then make a new practical judgment about this object (however hypothetical or fanciful) in front of the class in order to make this audience approach it differently in the future.
6. Remember a time you experienced a "contingency" as a child. (This does not have to be rhetorical.) Tell the story of your experience, trying to make it as vivid as possible so that your audience feels what you felt. The purpose here is to try to embody the *feeling* of contingency.
7. Find a print advertisement for some product. Who do you think is the target audience? What cues point you to this conclusion?
8. As in the examples presented in this chapter, think of an exigence that can take different forms according to the situation. Describe your exigence as a personal problem, a public problem, or a rhetorical problem. What factors determine it to be that specific type of problem?
10. Invent a new "crisis" that might face your community or the country as a rhetorical exigence. What would be the constraints to resolving this exigence rhetorically? Then create a short impromptu speech proposing a solution.
11. Think of an "occasion" with which you are very familiar and that recurs frequently. What are the rules and expectations (in terms of communication) at such an occasion? Can you think of a time when such expectations were violated? What were the consequences?

Ethos

This chapter discusses how a rhetorical public speaker develops a relationship with an audience. A "relationship" means more than simply letting an audience know a speaker's identity and his or her qualifications. A relationship is something personal that involves an emotional attitude toward another person or group and negotiates their reciprocal identities. This chapter explores the strategies that can be used to develop a relationship between speaker and audience that is most conducive to persuasion. Starting with the classical definition of ethos as a combination of goodwill, practical wisdom, and virtue that make us think a speaker is credible and trustworthy, this chapter moves into more specific concepts that help define ethos, including persona, evoked audience, identification, distinction, and polarization.

Perhaps what most distinguishes public speaking from any other form of persuasion is the fact that its effectiveness relies heavily on the character of the speaker. As an oral performer, a public speaker steps before an audience and effectively asks them a favor—to listen attentively as the speaker rewards their time and energy with a speech that is tailored specifically to their interests. An advertisement or a YouTube clip or an e-mail has no analogous constraint. Because of their reproducibility, these media can be watched or read at any time that is convenient to an audience and can be turned off or ignored just as easily without offending anyone. Yet when members of an audience ignore the speaker entirely or walk out of the room, we think of it as highly rude or antagonistic. That is why the choice to actually attend a public speech is usually a more personal and important decision than simply clicking on a video link. When we decide to be a member of an audience, we do so because we want to listen to the *speaker*, and we have done so because we have put trust in that speaker to reward our time commitment. Any successful public speech must therefore begin with the existence of mutual trust that forms a temporary relationship between speaker and audience. Without a sense of this "bond," a speaker's words fall on deaf ears.

For the purposes of rhetorical public speech, **ethos** represents this sense of public character that is recognized by an audience and influences their reception of the speaker's arguments. Ethos is thus the capacity to influence an audience based on the audience's perceptions of the credibility and character of the speaker in relationship to the audience's own interests and values. Importantly, even though the Greek word for ethos is "character," this does not have the modern connotation of being something private and inside of us that others cannot see.

That is why it is perhaps more appropriate to call it *public* character. Ethos in the rhetorical sense is not something absolute and stable that one carries around wherever one goes; it is determined by the relationship one has with an audience. The president of a country may possess great ethos with respect to his or her own constituency and yet be despised by a foreign population. This is because any act can be interpreted differently by different groups. A presidential declaration of war may be seen as a courageous defense of freedom by one side and a brutal act of imperialism by the other. To understand the possible effects of one's rhetoric, then, a person must understand how an audience perceives his or her character.[1] For the Greeks, people with ethos were those people who earned respect, admiration, and allegiance rather than those who simply possessed a good "soul" that went unseen by others.[2]

The concept of ethos has distinctly rhetorical implications because it deals with aspects of credibility and authority that influence our choice of whom to trust when faced with important decisions.[3] In other words, because we often do not have the time or resources to be able to make crucial judgments on our own, we look to those who possess strength of character, or ethos, to help guide our actions. For this reason, Aristotle believed that among the three forms of rhetorical proof (ethos, pathos, and logos), ethos was often the most powerful. He writes:

> There is persuasion through character whenever the speech is spoken in such a way as to make the speaker worthy of credence; for we believe fair-minded people to a greater extent and more quickly than we do others, on all subjects in general and completely so in cases where there is not exact knowledge but room for doubt. And this should result from the speech, not from a previous opinion that the speaker is a certain kind of person; for it is not the case as some of the handbook writers propose in their treatment of the art at fair-mindedness on the part of the speaker makes no contribution to persuasive this; rather, character is almost, so to speak, the most authoritative form of persuasion.[4]

The reason that ethos is the most authoritative form of persuasion is simply because we tend to accept the opinions of those people who we feel are more like us and who have our best interests at heart. Particularly when hundreds of different messages surround us every day, demanding our attention for this thing and that, ethos provides us an efficient and usually reliable way of selecting those few that we think are tailored specifically to our lives and our concerns. This is why public speaking, as an oral performance, still remains a powerful medium of persuasion in a digital age. It is the only medium that establishes a meaningful bond between speaker and audience and distills from the cacophony of popular and political culture a single message that creates a sense of shared experience between both speaker and audience and between audience members themselves.

---

[1] For more on speaker credibility, see chapter 5 of Gary C. Woodward and Robert E. Denton, Jr., *Persuasion and Influence in American Life,* 5th ed. (Long Grove, IL: Waveland, 2004).

[2] For more on the Greek notion of public life, see chapter 2 of Hannah Arendt, *The Human Condition,* 2nd ed. (Chicago: The University of Chicago Press, 1958).

[3] For excellent essays exploring the concept of *ethos,* see Michael J. Hyde, ed., *The Ethos of Rhetoric* (Columbia: University of South Carolina Press, 2004).

[4] Aristotle, *Rhetoric,* 1356a.

Because it is so central to the act of public speaking, establishing ethos is a complex process that involves more than simply offering an audience a list of accomplishments and admirable characteristics. Developing ethos in a public speech is not the same as presenting a written resume for a job application. The goal of developing ethos is to establish a relationship, not to document facts. Aristotle explains the difficulty of establishing ethos and its three components:

> There are three reasons why speakers themselves are persuasive; for there are three things we trust other than logical demonstration. These are practical wisdom (*phronesis*), and virtue (*arête*), and goodwill (*eunoia*): for speakers make mistakes in what they say through failure to exhibit either, all, or one of these; for either through lack of practical sense they do not form opinions rightly; or through forming opinions they do not say what they think because of the bad character; or they are prudent and fair-minded but let goodwill, so that it is possible for people not to give the best advice although they know what it is. These are the only possibilities.[5]

Understanding the subtleties of Aristotle's argument requires a clear distinction between these three components of ethos. By **practical wisdom**, he means a proven ability to size up problematic situations and make judgments that show prudence and forethought, as a military commander might possess due to actions during past battles. By **virtue**, he means excellence in performing particular activities that are held in high regard and embody the best cultural values, as one might think of the virtues of motherhood. By **goodwill**, he means the presence of conscious and thoughtful consideration of the audience's well-being, as we would expect from a good friend rather than from a stranger on the street.

In summary, we prove practical wisdom by boasting of our track record of past decisions, we prove virtue by showing how we have committed ourselves to certain noble habits of action, and we prove goodwill by addressing the concerns and interests of our audience and by revealing our willingness to sacrifice our own self-interest in service of their prosperity. As Aristotle remarks, however, it is difficult to show all three in a speech. For instance, a criminal may have demonstrated practical wisdom in his ability to rob banks, but lack virtue and goodwill. A reclusive monk might be well esteemed in virtue, but have little practical wisdom for everyday situations and perhaps might not care. And an old high school friend might have all the goodwill in the world toward you, but lack good sense and most components of virtue. In each case, we might have interesting conversations with each of these individuals, but rhetorically we would not necessarily look to them for counsel in times of crisis or uncertainty. It is during these times that ethos becomes a powerful persuasive tool because it focuses an audience's attention on the message that comes from one respected individual. Developing this rhetorical ethos will be the subject of the rest of this chapter.

Discussion: As indicated by many of the speeches included in this textbook, many times celebrities whose ethos comes from their acting ability try to also establish ethos in the political sphere. Which celebrity activist do you think has successfully established goodwill, practical wisdom, and virtue with respect to some political issue? And who do you think has done the opposite?

---

[5] Aristotle, *Rhetoric*, 1358a.

PERSONA

Most people step into any familiar social situation with an **inherited ethos,** which is the actual reputation that rhetors "carry with them" because of an audience's acquaintance with past behavior. When an inherited ethos is strong, such as the ethos of a mother for her child or that which close friends have with each other, the rhetor rarely has to spend any time establishing his or her reputation or credibility. It certainly would be strange for a mother to say to her child, "Because I have worked hard these many years learning how to cook healthy meals (good sense), because I care deeply for your future (goodwill), and because I am a just and honorable soul (virtue), please listen to my recommendation to eat your spinach." Having already established her ethos, she simply says "Eat your spinach." Inherited ethos is this kind of unspoken credibility that needs no mention to function. In Aristotle's language, it is "inartistic."

Ethos becomes a uniquely rhetorical concern of *art* only when rhetors, in some form, create or modify the perception of an audience about them. **Persona** is this rhetorical creation; it represents the constructed ethos that a rhetor creates within the confines of a particular rhetorical text. Persona, in other words, is more a creation of language rather than an inheritance of history. Like the costume that transforms an actor into a new personality on stage, rhetoric can create a "public face" that best suits the immediate needs of a rhetor. Unlike inherited ethos, which is the product of cumulative interactions or exposure over time with an audience, one's persona is always tied to a specific discourse and is completely contained within that discourse. For example, a convict before a parole board enters the hearing with an inherited ethos as a liar and a thief, and he attempts to counter that reputation by describing himself as a "changed man" who has seen the error of his ways. The decision of the board rests on whether the convict's persona of a "changed man" is more convincing than the inherited ethos of a liar and a thief.

Deciding when to construct a persona and when to rely on the strength of one's inherited ethos depends upon the presence and quality of one's reputation within an audience. On the one hand, when a speaker is unknown to an audience, creating a persona is necessary in order to present a favorable "first impression."[6] We are all familiar with those first job interviews when we must define ourselves as an ideal employee. On the other hand, when a speaker enters a situation as a respected leader, there is no need for such self-promotion; indeed, it would be seen as being in bad taste. Rarely do we enjoy listening to famous and powerful people talking about their fame and power. But most speaking situations usually fall somewhere in between these two extremes. In these cases, one must construct a persona that somehow addresses, modifies, and transcends the limits of one's inherited ethos.[7]

Because the construction of personae deals not just with possession of knowledge or skills, but with notions of character, it relies heavily on personal stories and the form of delivery. **Personal stories** are narrations of one's life experience that

---

[6]An interesting account of an actual scholarly persona is found in James Darsey, "Edwin Black and the First Persona," *Rhetoric & Public Affairs* 10, no. 3 (2007), 501–507.

[7]The relationship between rhetor and audience can be described in terms of the ratio between the level of credibility and the level of agreement. These considerations are explained in detail in chapter 7 of Woodward and Denton, *Persuasion and Influence in American Life.*

provide insight into the speaker's practical wisdom, virtue, or goodwill. Phrases like "The time I was behind enemy lines . . ." or "When I saved my sister's life . . ." or "Growing up in a tough neighborhood . . ." signify to an audience that a person is relating a story that offers a window into his or her deeper self. The **form of delivery** reveals character by using phrases, words, accents, or gestures commonly associated with certain "types" of people. Hence, a president often vacillates between acting "presidential" by speaking in firm, calm, and authoritative terms in formal settings and behaving as an "ordinary American" by doing volunteer work with rolled-up sleeves and telling jokes around a barbeque. Form of delivery is important because we trust those who speak like us, not just because it is familiar, but because it shows a mastery of the type of language that can only be acquired through life experience. It is thus an expression of goodwill.

The personae available for a rhetor are literally infinite. However, there are general types of personae that are always familiar and that conform to our social conventions. Take, for instance, just a few popular personae: the country lawyer, the wise sage, the teenage rebel, the religious prophet, the CEO, the father/mother figure, the loyal friend, the iconoclast, the president, the confidant, the drill sergeant, or the door-to-door salesperson. Any person attempting to create his or her own persona, of course, will always individualize his or her character such that no two personae will ever be alike. But these models provide general guides for action.

In their review of the research on the roles typically played by rhetors in rhetorical situations, Roderick Hart and Susanne Daughton identify four recurring personae: the apologist, the agent, the partisan, and the hero.[8] These roles represent fitting responses to situations that also take into account the personality and intentions of the speaker.

1. **Apologist**: The role of **apologist** is employed when speakers wish to rebuff attack, including both attacks on one's personal character and more often on one's position. The essential characteristic of the apologist is *righteous indignation*. The apologist does not actually "apologize." Like Socrates in front of the jury, the apologist instead corrects the mistaken impression of the audience and seeks to clarify the essential rightness of his or her position. The most powerful way to do this is by employing one of three strategies: *bolstering*, which supports one's case by "correcting" the erroneous facts and narratives held by the audience ("My accusers have been deceived by liars and are in turn distorting the truth about my position"); *differentiation*, which clarifies misunderstanding by more clearly separating, or differentiating, two issues that have been carelessly conflated ("My critics do not understand the difference between making policy statements and telling jokes."); and *transcendence*, which resolves tensions by invoking a higher principle that clarifies apparent contradictions ("I am accused of inciting violence, and yet the only thing I want is peace. But sometimes peace must be achieved through war."). Successful apologists appear noble because they're willing to suffer for their cause while seeking to clarify the truth.

---

[8]Roderick Hart and Susanne Daughton. *Modern Rhetorical Criticism,* 3rd ed. (Boston: Pearson, 2005), 220–221.

2. The **agent** speaks on behalf of some institution as a spokesperson of legitimate authority, thereby standing as a "representative" of a recognized institution, such as church body, a government, or a corporation. The essential characteristic of the agent is *enthusiastic loyalty*. Typical people who fit the role of agent in society are public relations specialists, priests, presidents, CEOs, chancellors, community leaders, and ambassadors of all kinds. What makes a successful agent is the fact that he or she charismatically can "stand in" for a larger institution, thereby putting a personal face on a sometimes abstract entity. It is difficult to have affection for the Catholic Church or the United States or Microsoft simply as institutions; but we can generate great enthusiasm at the prospect of meeting the pope or the president or Bill Gates. At the same time, our enthusiasm at meeting these individuals is only because they "stand for" a form of organized authority that is greater than them as individuals. In other words, a successful agent conveys personal charisma while at the same time being an effective representative of a larger and more powerful group that asks our allegiance.

3. The **partisan** is one who represents not a group or institution but an idea or ideal. This individual tends to thrive in heated debates during times of turmoil and upheaval, when people are looking for new directions based on new ideas. The essential characteristic of the partisan is *critical idealism*. Partisan are idealists because they are advocating a vision of society or politics or religion that is not yet real but that might be possible with faith and effort; and they are critical because in order to make this possibility a reality, they must remove many obstacles in the path, obstacles that are usually tied to tradition, law, or institutional inertia. Partisans are most influential, therefore, on the margins of politics, often as social movement leaders or public intellectuals or iconoclastic artists, musicians, and poets. The biggest difference, therefore, between the partisan and the agent is that the partisan can hypothetically stand alone, whereas the agent is always a representative of an established institution; ironically, then, when partisans actually succeed in promoting their ideas, they become agents.

4. Finally, the **hero** is defined as an individual who is willing to actively confront power in the name of helping others even if it means that great suffering might come upon him or her. The essential characteristic of the hero is therefore *romantic courage*. Heroes are "romantic" because, unlike the partisan, they do not have a coherent political vision they are promoting, but instead boldly stride into the unknown against all obstacles with the optimistic faith that things will work out for them in the end. And they are courageous because they do not simply "talk the talk" but also "walk the walk." Without a commitment to action, particularly the type of action that directly and physically confronts a more powerful foe, the hero is merely a big talker. It is for this reason that heroes are often spontaneously found or discovered in moments of crisis, because the hero reacts spontaneously to defend the weak and challenge the strong in the name of an abstract value that is shared by the community the hero fights for. Finally, what makes heroes capable of making such self-sacrifices is their confidence that even if they die in the struggle, their legacy will live on as martyrs.

It is important to also keep in mind that these roles are not mutually exclusive. Some of the greatest orations combined many or even all of these roles, with the speaker taking on new personae during different phases of the speech. For instance, an American president might assume the role of the apologist in defense of the wisdom of some military policy ("Those who question the wisdom of toppling this dictator do not properly understand the nature of evil"), then might take on the role of agent ("As the commander-in-chief of this nation, I will not allow its foreign policy to be determined by petty tyrants"), only to then transition to being a partisan ("Furthermore, this campaign is not simply about our national self-interest. I advocate this policy not simply because I am president, but because I believe that the true task of humanity is to spread freedom and democracy around the globe") and then end on a heroic note ("Finally, I can no longer stand to see children suffer and mothers weep; when evil shows its face it must be confronted at all costs if we are to live with ourselves"). A role is not something that locks us permanently into any type of performance; it is a type of script we perform to accomplish a specific rhetorical task.

Sojourner Truth: "Ain't I a woman?"

One of the most fascinating orators in American history is civil rights champion and former slave Sojourner Truth. Born Isabella Van Wagenen (a Dutch name given by her Dutch slave owners) in about 1797, Truth endured many years of abuse until finally achieving her freedom in 1827 and changing her name in 1843. Despite growing up illiterate, she was a woman of remarkable intelligence and presence. She was tall for her era—almost six feet—with a low and powerful voice that had a song-like quality to it. Her straight-talking and unsentimental style, combined with her imposing figure, made her a national symbol for strong women, both black and white. Her most famous extemporaneous address, "Ain't I a Woman?" was delivered at the Women's Convention in Akron, Ohio, on May 29, 1851. This type of convention was a major component of the early women's rights movement, which involved the organization of women's conferences to bring together feminists to discuss goals and strategies. However, many of these conferences attracted men (including several ministers) who came largely to heckle the speakers and to argue that women's proper place was one of being both subservient to and cared for by men.

It was the heckling of one of these ministers that inspired Truth to speak. Reacting to a black-robed minister who argued for male superiority based on "superior intellect" and "manhood in Christ," Truth argued that women were in fact more powerful than men and also that black women had been denied even the limited rights given to white women. Her argument constructs a persona that establishes her superior strength, capability, and authority. A firsthand account described how "Sojourner walked to the podium and slowly took off her sunbonnet. Her six-foot frame towered over the audience. She began to speak in her deep, resonant voice."

> Well, children, where there is so much racket there must be something out of kilter. I think that 'twixt the negroes of the South and the women at the North, all talking about rights, the white men will be in a fix pretty soon. But what's all this here talking about?

That man over there says that women need to be helped into carriages, and lifted over ditches, and to have the best place everywhere. Nobody ever helps me into carriages, or over mud-puddles, or gives me any best place! And ain't I a woman? Look at me! Look at my arm! I have ploughed and planted, and gathered into barns, and no man could head me! And ain't I a woman? I could work as much and eat as much as a man - when I could get it - and bear the lash as well! And ain't I a woman? I have borne thirteen children, and seen most all sold off to slavery, and when I cried out with my mother's grief, none but Jesus heard me! And ain't I a woman?

Then they talk about this thing in the head; what's this they call it? [member of audience whispers, "intellect"] That's it, honey. What's that got to do with women's rights or negroes' rights? If my cup won't hold but a pint, and yours holds a quart, wouldn't you be mean not to let me have my little half measure full?

Then that little man in black there, he says women can't have as much rights as men, 'cause Christ wasn't a woman! Where did your Christ come from? Where did your Christ come from? From God and a woman! Man had nothing to do with Him.

If the first woman God ever made was strong enough to turn the world upside down all alone, these women together ought to be able to turn it back, and get it right side up again! And now they is asking to do it, the men better let them.[9]

Truth masterfully combines elements of all four roles within her unique personae. First, her sheer act of standing up to speak at the convention implies she is an agent who speaks on behalf of the women gathered together. Indeed, her speech made many of the other women in the audience anxious because they were not sure that an imposing former slave with a thick accent was the best choice of representative for their group. Second, she acts the apologist by refuting the false accusations (made by the "man in black") that women are fragile and cannot take care of themselves without men. She accomplishes this by bolstering her assertion that women are equally competent to men by citing specific facts of her life that show her physical and emotional strength. Third, she plays the hero when she directly challenges the men in the audience, thus taking a real personal risk on behalf of other women who might not have had the courage to do so. Finally, she takes on the role of partisan by advocating the radical notion that it is women, not men, who are the true seat of power and authority because of the heritage of Eve (who turned the world upside down on her own) and Mary (who gave birth to Christ on her own). Anyone who doubts the power of *ethos* to leave a lasting rhetorical legacy need only recognize how this short and impromptu speech became one of the most famous orations in history almost entirely due to Truth's mastery of the power of personae.[10]

---

[9]Ibid.

[10]The changing narrative surrounding Truth's rhetoric is explored in Roseann M. Mandziuk and Suzzane Pullon Fitch, "The Rhetorical Construction of Sojourner Truth," *Southern Communication Journal* 66, no. 2 (2001), 120–137.

Discussion: Moving to a new place (either long term, such as for college or a new career, or short term, such as an exchange program or summer camp) often creates a new opportunity to create a novel persona that is no longer constrained by one's inherited ethos. Have you ever consciously tried to create a new persona after making such a move? Did you change your role as apologist, partisan, hero, or agent?

EVOKED AUDIENCE

If the persona is the image that the rhetor constructs of him- or herself as a speaker, the **evoked audience** is the attractive image that the rhetor constructs of and for the audience. If the speaker's constructed self-image can be considered as the "first" persona (in which the speaker tells the audience who "I" am), then the evoked audience can be considered as the "second" persona (in which the speaker tells the audience who "you" are). The concept of the second persona was advanced by Edwin Black. For him, an astute rhetorical critic can thus see "in the auditor implied by a discourse a model of what the rhetor would have his real auditor become."[11] The function of the evoked audience, or this "second persona," is to create an attractive image of unity that makes members of an audience desire to be a part of a common group rather than an aggregate of separate individuals.

In its most general form, we find politicians using evoked audiences whenever they speak of the *American people* as a collective body of people who love liberty, freedom, and democracy. By creating a category of identity that can unify a group of separate individuals, an evoked audience creates the possibility of cooperative action because it contributes to the creation of a sense of unity that may not have existed before the speech. For example, we often take for granted that everyone who is born within the geographic boundaries of the United States is an "American," but prior to the revolution, people identified themselves more with their local city or region. For revolutionaries to start using the term *American* thus helped make possible a national identity that stood apart from the British Empire.[12]

Like the concept of persona, the evoked audience is a partly fictional identity that usually overstates the unified character of the people listening to a speech (who in reality are far more diverse). Like persona, the evoked audience often is what a rhetor *wants* an audience to be rather than what it literally *is*. Yet this ideal often brings a new reality into existence. For instance, a collection of teenagers may all be talented at a certain sport, but they do not think of themselves as a "team" until the coach starts telling them to act like one ("Go Tigers!"). The coach's rhetoric creates a sense of commonality by evoking the team spirit within the individual players that may not have been fully present before. The most typical sign that such a team spirit is being attempted by a speaker is the repetitive use of "we" or "you," such that an audience feels it is being grouped together under a single category. One can imagine a parent telling his or her children, "If we are a family, then we will eat

---

[11]Edwin Black, "The Second Persona," *Readings in Rhetorical Criticism,* ed. Carl R. Burgchardt (State College, PA: Strata Publishing Co., 1995), 90.

[12]For more on the "public" as an evoked audience, see Michael McGee, "In Search of the People," *Quarterly Journal of Speech* 71 (1975), 235–249.

together at the dinner table." The implicit choice now placed upon the audience is whether or not to accept that group membership.

Therefore, although there is a fictional quality about an evoked audience, this does not mean that it is an illusion. Clearly, a speaker who speaks to an audience of school children as if they were all members of Congress is not literally accurate. However, motivational teachers *can* speak to them as "future leaders of America" and anticipate an energetic response. In other words, the evoked audience should always select and amplify shared qualities that are already present (or at least potentially present) within an audience. The average audience of college students, for instance, can be referred to as "university students," or "citizens," or "eager young people," or "future leaders," or "party-goers." Each of these designations may be partly true, but each of them only speaks to one portion of that group's identity. Consequently, deciding what identity to evoke in an audience has different consequences for rhetorical persuasion.

Despite what has been said, however, one should not think that the evoked audience is something that the speaker always *does* to the audience. Many times, an audience goes to a speech, as with a "rally," precisely to feel a part of a common identity. In this case, the evoked audience is merely the vehicle through which this desire is actualized. In other words, the audience must be *active,* not *passive,* in generating its sense of common identity. It is this constitution of a common emotional bond between members of an audience that makes public speaking, as an oral performance, so powerful.

Tecumseh: "Brothers, we all belong to one family."

One of the greatest Native American leaders and warriors was Tecumseh, a Shawnee leader who resisted colonization of native lands by uniting the various tribes into a Native Confederacy spreading from the Great Lakes to Mexico. As part of this campaign, Tecumseh supported the British during the War of 1812, hoping that alliance with the enemies of the United States might stem the tide of settlers. This speech to the Osages in winter of 1811–1812 attempted to create a common identification between tribes as a necessary means of self-defense by evoking an audience who saw themselves as "brothers" of one "family":

> Brothers we all belong to one family; we are all children of the Great Spirit; we walk in the same path; slake our thirst at the same spring; and now affairs of the greatest concern lead us to smoke the pipe around the same council fire!
>
> Brothers, -We are friends; we must assist each other to bear our burdens. The blood of many of our fathers and brothers has run like water on the ground, to satisfy the avarice of the white men. We, ourselves, are threatened with a great evil; nothing will pacify them but the destruction of all the red men...
>
> Brothers, -We must be united; we must smoke the same pipe; we must fight each other's battles; and more than all, we must love the Great Spirit; he is for us; he will destroy our enemies, and make all his red children happy.[13]

---

[13]Tecumseh, available at <http://www.historyisaweapon.com/defcon1/tecumosages.html> (accessed 6 September 2012).

Although Tecumseh's speech also had explicit deliberative intent insofar as it advocated an explicit policy, the primary function of the speech was to construct a common identity as "brothers" who all share a kinship with the Great Spirit. Consistent with speeches of identification, Tecumseh speech spends a great deal of time talking about the common characteristics of his audience that make them all "one," including a shared environment, a shared history, shared rituals, shared appearance, and a shared spirituality. From his perspective, only by evoking an audience capable of sharing a common identity and purpose can any of them stop their inevitable annihilation.

Discussion: The creation of "team" spirit has become as common a goal in business as in athletics. When have you participated in some activity as an employee that was intended to evoke a group identification with fellow employees? Did the activity have any unintended consequences in actual practice?

IDENTIFICATION

When we "identify" with someone, we see ourselves as sharing some quality or experience with another person or group. Usually this feeling comes after the revelation of a life experience that we see as similar to our own. The process of making friends with people often begins with this step of identification in which two strangers find themselves sharing in some common interest, habit, belief, or feeling. In this sense, the process of identification is how two or more people come to form a bond that generates commonality out of what might seem, at first, to be different perspectives. What we "identify," then, is some quality in another person that he or she shares with us. Identification is not merely labeling something; it is identifying the qualities in others that we find in ourselves as well.

In rhetoric, **identification** is the strategy of creating a common bond with an audience by drawing parallels between the characteristics of speaker and audience. For Kenneth Burke, *identification* is a broad term that ranges from the simple schoolyard attempt to make friends by asserting a common quality or interest (e.g., "we are all baseball lovers") to religious or nationalistic attempts to create a unified group with common goals and characteristics.[14] What each of these examples has in common is a sense that two or more distinct and unique individuals share in some "essence" or "quality" that transcends their individuality (love of farming, class identity, and divine origin, respectively). This sense of commonality thus leads to people uniting in a common purpose. For instance, when Sojourner Truth argues that she also possesses "masculine" qualities, she creates a commonality between men and women that had not previously been present. In short, identification represents the persuasive attempt on the part of the rhetorical agent to say "I am one of you" in order to create a sense of "we." The justification for such a strategy is that we tend to prefer listening to people who feel and think like we do.[15]

---

[14]For more on identification, see Kenneth Burke, *A Rhetoric of Motives* (Berkeley: The University of California Press, 1969), xiv.

[15]For more on identification, see Gary C. Woodward, *The Idea of Identification* (Albany: State University of New York Press, 2003).

Benjamin Banneker: "We are all of the same family"

As the Tecumseh example demonstrates, identification can be used to solidify a preexisting similarity. However, identification can also be one way in which previously marginalized groups attempt to include themselves as active parts of the general public. For instance, after the American victory in the Revolutionary War, many opponents of slavery—particularly the slaves themselves—hoped it would lead to an end of that oppressive institution. One such person was Benjamin Banneker, a child of a freed slave who taught himself mathematics and astronomy and eventually published several successful almanacs. On August 19, 1791, he sent one of his almanacs to Thomas Jefferson along with a letter that rebuked Jefferson for his proslavery views. He went on to compare black slavery to the British rule over the colonies. One strategy Banneker used to convince Jefferson of the evils of slavery was identification. However, the power of his identification comes only after beginning with the appearance of difference and division:

> I suppose it is a truth too well attested to you, to need a proof here, that we are a race of beings, who have long labored under the abuse and censure of the world; that we have long been looked upon with an eye of contempt; and that we have long been considered rather as brutish than human, and scarcely capable of mental endowments.
>
> Sir I hope I may Safely admit, in consequence of that report with hath reached me, that you are a man far less inflexible in Sentiments of this nature, then many others, that you are measurably friendly, and well disposed towards us, and that you are willing and ready to Lend your aid and assistance to our relief from these many distresses and numerous calamities to which we are reduced.
>
> Now Sir, if this is founded in truth, I apprehend you will embrace every opportunity, to eradicate that train of absurd and false ideas and opinions, which so generally prevails with respect to us; and that your sentiments are concurrent with mine, which are, that one universal Father hath given being to us all; and that he hath not only made us all of one flesh, but that he hath also, without partiality, afforded us all the same sensations and endowed us all with the same faculties; and that however variable we may be in society or religion, however diversified in situation or color, we are all of the same family, and stand in the same relation to him.[16]

Banneker's persuasive strategy clearly is meant to draw from the very principles of equality that Jefferson had enshrined in the Declaration of Independence. In short, he argues that Jefferson's statement of "all men are created equal" clearly includes all human beings, including African-American slaves. Notably, Banneker makes his case by "identifying" the qualities that are shared by human beings despite their skin color, including possessing the same flesh, the same sensations, the same faculties, and ultimately the same relation to God. This shows that a strategy of identification requires more than simply saying "we are all in this together." It requires identifying the specific characteristics that a speaker shares with an audience and that members of an audience share with each other.

---

[16]Benjamin Banneker, available at <http://mith.umd.edu/eada/html/display.php?docs=banneker_letter.xml&action=show> (accessed 6 September 2012).

However, this particular example also shows the limits of this strategy when it does not occur in a face-to-face oral environment. Banneker writes a *letter* to Jefferson, thereby allowing Jefferson to read the letter at his convenience or even skim over the parts that make him uncomfortable. Consider how different this message would have been received had Banneker stood before Jefferson and shook his hand while looking him in the eye. The fact that Jefferson never acknowledged Banneker's letter or directly confronted the institution of slavery shows how even the most brilliant minds find it easy to rationalize their own behavior when they are left to their own resources in the comfort of their private homes.

Discussion: Politicians notoriously strive to be all things to all people, trying to find parts in their lives that somehow connect to a particular constituency. What are the most common identifications made between politicians and American audiences? And what does the ubiquity of the strategies say about the actual character of the American public?

DISTINCTION

Identification is a mainstay of rhetorical persuasion, but it is not always sufficient. Especially in times of uncertainty in which we seek good advice rather than loyal friendship, we often look to those people who are very *unlike* us because they possess uncharacteristic excellence in character or special expertise in a very specific subject. In other words, we often want speakers not to "fit in" but to "stand out." In this case, we look not for identification but for **distinction**, which is the attempt to establish credibility by the possession of special knowledge and/or unique experience that are superior to those of the audience. **Special knowledge** refers to the kind of knowledge one receives by learning technical discourses and procedures, such as the knowledge one receives from attending a university. Whether experts are scientists, theologians, ethicists, economists, or movie critics, they all base their arguments on knowledge not accessible to the general public. **Unique experience** refers to the kind of expertise one acquires by having "been there" or "gone through that." For example, it is a common dramatic technique used in all war movies that the highly educated new officer always defers to the practical experience of the veteran soldier once combat begins. The officer might be more capable to discuss broader military strategy (thus having special knowledge), but the enlisted soldier usually knows better what to do in the heat of battle (thus possessing unique experience). The ideal, of course, is a fusion of both qualities within a single person.

In cases of *distinction*, the persona of the rhetor stands apart from the evoked audience; in cases of *identification*, it is aligned with it. Both represent forms of credibility, but distinction is credibility from *difference* (even if it is just difference in degree), whereas identification is credibility from *likeness*. Frequently, some combination of the two is most useful.[17] To continue the military metaphor, a four-star general cites the possession of superior knowledge and broader experience in

---

[17]The desirability of a mixture of both qualities is exemplified by the notion of "source credibility" as explained by Jack Whitehead in "Factors of Source Credibility," *Quarterly Journal of Speech* 54 (1968), 59–63.

order to justify leading a campaign, but he or she usually makes an effort to also establish how he or she is still a common soldier "at heart" in order to command loyalty. Presidential candidates, too, often spend a great deal of time touting their expertise while simultaneously spending most of their days eating hot dogs, going bowling, or kissing babies. They want to appear as ordinary citizens and extraordinary leaders simultaneously.

Gorgias: "What is there greater than the word?"

Perhaps the original masters of speeches of solicitation were the Greek Sophists themselves. As the practitioners of a new art of rhetoric, they had discovered a new commodity that was in much demand in the new democracies of the fifth century B.C.E. It was therefore natural that they also would use their own persuasive skills to market themselves much in the way that contemporary universities compete for students. However, their aggressive salesmanship and at times arrogant tone did not sit well with aristocrats like Plato, who thought that paying fees to acquire wisdom and virtue corrupted the very nature of wisdom and virtue. However, before criticizing the Sophists in his dialogue, Plato has the fictionalized portrayal of Socrates question Gorgias about what he teaches and why he considers himself an expert in his field. Gorgias's answer employs the strategy of distinction to set himself (and his art) above others:

SOCRATES   What is that which . . . is the greatest good of man, and of which you are the creator? Answer us.

GORGIAS   That good, Socrates, which is truly the greatest, being that which gives to men freedom in their own persons, and to individuals the power of ruling over others in their several states.

SOCRATES   And what would you consider this to be?

GORGIAS   What is there greater than the word which persuades the judges in the courts, or the senators in the council, or the citizens in the assembly, or at any other political meeting? If you have the power of uttering this word, you will have the physician your slave, and the trainer your slave, and the money-maker of whom you talk will be found to gather treasures, not for himself, but for you who are able to speak and to persuade the multitude....

SOCRATES   I had that in my admiring mind, Gorgias, when I asked what is the nature of rhetoric, which always appears to me, when I look at the matter in this way, to be a marvel of greatness.

GORGIAS   A marvel, indeed, Socrates, if you only knew how rhetoric comprehends and holds under her sway all the inferior arts. Let me offer you a striking example of this. On several occasions I have been with my brother Herodicus or some other physician to see one of his patients, who would not allow the physician to give him medicine, or apply a knife or hot iron to him; and I have persuaded him to do for me what he would not do for the physician just by the use of rhetoric. And I say that if a rhetorician and a physician were to go to any city, and had there to argue in the Ecclesia or any other assembly as to which of them should be elected state-physician, the physician would have no chance; but he who could speak would be chosen if he wished; and in a contest with a man of any other profession the rhetorician more than any one would have the power of getting himself chosen, for he can speak more persuasively to the multitude than any of them, and on any subject. Such is the nature and power of the art of rhetoric.[18]

In the voice of Gorgias we hear the voice of distinction insofar as he offers proof—through both knowledge and experience—of his possession of a skill that gives its possessor power and money and freedom. Like any good salesman in a speech of solicitation, Gorgias does not deny that he is selling something for his own personal gain; he simply wishes to make very clear, through exaggerated examples that mark his distinction, that what he is selling will bring even more benefit to the one spending money.

Discussion: One way to think about the strategy of distinction is the effort to be the "best of the best" (rather than the good amidst the bad). Distinction is to have a special quality of excellence that is admired by those with comparable virtues. In what context are speeches of distinction the most common? What kind of audience is most receptive to the speeches in a way that does not produce resentment?

POLARIZATION

Understanding of the complex ethics behind strategies of ethos would not be complete without a consideration of polarization (or "division"). Just as any action has a reaction, any attempt to establish unity inevitably also creates a division between "in" groups and "out" groups that results in inevitable polarization. For something to be "polarized" is to have two objects that repel each other from a distance. For instance, the North Pole and the South Pole represent two sides of the earth, but they are not antagonistic toward one another. They are simply far apart. Two magnets of the same polarity, however, will literally repulse each other when brought together. Similarly, two friends separated by thousands of miles are not polarized, but simply distant; two enemies in the same room, however, will create a palpable tension. Polarization thus represents a division based on antagonism. For example, we are often forced to choose between aligning ourselves with one group or another with little room for compromise. Either we are "with them or against them." And those who seek compromise in this situation are thus usually attacked from both sides for being wishy-washy. In a polarized environment, the decision not to choose is also a choice that puts us at risk of being abandoned, rejected, or ignored.

By its nature as an art that thrives in conflict and uncertainty, rhetorical discourse often magnifies these choices and uses the contrast to force a decision. In rhetoric, **polarization** is the strategy of dividing an audience into a positive "us" and a negative "them" in order to create unity through difference. The "them" in this case is usually a **criticized audience** that represents a group antagonistic to the rhetor's interests, such as another political party, or simply a demonized audience

---

18 <http://classics.mit.edu/Plato/gorgias.html>.

that is used as a convenient foil, such as a group of "traitors" or "evil-doers." The strategy is then to argue that if one does not follow the path preferred by the rhetor (a path that ends in belonging to an evoked audience), then this person will align him- or herself with a group of people who lack ethical or practical judgment. Most children become acquainted with this strategy early on in their lives when they are encouraged to behave during the year so that Santa Claus includes them on his "nice" list rather than his "naughty" list. This same model can be applied effectively in the analysis of contemporary partisan politics.[19] In summary, if the first persona presents the "I" who is speaking and the second persona defines the "you" who is being spoken to, polarization defines a "third" persona representing the undesirable "they" who are not present but who are used to define who the "I" and "you" are not.[20]

Including "polarization" within a public speaking textbook may appear to border on the unethical. After all, are we not usually advised to invite as many people as possible to hear our speech? Is it not completely inappropriate in a tolerant age to pick out a group of people (or a type of person) to criticize or condemn? The work of Kenneth Burke is instructive here. Throughout his writings, Burke lamented the tendency for **scapegoating** in public rhetoric, in which all of a public's "sins" are placed upon a largely defenseless group that is then run out of town. At the same time, however, Burke also recognized that division is a natural state of human nature, and that rhetoric arises whenever individuals and groups are in conflict with one another. Moreover, rhetorical action cannot avoid the effects of polarization. For instance, even the statement "we should all love one another" can be used to divide those who love from those who hate. Burke's point is that we must be aware of the implicit acts of polarization that occur in all our identifications, make them explicit, and do our best to make our criticisms of others intelligent, precise, just, and sympathetic.

One common strategy to make polarization less ethically problematic is to base it more on hypothetical values or attitudes than on actual characteristics of specific social groups. Certainly, parents who ask their children whether they want to be a "doctor" or a "couch potato" are using polarization primarily to inspire them to do their best. In this case, the negative audience is not real but hypothetical—it represents a "type" of behavior we find distasteful. This still involves ethical responsibility, but it often can be used for purposes of genuine encouragement. The responsibility of speakers is thus to identify all possible divisions and to avoid unnecessary or unintentional castigation of other groups, even in the name of the most noble and respectable goal or virtue. As history has shown, many of the greatest

---

[19]Some examples discussing the rhetoric of polarization include Andrew King and Floyd Douglas Anderson, "Nixon, Agnew, and the 'Silent Majority': A Case Study in the Rhetoric of Polarization," *Western Speech* 35, no. 4 (1971), 243–255; William D. Harpine, "Bryan's 'A Cross of Gold': The Rhetoric of Polarization at the 1896 Democratic Convention," *Quarterly Journal of Speech* 87, no. 3 (2001), 291–304; and David E. Foster, "Bush's Use of the Terrorism and 'Moral Values' Issues in His 2004 Presidential Campaign Rhetoric: An Instance of the Rhetorical Strategy of Polarization," *Ohio Communication Journal* 44 (2006), 33–60.

[20]See Philip Wander, "The Third Persona: An Ideological Turn in Rhetorical Theory," *Central States Speech Journal* 35 (1984), 197–216.

atrocities were committed by those who truly believed they were fighting in the name of truth and freedom and goodness. As important as it is to be motivated by noble values and inspiring identifications, it is also important to analyze who is being excluded or condemned.

Clarence Darrow: "The cruel and the thoughtless will approve"

Polarization becomes a particularly potent strategy when an audience is faced with an absolute decision to say "yes" or "no" to something without the possibility of middle ground. When we are faced with an either/or decision, our alternatives are immediately polarized into two competing paths from which we must choose. Not surprisingly, then, courtroom arguments are often the most polarized of all arguments. The prosecution warns us that a judgment of innocence will render us dupes; the defense ominously predicts that a judgment of guilt will convict the jury of cruelty and thoughtlessness. A prime example of the strategy was given by Clarence Darrow on May 29, 1924, in defense of two wealthy and highly educated university students from Chicago named Nathan Leopold, Jr., and Richard Loeb. These two young men had kidnapped 14-year-old Bobby Franks by luring him into a car and had then subsequently killed him, taking care to cover their tracks by burning the body and pretending the boy had been taken for ransom. In reality, the two students had murdered Franks to test a theory that they were "Nietzschean supermen" who could commit a perfect crime without being caught. Predictably, when the method and motives of their crimes were revealed after their capture, there was widespread public demand for their execution.

In the midst of this turmoil, lawyer Clarence Darrow took the case for their defense. His intention was not to prove their innocence but rather to put capital punishment itself on trial. After convincing his clients to plead guilty, he embarked on a defense that the two young men weren't completely responsible for their actions, but were the products of the environment in which they grew up, an environment that condoned intolerance and cruelty. At the conclusion of his summation, Darrow polarized two competing value systems in an effort to make his audience choose the path of "love" over that of "hatred." The first path he described as the path of execution:

> The easy thing and the popular thing to do is to hang my clients. I know it. Men and women who do not think will applaud. The cruel and the thoughtless will approve. It will be easy today; but in Chicago, and reaching out over the length and breadth of the land, more and more fathers and mothers, the humane, the kind, and the hopeful, who are gaining an understanding and asking questions not only about these poor boys but about their own, these will join in no acclaim at the death of my clients. These would ask that the shedding of blood be stopped, and that the normal feelings of man resume their sway . . .
>
> I know the easy way. I know Your Honor stands between the future and the past. I know the future is with me, and what I stand for here; not merely for the lives of these two unfortunate lads, but for all boys and all girls; for all of the young, and as far as possible, for all of the old. I am pleading for life, understanding, charity, kindness, and the infinite mercy that considers all.

I am pleading that we overcome cruelty with kindness and hatred with love I . . . am pleading for the future; I am pleading for a time when hatred and cruelty will not control the hearts of men. When we can learn by reason and judgment and understanding and faith that all life is worth saving, and that mercy is the highest attribute of man.[21]

According to Darrow, pursuing the easy path of cruelty has long-term negative consequences for "the humane, the kind, and the hopeful" who are struggling to raise their children in a peaceful country. For this virtuous group of people, crime needs to be punished without falling victim to the very forces of cruelty that motivated the criminals. Hence, he effectively polarizes two groups of people—those who would hate and those who would love—and implies that a judge or jury who would condemn murderers to death belong to the same group as the murderers themselves. This is certainly not a fair fight by the end. On the one side stands the "easy way" of cruelty and hatred; on the other side stands the "future" of life: understanding, charity, kindness, infinite mercy, love, reason, judgment, and faith. Who would chose to be a party to the first group? Certainly not the judge, who decided to sentence the two boys to life in prison—where they were subsequently murdered by other inmates who chose the other path.[22]

Discussion: When do you think polarization is ethically warranted? We often do not think that it is ever right to speak in terms of "us" versus "them," and yet nothing is more common in political and moral discourse. How can you tell between an ethical and unethical use of polarization?

[21]Clarence Darrow, available at "PBS: American Experience," <http://www.pbs.org/wgbh/amex/monkeytrial/filmmore/ps_darrow.html> (accessed 3 September 2012).
[22]For more on Darrow's courtroom rhetoric, see Martin Maloney, "The Forensic Speaking of Clarence Darrow," *Speech Monographs* 14, no. 1 (1947), 111–126. For more on the trial of Leopold and Loeb, see Charles E. Morris III, "Passing by Proxy: Collusive and Convulsive Silence in the Trial of Leopold and Loeb," *Quarterly Journal of Speech* 91, no. 3 (2005), 264–290.

KEY WORDS

SUMMARY

Ethos is something given to a speaker by an audience based on how a speaker displays himself or herself within a particular rhetorical situation. We should therefore not confuse ethos, as a rhetorical concept, with personal concepts such as affection or trust or reputation. Each of these things is certainly relevant to considerations of ethos, but they are not determining conditions. Indeed, sometimes we grant ethos to people we hate, distrust, and think of low repute. These situations occur, for example, when these individuals testify against their own best interests about something that they have specialized knowledge about, as when an executive convicted of insider trading testifies at a congressional committee about the need to regulate insider trading. As Anthony Pratkanis and Elliot Aronson observe, "a communicator can be an immoral person and still be effective, as long as it seems clear that the communicator is not acting in her or his self-interest by attempting to persuade us."[23] Although this particular strategy is only relevant to a small class of people in extraordinary circumstances, it nonetheless shows that we should consider *ethos* not as a quality of a person's character but as a criterion for judgment in a specific speech situation.

In most of our everyday interactions, the Aristotelian categories of goodwill, practical wisdom, and virtue are usually sufficient for acquiring ethos. Goodwill represents an emotional attitude of the speaker toward the audience such that he or she appears to wish the very best for the person or people to whom the rhetor is speaking. We tend to think people have goodwill toward us when they make sacrifices on our behalf, sometimes in the moment but usually over a longer course of a relationship. Practical wisdom represents an intellectual capacity to make decisions in complicated situations that make those situations turn out for the better far more often than they turn out for the worse. Those with practical wisdom are people with much experience and knowledge to whom we look for specific advice. Whereas our close friends might give us the emotional support of goodwill, oftentimes we look to professionals or even strangers for counsel about complicated judgments. Finally, virtue represents a condition of character that embodies multiple values, such as courage, temperance, generosity, humility, and the like. We look to people with character because they seem to be "well rounded" and thoughtful, thus assuring that their counsel will not be based on narrow criteria but broader considerations. It is no accident that we often associate virtue with age, as it takes a great deal of time and diverse life experience to accumulate multiple virtues in a coherent and stable character.

Developing a message that also supports one's ethos requires further conceptual strategies, however. Persona provides a way of developing a specific presentation style that can balance the needs of a specific situation with the imperative to maintain consistency in character. *Persona* should not be considered a way of simply "acting," and thereby putting on a mask, for narrow purposes of persuasion; rather, it should be considered a method of amplifying or diminishing certain characteristics in one's own personality in order to best respond to

---

[23]Anthony Pratkanis and Elliot Aronson, *Age of Propaganda: The Everyday Use and Abuse of Persuasion* (New York: Henry Holt, 2001), 134.

a situation and an audience. Similarly, the evoked audience is not a purely fictional creation that is offered to an audience as in a fantasy role-play exercise. An *evoked audience*, like persona, is rather a selective amplification of certain qualities that are already shared by members of an audience and then given a concrete name and identity that serves as an appropriate response to a rhetorical situation. Turning a group of teenagers interested in basketball into the "Fighting Tigers" does not invent their interest in being a part of an athletic team out of the blue; it simply solidifies this interest and gives it a concrete manifestation. Identification is thus a natural bridge between persona and the evoked audience, as it represents a way of creating a common "we" out of an "I" and "you," even while retaining certain differences. A general may still be a general and a platoon a platoon, but they are all soldiers fighting for their nation and for "freedom."

The categories of distinction and polarization, being categories of difference, are usually only effective once such a common identification has been made. Distinction takes for granted the assumption of identification but seeks to add extra qualities to make the speaker stand out from the group. For instance, once the "Fighting Tigers" have been identified and their emotional bond solidified through various practices and rituals, it comes time to select a team captain. This is the time for speeches of distinction, in which each member of the team justifies why he or she stands apart from others (while still retaining the members' common unity). Distinction is thus a delicate balancing act of sameness and difference.

Last, polarization occurs when a speaker attempts to further solidify the identification of a group by comparing its members with an outsider group that represents the opposite in values and goals. Polarization presents an unsavory "other" (real or fictional) that usually serves to increase competitive motives. Of all the strategies, therefore, polarization has the most potential for ethical abuse, as speakers all too easily descend into vicious caricature of competing groups. As with all strategies of ethos, one must be careful of exaggerating one's own virtue while condemning the vice of others for narrowly selfish ends. Some degree of polarization is virtually inevitable in any speech, but one must at all times be careful to reduce its possible negative impacts to a minimum. We can have goodwill, after all, even toward those who disagree with us or are unlike us.

CHAPTER 4 EXERCISES

1. Analyze your rhetorical artifact selected in chapter 1. Which was the primary strategy used to constitute ethos with the audience? Choose one and explain, using quotations from the speech for support.

2. Break into groups of two and briefly interview your partner about the accomplishments in his or her life, drawing on specific examples. Then give impromptu speeches of introduction for each other, creating for the partner an exaggerated persona (by using the strategy of distinction) that presents him or her in a heroic light. Did the speech about yourself sound anything like you?

3. Divide yourselves into groups either by year (freshman, sophomore, etc.) or by major. Have each group come up with a speech that argues why its year or major has distinction and then use polarization to show why it is better than the others. Were any elements of these speeches persuasive to the other groups?

4. Randomly break into groups of four. For a few minutes, try to find what you have in common. Then create a name for a "club" to which you all belong and give a list of characteristics (which you all possess) that are necessary to be part of that club. (The name of the club should also reflect something about these shared qualities.) Present your club and its characteristics to the class. How many other people belong to that club? Which club is the most exclusive and which is the most inclusive?

5. Come up with some absurd ethical argument (e.g., clothing should be optional when coming to class). Now create an impromptu speech that relies on creating an evoked audience that would naturally favor this argument (e.g., we are all "free spirits" who reject any kind of constraint on our freedom). Which speech was the most persuasive? Why?

Logos

This chapter addresses the forms of reasoning that can be used to persuade an audience based on factual evidence. Of all forms of proof, those from reasoning are the most cognitive (as opposed to "affective" or "emotional"). In rhetoric, reasoning is the capacity to interpret and organize elements of a problematic situation in order to prove certain practical judgments to be more prudent than others. The relevant concepts for logical reasoning are the relationships among claims, grounds, and warrants; the list of most common warrants (generalization, sign, causal, principle, authority, analogy); and the list of common fallacies. The goal of this chapter is to show how to develop rational arguments, based on the best available evidence, that are also clear and persuasive by being related to audience beliefs and attitudes.

When citizens of Classical Greece used the word *logos,* they usually used it to mean *words, arguments,* or *reason.* For example, the term *dissoi logoi* (meaning "double arguments") was a common phrase that referred to the Greek belief that there were always two or more arguments opposed on every issue. The Greeks acquired this belief largely because of their reliance on courts of law to decide almost any dispute. Any time two people came into conflict, their instinct was to bring this conflict into court in order to hear both sides and come to a practical judgment. In these sorts of rhetorical contexts, **logos** refers to the use of rational arguments and evidence to persuade an audience of the reasonableness of one's position. It is based on the belief that human beings are rational beings with the potential to make decisions based on logic, principles, and evidence.[1] John Dewey offers the following narrative of how logic, as the conscious study of the structure of logos, originated as a conscious art:

> The conditions under which logical theory originated are indicated by the two words still generally used to designate its subject matter—logic and dialectic. Both of these words have to do with speech, not of course with speech in the form of mere words but with language as the storehouse of the ideas and beliefs which form the culture of a people. Greek life was peculiarly characterized by the importance attached to discussion. Debate and discussion were marked by freedom from restrictions imposed by

---

[1] For the various meanings of *logos,* see George B. Kerferd, *The Sophistical Movement* (Cambridge, UK: Cambridge University Press, 1981), 83.

priestly power and were emphasized with the growth of democratic political institutions. In the Homeric poems the man skilled in words which were fit for counsel stands side by side with the man skilled in martial deeds. In Athens not merely political but legal issues were settled in the public forum. Political advancement and civic honor depended more upon the power of persuasion than upon military achievement. As general intellectual curiosity developed among the learned men, power to interpret and explain was connected with the ability to set forth a consecutive story. To give an account of something, a logos, was also to account for it. The logos, the ordered account, was the reason and the measure of the things set forth. Here was the background out of which developed a formulated theory of logic as the structure of knowledge and truth.[2]

The study of rhetoric corresponded with the study of logic. It was simply considered a "practical" logic of law or politics, a logic directed toward providing "ordered accounts" of contingent situations in order to suggest rational courses of action to resolve them. In other words, rhetoric no less than logic is grounded in the faith that human beings are rational creatures who seek reasons for their actions. Without the faith that people make better practical judgments when presented with more comprehensive and accurate facts, we would be forced to rely purely on either habit, passion, or luck. However, this faith in human rationality should not be interpreted to be somehow in competition with the other rhetorical appeals of ethos and pathos. Reason plays a vital role in human decision making, but it is rarely, if ever, sufficient for making good decisions. Often, our emotions are necessary to judge right from wrong, effective from ineffective, and pleasure from pain. Likewise, our ability to discern who is a more reliable advisor during times of crisis can rarely be made by logic alone. In fact, our need to trust other people usually arises precisely when logic reaches its practical limit. The very idea of the rhetorical situation supports this conclusion—for if we had all the facts that we needed to make a decision, we would hardly need to be persuaded of anything. Only when we lack sufficient reason do we usually seek out a path based on a more intuitive form of judgment.

The difference between rhetoric and logic is that whereas logic examines the validity and coherence of argumentative propositions apart from situated context of action, rhetoric is concerned with how arguments affect specific audiences in specific times and places. This distinction comes from Charles Peirce, one of the founders of the study of logic in the United States. He defines logic as "the science of the conditions which enable symbols in general to refer to objects," and rhetoric as "the science of the formal conditions of intelligibility of symbols."[3] The distinction is not as complicated as it sounds. Peirce defines logic in terms of the formal relationship between symbols and objects, such as the difference between how a photograph and a name refer to the same thing. However, he defines rhetoric in terms of the "intelligibility" of symbols, meaning the intelligibility to specific people in specific situations. A young student, for instance, might look at a periodic table of the elements for

---

[2]John Dewey, "Logic," in *John Dewey: The Later Works*, vol. 8, ed. Jo Ann Boydston (Carbondale: Southern Illinois UP, 1986; original work published 1933), 4.

[3]Charles Peirce, "Harvard Lecture 1, 1865," in *The Writings of Charles S Peirce: A Chronological Edition, Vol. 1*, ed. Max Fischh, 175 (Bloomington: Indiana University Press, 1982), 175.

the first time and have no idea what it refers to, and the job of the chemistry teacher is to make the logic of the periodic table "intelligible" to that particular student by adapting the message to his or her particular experiences, interests, and expectations.

What the study of logic brings to rhetoric is, in Peirce's words, the increased capacity to make our ideas clear, both to ourselves and to our audience. Unfortunately, it is a bad habit of virtually all human beings to assume that they make more sense than they actually do, which is only made worse by the accompanying assumption that other people's thoughts are more muddled than their own. Peirce wryly observes that "few persons care to study logic, because everybody conceives himself to be proficient enough in the art of reasoning already. But I observe that this satisfaction is limited to one's own ratiocination [rationality], and does not extend to that of other men." Yet the fact is that we are all in the same boat: "We come to the full possession of our power of drawing inferences, the last of all our faculties; for it is not so much a natural gift as a long and difficult art."[4] Although effective public speaking is not the same thing as mastery of logic, understanding the basic process of logical inference and recognizing that logic is not an innate faculty but a long and difficult art makes us more careful in the research, composition, and performance of our speeches. This chapter hopes to provide the rudiments of logical reasoning in order to improve the clarity of our public speeches.

In rhetoric, **logical reasoning** comes into play any time we use inferences and proofs to establish relationships among propositions that warrant specific conclusions. Whenever we debate with ourselves or with others about why one thing or action is better than another, and use evidence and proof to defend or arrive at our conclusion, we engage in the process of logical reasoning. Put more simply, logical reasoning occurs any time we give a "reason why." A bare assertion ("It is sunny today"), request ("Let's get going"), or definition ("The best beach is one with the best waves") does not engage us in logical reasoning. Only when we provide a reason to these utterances do we start the process of making **inferences**, which is the act or process of deriving conclusions from premises known or assumed to be true. For instance, let us say I wake up and say "It is sunny today, because I see light coming through the window shades" or "Let's get going, because we don't want to get caught in traffic" or "The best beach is the one with the best waves, because then we can body surf." Each of these arguments seems to make sense without further need for elaboration, but in fact we are drawing inferences to make these comprehensible. Consider, for instance, the following possible conditions that show our inferences to be false: that the light is from the neighbor's car, that the cottage is within walking distance of the beach, and that you are talking to someone who has a leg cast.

One way to explain this process is through the Aristotelian-inspired model developed by Stephen Toulmin.[5] For him, logical arguments consist of the relationship between three things: the claim, the grounds, and the warrant. A **claim** is the

---

[4]Charles Peirce, "The Fixation of Belief," in *The Philosophy of Peirce*, ed. Justus Buchler, 5–22 (New York: Harcourt, Brace, and Co., 195), 5.
[5]This model is elaborated in Stephen Toulmin, *The Uses of Argument* (Cambridge, UK: Cambridge University Press, 1958). See also Wayne Brockriede and Douglas Ehninger, "Toulmin on Argument: An Interpretation and Application," *Quarterly Journal of Speech* 46 (1960), 44–53.

primary position or conclusion being advanced by a speaker ("We should drink more red wine."). The **grounds** are the supporting evidence for the claim ("Because we want to savor the good life."). The **warrant** is the inferential leap that connects the claim with the ground, usually embodied in a principle, provision, or chain of reasoning ("Wine is a necessary condition for bringing about the good life."). What makes this relationship subtle is the fact that the warrant is usually left unstated because it is taken for granted. Except in very complex chains of reasoning, we usually assume is that audience members will "fill in" warrants for themselves by drawing from their own resources of common sense, experience, and education. For instance, if we say "you should drink some water, because you are probably thirsty," we leave out the warrant "water quenches thirst" because it is obvious. But invoke an absurd or false warrant and it immediately becomes obvious to us. If I said "you should drink some whiskey, because you are probably thirsty," we would probably laugh because nobody drinks whiskey for quenching thirst. That is what makes it funny.

One way to think about the function of a "warrant" is as a bridge. A warrant simply connects the claim to the ground. A warrant does not make a new argument or provide new evidence. It simply is the connecting link that makes an argument "make sense." Think of a warrant, therefore, as one would think of a bridge between two places that would otherwise be kept apart. How do I get from the claim "we should get married" to the grounds "because we love each other"? And how is this path different than the one between the same claim "we should get married" and the different grounds "in order to appear respectable"? In the first case, the warrant is "you should marry the one you love." In the second case, the warrant is "marriage provides cultural respectability." Both of these are reasonable paths and are logically coherent (as opposed to the path that connects the claim "we should get married" with the grounds "because we need a good laugh"). Rhetorically, however, certain paths, no matter how logically coherent, nonetheless appeal to certain types of people more than others. A young couple unconcerned with material success and who fall in love while hitchhiking through Europe would find the first path more agreeable, whereas two successful adults with great political ambition might find the second warrant very persuasive. The art of crafting a rhetorical argument, therefore, includes creating attractive bridges between claims and grounds that are constructed for a particular audience to generate movement in thought and action.

The first step in crafting an argument is distinguishing the six types of warrants that are used in logical argumentation: *principle, causal, sign, analogy, generalization*, and *authority*. The easiest way to distinguish these types of warrants is by imagining each of them as a type of algebraic formula. A principle warrant either tells me what something is (All X's are Y's) or tells me how to act in response to something (Whenever you encounter X, do Y). A causal warrant tells me what something brings about (X causes Y). A sign warrant tells me what something indicates (X is indicative of Y). An analogy warrant tells me what I can treat something like (We can treat X like we treat Y). A generalization warrant tells me how universal something is (We can treat all Xs like this X). And an authority warrant tells me whom to trust (Always trust X).

All warrants follow this general pattern. If a warrant cannot be rephrased in one of these ways, it is probably not a warrant but a claim or a ground. Here are some examples:

Principle:	Claim: "We need to outlaw abortion."
	Grounds: "Because abortion is murder."
	Warrant: "All murder should be outlawed."
Causal	Claim: "Stop smoking."
	Grounds: "Because you want to be healthy."
	Warrant: "Stopping smoking makes a person healthier."
Sign	Claim: "We are clearly headed toward a recession."
	Grounds: "Because job growth has slowed considerably."
	Warrant: "Slow job growth indicates a coming recession."
Analogy	Claim: "I don't want to go to the football game."
	Grounds: "Because I hate gladiator contests."
	Warrant: "We can treat football games like gladiator contests."
Generalization:	Claim: "I'm never buying this make of car again."
	Grounds: "Because the one my father had kept breaking down."
	Warrant: "We can treat all similar cars like my dad's car."
Authority:	Claim: "Don't climb that ladder."
	Grounds: "Because my dad told me not to."
	Warrant: "We should always trust my dad."

In each of these cases, the warrant acts as a "bridge" between the claim and the grounds and remains unstated because it draws from common knowledge or obvious inferential leaps that would be redundant to make explicit. The warrant simply answers the question, "Why does this use of grounds support the claim?" It explains why these two statements (the claim and grounds) appear together as a "unit" and not as two separate entities.

The most important thing to keep in mind when studying warrants is that their persuasive power comes precisely from their invisibility. A good public speaker should make argumentation look and feel "easy" to an audience. But this effect only is produced through a great deal of conscious labor beforehand. As indicated in the example of the marriage proposal, the art of the well-crafted argument is in identifying the warrants that a particular audience already believes and is ready and willing to draw upon in filling out the logical assertion. As Aristotle long ago pointed out, the most successful arguments are those in which the speaker gives the audience just enough for them to complete the argument on their own. Too much information makes a speech tiring and pedantic; too little information makes a speech obscure and confusing. But if the speaker can craft an argument that invites warrants that the audience is ready and willing to contribute to the completion of the logical proposition, then audience members become active participants in the construction of meaning, which brings about a pleasurable feeling of learning without even realizing they are doing so.

As the goal of a rhetor (as opposed to a rhetorical critic) is less to logically analyze the arguments of others and more to create arguments that engage and persuade an audience, the goal of this chapter is to provide a method of construction. When inventing arguments, *first* think about the perspective of your audience and consider what types of beliefs, attitudes, values, and shared experiences they possess. *Second*, think about which of these resources can be phrased as a logical proposition in the form of a warrant. *Third*, select from these warrants the ones you think are most relevant to your case and can be embedded within an argument. *Last*, carefully pair claims with grounds that "call forth" these warrants without having to state them explicitly. For instance, let us take the position of the young couple who decide to get married while hitchhiking through Europe. How do they explain their decision to the husband's practical-minded father? They might assume that he might accept the causal warrant that "marriage tends to produce maturity." In that case, they carefully put together a claim and a ground that would stimulate this warrant in the father: "We got married because it is time for me to grow up." This simple process of thinking *through* the audience instead of *at* the audience is the most essential step in creating a trusting rather than an antagonistic relationship. Logic, in other words, is first and foremost an *ethical* practice when it comes to rhetoric, for it requires us to think first of others before we speak to them about their fears, desires, and interests.

To understand what makes a "legitimate" argument, then, it is helpful to also know what makes an "illegitimate" one. **Fallacies** represent arguments that, when analyzed in isolation, do not "hold up," in the sense of maintaining logical coherence. Practically, logical fallacies are precisely those quotes that, when taken out of context and broadcast on the news, force politicians and celebrities and other public figures to explain themselves. This demand on the part of the public for such speakers to "justify" their fallacious statements is central to understanding the nature of fallacies. Although it is often common to hear fallacies defined as "errors in logic," it is more accurate to describe them as incomplete arguments that have attempted to do too much in a short amount of space. Logician Charles Peirce, for example, denies that there are such things as purely false logical oppositions. Rather, "logical fallacies produce propositions, false, indeed, as they were intended, but yet with a modified meaning, true.... This fact, that human errors are always those which addition or amendment will rectify."[6] In other words, even the most ridiculous statement can be corrected by filling in all of the gaps that had initially been left empty.

The determination of a fallacy should thus address the following questions: (1) *Understood purely on the level of symbolic relationships, do the assertions*

---

[6]Charles Peirce, "Private Thoughts Principally on the Conduct of Life," in *The Writings of Charles S Peirce: A Chronological Edition, Vol. 1*, ed. Max Fischh, 4–9 (Bloomington: Indiana University Press, 1982), 5.

contained in warrant, claim, and grounds add up to a coherent whole? (For example, there is no simple warrant that connects the claim "I should buy a cat" with the grounds "because I hate animals." However, this might make more sense if the person explained he or she is trying to learn to love animals and that a cat seems easier to take care of than a dog.) (2) *Understood as a practical tool to address a problematic situation, does the argument conscientiously address the realities of the situation?* (For example, the argument "you should take a risk, because life is short" [invoking the warrant from the principle "those with short lives should take risks"] may be reasonable advice for a person planning a trip to France, but it is highly unethical to say to a child who wishes to dive off a bridge.) (3) *Understood as an empirical claim, does the argument invoke a valid warrant or refer to verifiable grounds?* (For example, the argument "you should eat more candy because you want to stay healthy" invokes the causal warrant "candy increases health," which is clearly false [except under extraordinary circumstances], and the argument "people are Gods because they never die" is clearly false because people are mortal [unless this argument is to be taken metaphorically]).

Perhaps the simplest way to identify a fallacy from a rhetorical standpoint is simply to ask which arguments, when taken in isolation, simply don't make sense to an audience or strike them as absurd. It is the responsibility of the rhetor to make claims that an audience can understand and then act upon. Speaking without having understood the facts of the situation, having properly analyzed the audience, and having taken the time to construct arguments that are internally consistent and ethically responsible leads to misunderstanding at best and misdirection at worst. Therefore, each examination of the forms of reasoning will also include mention of common fallacies associated with each form.

Discussion: One of the best ways to understand the function of a warrant is through jokes. A major component of humor is how we are able to participate in constructing absurd arguments that somehow make sense. For instance, take the bad joke: "A man walked into a bar and said 'ouch!'" In effect, this can be rewritten as an argument: "A man said 'ouch' (the claim) because he walked into a bar (grounds)," thus invoking the causal warrant "walking into a hard metal object causes pain" instead of the expected warrant concerning what happens when one walks into a place that sells alcohol. What other jokes can you think of that rely on unspoken warrants for their humor?

AUTHORITY

Arguments from authority are the simplest and often the most powerful persuasive tools for a speaker. An argument from authority grounds a claim by attributing the source to an authority who is respected by the audience. Methodologically, a speaker must therefore identify this authoritative source and then attempt to find within it some belief or value or attitude that supports the speaker's position. This is a fairly common tactic amongst politicians as they attempt to adapt their messages to different audiences. In debates over civil rights, they quote the Declaration of Independence; when speaking in Christian churches, they quote the Bible; when giving commencement speeches they draw from American literature, when speaking to children, they tell stories about Dr. Seuss. In each case, the basic claim might be the same (e.g., "All people love freedom") but the particular grounds that are chosen (e.g., "as is it expressed by Thomas Jefferson in the Declaration" or "as Walt Whitman wrote in *Leaves of Grass*") call up different warrants (e.g., "We should trust what the Declaration says" or "Walt Whitman is an authority on the human condition"). As with all warrants, keep in mind that the warrant is almost always left unsaid, and is called up by the combination of the claim and the ground together.

One type of abuse of this type of argument results in the fallacy of **misleading authority**. There are two primary forms of this fallacy. The first form attributes authority to someone who has no special knowledge or experience to offer. For instance, many celebrity endorsements of products make the implicit argument that "you should purchase this because I think it is a good product," invoking the warrant "always trust what I say about products." But clearly most celebrities have no insight into the products they are paid to promote, thereby making their endorsement purely superficial. The other form makes an appeal to authority (usually with the backing of force) as a means of cutting off other forms of justification. These types of fallacies function in authoritarian situations in which an audience is made dependent on a leader or class or institution that demands obedience and feels further justification unnecessary. In both cases, however, appeals to authority generally function to short-circuit the process of investigation and verification.

Another type of fallacy associated with authority is the inverted logic of **ad hominem**. Latin for "to the man," this fallacy effectively makes a negative statement rather than a positive one, thus making the warrant "do not trust what X says." Whereas positive arguments from authority ask us to accept a position simply because it came from a certain person, ad hominem demands that we reject it simply because it came from a certain person. These types of attacks are fairly common in political campaigns and are associated with "negative ads" of the type that directly attack a candidate's character rather than a specific position taken by that candidate. The argument that "you should not vote for this bill concerning regulating wastewater because it was sponsored by an adulterer" invokes the warrant "Don't trust adulterers." Although there are certainly times that a person's character may be the reason for mistrusting his or her statements, rarely is it a reason to question the legitimacy of a law that should stand or fall on its own merits. The risk of ad hominem is that it distracts attention from the issues and encourages us to make our decisions based purely on personal affection or dislike for a person.

John Brown: "The court acknowledges the validity of the law of God."

Arguments from authority are particularly important when a speaker is attempting to justify a morally questionable or even illegal action. By citing respected authorities, a speaker (in this case, playing the role of apologist) attempts to bolster his or her claim or even achieve a degree of transcendence. This was the case with abolitionist and revolutionary John Brown. On October 16, 1859, Brown and a group of twenty-one others captured a cache of weapons stored at the U.S. Arsenal at Harpers Ferry, Virginia, in an effort to arm liberated slaves and therefore destroy the slave system of the South. Although successful in the initial raid, they were eventually surrounded by federal troops and Brown was captured after a firefight. During his trial on December 2, 1859, Brown predictably attempted to justify his actions by citing the standard for moral authority in the United States at that time: the Bible. In this excerpt from his final speech after his conviction, Brown actually acknowledges the warrant before then embodying it in an argument:

> This court acknowledges, as I suppose, the validity of the law of God. I see a book kissed here which I suppose to be the Bible, or at least the New Testament. That teaches me that all things whatsoever I would that men should do to me, I should do even so to them. It teaches me, further, to "remember them that are in bonds, as bound with them." I endeavored to act up to that instruction. I say, I am yet too young to understand that God is any respecter of persons. I believe that to have interfered as I have done as I have always freely admitted I have done in behalf of His despised poor, was not wrong, but right. Now, if it is deemed necessary that I should forfeit my life for the furtherance of the ends of justice, and mingle my blood further with the blood of my children and with the blood of millions in this slave country whose rights are disregarded by wicked, cruel, and unjust enactments, I submit; so let it be done![7]

Typical of arguments from authority, Brown begins with the warrant in order to establish identification with an audience before making his specific claims concerning the justification for violence. Slightly reworded, he effectively justifies the claim "my shedding of blood is a righteous act" with the grounds "because the Bible justifies violence in the face of injustice." The warrant, conveniently, is actually stated in his first sentence. Reworded, it says: "We all acknowledge the validity of the law of God as written in the Bible." Brown therefore makes explicit his method of persuasion. He sees people acknowledging the validity of the Bible, and then seeks to draw from that text a passage that he believes justifies his own actions, in effect drawing from the same source that the court uses to condemn him to in turn condemn the court.

Discussion: Some consider any warrant from authority to be inherently a fallacy because it appears to defer responsibility for thinking to another person. Do you think this is true? When do you think that appealing to warrants from authority is the responsible thing to do?

GENERALIZATION

Rhetors use arguments from generalization when they try to draw general conclusions from single powerful examples or anecdotes. **Generalization** therefore entails drawing a general conclusion about a class of people, events, objects, or processes based on specific examples drawn from experience. In other words, the claims made in arguments from generalization therefore always demand that we treat a great number of things in a certain way, and the grounds for this sweeping judgment is that a single case can stand in for the whole. For instance, "as my grandfather

---

[7]Available from "Africans in America," http://www.pbs.org/wgbh/aia/part4/4h2943t.html (accessed 11 April 2012).

witnessed in World War II, all wars devastate the civilian population." The claim invites us to treat all wars the same way (as devastating to civilians) based on the particular experience of a particular person in a particular war. The warrant for this claim is that "my grandfather's experience with one war is representative of everybody's experiences with all wars." Clearly, however, this warrant would likely be challenged by military veterans who may have fought in more modern wars, which tend to use precision weapons and avoid at all costs mediated images of civilian deaths. They might respond "wars have changed since your grandfather's day," thereby challenging the representativeness of his experience.

One way to think about arguments from generalization is to think of the grounds in terms of an individual spokesperson for a larger group. The question for the audience, then, is why they should trust *this particular* spokesperson. What makes he/she/it such an authority? Clearly, not all particular things can stand in for the whole. Simply accepting any case as representative leads to the worst type of stereotyping. For instance, if I am walking down the sidewalk and a man in an "I love NY" T-shirt rudely bumps into me without apologizing, I do not then blurt out the argument "All people from New York are rude because that guy in the T-shirt was rude to me!" The warrant that "this one man in an 'I love NY' T-shirt stands in for the entire population of the state of New York" is absurd. However, if I buy a particular make of car and it constantly has engine problems due to no fault of my own, there seems justification for saying that "this make of car is terrible because I bought one and it kept having engine trouble." Because manufacturing produces each car effectively the same way, there is warrant for assuming that "my car is representative of every car of this make." The difference between these two examples is simply that whereas no two people are ever alike, two industrially manufactured products are virtually identical. The challenge with making arguments from generalization is therefore to determine how reliably a single example can stand in for multiple examples.

The most frequent fallacy associated with warrant from generalization is, predictably, **overgeneralization**. Overgeneralization is simply any time one makes too broad a leap from the particular to the general, such that the warrant "this X stands for all Xs" simply does not hold up. Simply because a person has the bad luck to pick a rotten apple out of a bin does not mean that the entire selection of apples is rotten. Similarly, simply because one has met a single person who is associated with a certain group (or has seen such a person represented in the media) does not mean that he or she represents the entire group. Unfortunately, overgeneralizations are easy to slip into because single cases might be so vivid and powerful that they capture our imagination and our emotions in a way that distorts our judgment. Oftentimes, a single powerful anecdote has the potential to motivate people in a way that even the most accurate statistics can never do.

Russell Conwell: "There was a poor man out of work in Massachusetts."

A master of the **narrative** form of argument was Russell Conwell, famous for his lecture "Acres of Diamonds." Between 1870 and 1924, Conwell delivered this speech more than 6,000 times until it became the gospel of the American entrepreneur. Conwell was a preacher and academic who saw the solution to the problems of industrialization in the ability of individuals to rise out of poverty through the power of creative thinking and marketing. But his primary method of persuasion was through the use of a powerful example that could be generalized to all people. For instance, this example of a man in Hingham, Massachusetts, is meant to convey a certain method that any American entrepreneur can use to create and sell products:

> There was a poor man out of work living in Hingham, Massachusetts. He lounged around the house until one day his wife told him to get out and work, and, as he lived in Massachusetts, he obeyed his wife. He went out and sat down on the shore of the bay, and whittled a soaked shingle into a wooden chain. His children that evening quarreled over it, and he whittled a second one to keep peace. While he was whittling the second one a neighbor came in and said: "Why don't you whittle toys and sell them? You could make money at that." "Oh," he said, "I would not know what to make." "Why don't you ask your own children right here in your own house what to make?" "What is the use of trying that?" said the carpenter. "My children are different from other people's children." (I used to see people like that when I taught school.) But he acted upon the hint, and the next morning when Mary came down the stairway, he asked, "What do you want for a toy?" She began to tell him she would like a doll's bed, a doll's washstand, a doll's carriage, a little doll's umbrella, and went on with a list of things that would take him a lifetime to supply. So, consulting his own children, in his own house, he took the firewood, for he had no money to buy lumber, and whittled those strong, unpainted Hingham toys that were for so many years known all over the world. That man began to make those toys for his own children, and then made copies and sold them through the boot-and-shoe store next door. He began to make a little money, and then a little more, and Mr. Lawson, in his *Frenzied Finance* says that man is the richest man in old Massachusetts, and I think it is the truth. And that man is worth a hundred millions of dollars today, and has been only thirty-four years making it on that one principle—that one must judge that what his own children like at home other people's children would like in their homes, too; to judge the human heart by oneself, by one's wife or by one's children. It is the royal road to success in manufacturing.[8]

The use of the single example helps make what might otherwise be a dry, analytical process into lively and engaged creative activity. It would have been easy for Conwell simply to have told people that he once knew a man who earned a million dollars by selling the toys that he made for his children. Instead, he told the example in all its detail, including actual dialogue between the man and his neighbors, in such a way that the method can easily be recalled to memory. And at the end of it he implies the following argument: "Making products that satisfy the desires of those closest to you is the royal road to manufacturing (claim) because I knew a man who made $1 million selling toys that his own children liked (grounds)," with the implied warrant being "this man's experience is representative of every person's

---

[8]Available from American Rhetoric at http://americanrhetoric.com (accessed 28 April 2010).

experience who uses this method." The success of this specific type of argument, of course, relies upon the audience's identification with the person in the story to the extent that they believe they are part of the class of "entrepreneurs," thus implying an identification behind the generalization.[9]

Discussion: The warrant for generalization often comes from the nature of the thing being generalized. We have a feeling that generalizing about certain classes of human beings based on one experience is the worst kind of stereotyping, yet we don't mind at all generalizing about entire classes of commodities based on a single experience. What kinds of experiences do you think are generalizable and which are not? How do we know the difference?

ANALOGY

Arguments from analogy invite us to accept a claim by inviting us to treat something unfamiliar as we would treat something more familiar. An **analogy** warrants us to treat two essentially unlike things the same way because they share a vital similarity that is particularly relevant to the case at hand.[10] Importantly, arguments from analogy do not actually make explicit *claims* that we should treat two things alike. For instance, the argument that "alligator is like chicken because I couldn't tell the difference when I was served it yesterday" is actually an argument from generalization, the warrant being "all dishes served with alligator are similar to the one that I ate." As with all warrants, arguments invoke analogy only when the comparison is *implied* when a certain type of ground is used to justify a claim. The typical claim used in this type of argument asks us to approach something in a certain way, thus suggesting an attitude. The grounds then switches some subject or object made in the claim with another subject or object without necessarily justifying the "switch." For example, For instance, "you should support gay marriage because you support civil rights" or "I think we should pass a balanced budget amendment because every household needs to balance its checkbook." The warrant for the first argument is "we can treat gay marriage as we treat civil rights" and for the second is "we can treat the federal budget as we treat a personal checking account." In effect, arguments from analogy ask us to take an attitude that we have developed toward one thing and simply apply it to something else that we think is equivalent.

What makes arguments from analogy persuasive is that they allow the audience to draw the parallel between two unfamiliar objects in their own way. Consequently, analogies often have the aura of humor because of the sudden resolution of incongruity in the imagination. For instance, let us say that your friend picks you up in a loud and rusty 1972 pickup truck, and you say "Just be on the lookout for

[9]For more on Conwell's speech, see A. Cheree Carlson, "Narrative as the Philosopher's Stone: How Russell H. Conwell Changed Lead into Diamonds," *Western Journal of Speech Communication* 53 (1989), 342–355.

[10]For more on argument by analogy, see James R. Wilcox and Henry L. Ewbank, "Analogy for Rhetors," *Philosophy and Rhetoric* 12 (1979), 1–20; James S. Measell, "Classical Bases of the Concept of Analogy," *Argumentation and Advocacy* 10 (1973), 1–10.

angry cavemen, because I hear Fred Flintstone wants his car back." The warrant for this is that we can treat your friend's old truck as we treat Fred Flintstone's prehistoric car. The logic is no different from when Franklin Delano Roosevelt, in his indictment of the financial industry that he believed helped bring about the Great Depression, said that "the money changers have fled from their high seats in the temple of our civilization. We may now restore that temple to the ancient truths." His argument that the nation can restore ancient truths because the money changers have fled the temple effectively asks us to treat corporate financiers in twentieth-century America as Jesus treated the money changers in the temple in Jerusalem 2,000 years ago. What makes this argument persuasive is that it is pleasurable to figure out the parallels between two unfamiliar objects (at least when they are not so different as to produce confusion or so similar as to be banal).

False analogy is the fallacy associated with this form of argument. Put simply, false analogy either makes logically absurd or ethically dubious associations between two things that have very little relationship to one another, such that the warrant "we can treat X like we treat Y" simply makes no sense. Sometimes the fallacy is due to lack of understanding. The skeptical argument that "I'm not going to see a doctor because I don't believe in magic" invokes the (false) analogical warrant "we can treat modern medicine as we treat magic." Other times the fallacy is clearly not meant to be empirically true but is nonetheless ethically dubious. Ironic arguments that compare certain social groups with animals or things are not meant to be taken literally but nonetheless convey meanings that are offensive and untrue. Perhaps more than any other fallacy, false analogy has led to many embarrassing moments for many public figures.

Socrates: "Unrighteousness runs faster than death."

One of the most famous speeches in the Greek world, which set the model for heroic rhetoric for ages to come, was the "apology" of Socrates at his trial in 399 B.C.E. Socrates had been accused of corrupting the youth and of being not pious to the gods because of his dedication to the philosophical method he associated with critical questioning and uninhibited inquiry into all human affairs. The trial came at the end of thirty years of war in which the great empire of Athens was defeated by Sparta and its allies, and Socrates was a convenient scapegoat for their failure. At his trial, Socrates once again showed his talent for argument by analogy, in which he tried to explain complex affairs through references to common objects and actions. In this excerpt from his defense (hardly an "apology" in a literal sense), Socrates responds to the decision to condemn him to death by drinking hemlock and defends his decision not to grovel and weep before the jury in order to spare his life, but instead to speak the truth as he knew it:

> You think that I was convicted through deficiency of words—I mean, that if I had thought fit to leave nothing undone, nothing unsaid, I might have gained an acquittal. Not so; the deficiency which led to my conviction was not of words—certainly not. But I had not the boldness or impudence or inclination to address you as you would have liked me to address you, weeping and wailing and lamenting, and saying and doing many things which you have been

accustomed to hear from others, and which, as I say, are unworthy of me. But I thought that I ought not to do anything common or mean in the hour of danger: nor do I now repent of the manner of my defence, and I would rather die having spoken after my manner, than speak in your manner and live. For neither in war nor yet at law ought any man to use every way of escaping death....The difficulty, my friends, is not in avoiding death, but in avoiding unrighteousness; for that runs faster than death. I am old and move slowly, and the slower runner has overtaken me, and my accusers are keen and quick, and the faster runner, who is unrighteousness, has overtaken them. And now I depart hence condemned by you to suffer the penalty of death, and they, too, go their ways condemned by the truth to suffer the penalty of villainy and wrong; and I must abide by my award—let them abide by theirs.[11]

Socrates spells out an argument by principle to justify his acceptance of death, arguing, in effect, "I cannot escape death (claim) because I am a man (grounds) and all men die (warrant)." However, he uses argument by analogy to explain why he has been condemned based on lies and false accusations. Reworded, his argument amounts to "I have succumbed to death (conclusion) because I cannot run faster than unrighteousness (grounds)," with the warrant being "we can treat life as a race between death and unrighteousness." Using argument from analogy thus allows Socrates to continually draw unexpected conclusions, often accompanied by laughter, because it forces the audience to figure out the analogical basis for his claims.

Discussion: We search for analogies to make something unfamiliar seem familiar. Unfortunately, some analogies are rarely helpful in bringing clarity to a situation. For instance, one of the most common analogies used in partisan politics is that of Hitler and the Nazis, usually used to describe the leadership and policies of the opposing party. Why do you think this analogy is used so frequently? What do you think people mean when they use it? And why do you think it is generally inappropriate?

SIGN

Arguments from signs urge us to accept the existence of something that is not immediately present to our senses but that has left evidence of its existence that can be interpreted by a discerning eye. Therefore, **sign** warrants encourage us to believe in something that cannot immediately be seen based on the appearance of external clues or indicators. This warrant is similar to generalization insofar as it draws a general conclusion based on the analysis of particular things. However, generalization attempts to unite many specific things under a general class or "heading," as if the goal was to place items in their right boxes. Sign is more interested in identifying what lies *behind* the examples and causes them to appear, much as a doctor is not interested in classifying a skin rash so much as determining what

---

[11]Socrates, "Apology," available from http://classics.mit.edu/Plato/apology.html (accessed 7 Sept. 2012).

kind of infection or condition brought it about. Warrants based on sign are usually called for in situations when people are concerned with identifying the nature of a problem—in attempting to make the "unseen" into something tangible and objective. Consequently, arguments from sign are most commonly used either in forensic argumentation that deals with proving the guilt or innocence of a person based on what evidence shows the individual has done in the past, or in deliberative policy discussions that require us to make predictions of the future based on the reading of present indicators.

Arguments from sign follow a very simple pattern. The claim always makes a tangible statement that some state of affairs exists, and the grounds support this claim by pointing specifically to particular things that are either an incontrovertible facts or phenomena that are readily available to sense perception. For instance, the prosecution in a court trial might argue: "the defendant was clearly present in the room at the time of the shooting because the blood stain on the carpet matched the defendant's DNA." This claim actually requires two warrants, the first being that "a DNA match indicates that a blood sample comes from that individual" and that "a person's blood stain on the carpet indicates the presence of that person in that room." However, the defense attorney would challenge both of those warrants, first questioning the accuracy of DNA testing and second arguing that the actual killer may have simply planted the blood to frame her client. Or, to use a political example, a president running for reelection might argue that "the state of the union is getting stronger because we see unemployment dropping and increased consumer confidence." The warrants here are that "decreased unemployment and increased consumer confidence are reliable indicators of a strengthening economy." However, the opposing party might accuse the president either of cherry picking only positive indicators while neglecting negative ones or simply misreading the signs in order to rationalize existing policies.

The fallacy associated with this warrant is **faulty sign**. A faulty sign is simply an appeal to an indicator that does not actually point to what the rhetor claims that it does. One way faulty signs are effective is when they appeal to unreflective commonsense associations to either advance or reject intricate diagnoses of situations of incredible breadth and complexity. The claim that "our nation's morals are declining because of all the violence on television police dramas" implies the faulty sign that "rising violence on television is indicative of rising violence in actual life." Another way they are effective is when they are used as shorthand indicators of value based on price or packaging or popularity. The popular **bandwagon** fallacy is a variant on faulty sign that takes the form of the warrant "the popularity of a thing is a sign of its value." Whenever we purchase a product because it is the "#1 Bestseller" and comes in an attractive package, we purchase it because we believe these things are indicators of its worth.

Chief Seattle: "Not a single star of hope hovers above his horizon."

Arguments from sign infer the existence of tendencies or characteristics from evidence that can be seen, touched, smelled, tasted, or heard. Sometimes arguments from sign make inferences about *particular* tendencies, such as that a storm is coming based on changes in the wind, or about *particular* characteristics, such as that a man is a soldier because he is carrying a gun. But other times these arguments read the "signs of the times," as it were. This was the sorrowful task for Chief Seattle of the Duwamish tribe, who lived in what is now the state of Washington. Faced with the prospect of his tribe being driven from their native lands, Chief Seattle spoke before an assemblage of both Native American and white settlers that included territorial governor Isaac Stevens. The purpose of the meeting was to formally accept the U.S. government's terms for buying tribal lands and establishing a reservation, but in the version of the speech written by Dr. Henry A. Smith, Chief Seattle took the opportunity to address the future of his people and their relationship to the culture of the white settlers:

> Your God is not our God! Your God loves your people and hates mine. He folds his strong protecting arms lovingly about the pale face and leads him by the hand as the father leads his infant son; but He has forsaken His red children—if they really are his. Our God, the Great Spirit, seems also to have forsaken us. Your God make sure people wax strong every day. Soon they will fill all the land. Our people are ebbing away like the rapidly receding tide that will never return. The white man's God cannot love our people or he would protect them....We are two distinct races with separate origins and separate destinies. There is little in common between us...
>
> Day and night cannot dwell together. The red man has ever fled the approach of the white man, as the morning mist flees from the morning sun. However, your proposition seems fair and I think that my people will accept it and will retire to the reservations you offer them. Then we will dwell apart in peace, for the words of the great white chief seem to be the words of nature speaking to my people out of the dense darkness. It matters little where we passed the remnant of our days. They will not be many. The Indians' night promises to be dark. Not a single star of hope hovers above his horizon. Sad-voiced winds moan in the distance. Grim fate seems to be on the red man's trail, and wherever he goes he will hear the approaching footsteps of his fell destroyer and prepare stolidly to meet his doom.[12]

Chief Seattle uses arguments by sign to prove two different claims. First, he first makes the assertion of a general characteristic that "your God loves your people and hates mine," backed with the grounds that "your people wax strong every day" and "our people are ebbing away." These two signs invoke the warrant from sign: "the prosperity and decline of races is indicative of being blessed or hated by the gods." He then adds misery upon misery when he asserts the existence of a general tendency that "The Indian's night promises to be dark," backed with the grounds, "sad voiced winds moan in the distance." The warrant from sign is that "sad-voiced winds in the distance are indicative of a disastrous fate to come." Chief Seattle thus reads the signs of the times and has resigned himself to stolidly meeting his doom.[13]

---

[12]Chief Seattle, available from http://www.halcyon.com/arborhts/chiefsea.html (accessed 3 Sept. 2012).
[13]For more on Chief Seattle, see Arnold Krupat, "Chief Seattle's Speech Revisited," *American Indian Quarterly* 35, no. 2 (2011), 192–214.

Discussion: The entire attraction of the fortuneteller is based on the notion that certain cryptic signs (such as lines in a palm or the design of tea leaves) are indicative of future events. Do you think that political economists often sound like fortunetellers in their rhetoric? How do they account for their predictions when things do not turn out the way they foretold?

CAUSATION

Arguments from causation justify practical conclusions based on the likely effects brought about by some underlying cause. **Causation** therefore encourages us to accept or reject a course of action based on its perceived consequences.[14] The claim of a causal argument is usually explicitly normative, telling us to do or not do something (rather than telling us what something is or isn't). The ground for the claim is then a statement of positive or negative effects of our action or inaction. For instance, "Put on your coat because you don't want to get cold." The warrant here is simply "wearing a coat will cause you to keep warm." Note that it is especially tempting in causal arguments to go beyond the bounds of the claim and think that the warrant might be something like "it is raining or snowing outside, which is why it is cold." But the claim says nothing about the actual environment. It only talks about coats and being cold. Consequently, the warrant cannot import any extra "content." It can only establish a *relationship* between coats and coldness. It is important to remember that warrants cannot go beyond the bounds of what is already in the claim or the grounds. A warrant's only function is to connect the two together. Any statement about the reason *why* it is cold becomes a separate argument altogether.

Causal reasoning is employed wherever we are encouraged to act (or not act) based upon *accepted* beliefs about cause-and-effect relationships. Causal arguments do not introduce new explanatory concepts, but rather rely on explanations already in place. Superstition, for instance, relies heavily on accepted causal accounts, no matter how fallacious. "Don't step on that crack if you don't want to break your mother's back" invokes the warrant "stepping on cracks causes your mother's back to get broken." As arguments become more complex, the type of audience that is influenced by causal warrants becomes more specialized. For instance, a conservative economist might argue that "we need tax cuts on capital gains in order to increase investment in new business." The warrant for this claim is simply that "capital gains tax cuts increases investment." But a liberal economist might argue that "without government stimulation of a depressed economy,

---

[14]In concentrating on matters of empirical relation, causation thus is similar to warrant by sign. However, sign concentrates on diagnosing an unknown condition based on effects or symptoms already present. Causation focuses more on predicting the future effects based on present causes already known. For instance, an argument by sign says "you have chickenpox because of the red dots all over your body," the warrant being "red dots are indicative of chickenpox." A causal argument would say "don't visit your friend with chickenpox because you don't want to catch it yourself." The warrant here is that "being exposed to chickenpox makes you susceptible to catching it." Sign indicates the presence of something that is already there, whereas cause predicts that something will happen if certain conditions are in place.

consumer confidence will continue to decline." The warrant for this claim is "government stimulation of the economy increases consumer confidence." Both of these arguments would be applauded when delivered to friendly audiences that willingly "fill in" the warrant to connect the claim and the grounds. When delivered to unfriendly audiences, the warrant is immediately exposed and challenged: "cutting capital gains only gives away money to the rich" or "government stimulation only increases debt to pay for wasteful projects." Consequently, speeches that use causal reasoning for a mixed audience almost always rely on expert research to establish their accuracy. Once a causal argument is made, rhetors almost always try to justify the warrant that has been invoked using testimony or statistics.[15]

If I wish to *challenge* the implied warrant, however, I do not myself invoke a causal warrant. Once a warrant itself becomes a problematic assertion and topic of debate, it changes its function from warrant to claim. For instance, let us say that I attempt to refute the claim that one should knock on wood to avoid bad luck by saying "failing to knock on wood does not produce bad luck, because laboratory studies have shown it has absolutely no effect." This is actually an argument by generalization that invokes the warrant that "controlled studies in the laboratory stand in for all cases of knocking on wood." As with all logical arguments, it is important not to confuse the content of the claim with the function of the warrant. What constitutes a claim, a ground, or a warrant has nothing to do with the content of the assertion; it has to do with its particular function within an argument based on its relationship to other assertions. A causal warrant is always something contributed by the audience and only implied by the speaker.

The fallacy of **false cause** occurs any time a causal argument is made that invokes a clearly incorrect or exaggerated causal sequence. As it has already been pointed out, the most pervasive arguments from false cause occur in superstition. The claim that "I knew my good luck would come to an end because I didn't knock on wood" invokes the causal warrant that "failing to knock on wood produces bad luck." But more serious cases of false cause often occur when people act on the basis of traditional and prescientific causal attributions, such as arguments that one should consume ground-up rhinoceros horn in order to increase sexual potency or that interracial marriage should be outlawed in order to protect children from psychological harm. As with the fallacy of faulty sign, however, those of false cause are attractive precisely because they provide easily comprehensible explanations for sometimes bewilderingly complex affairs. The frequent explanation that various plagues or diseases (such as AIDS) have been caused by some type of moral failing or divine retribution is indicative of the human craving for simple explanations.

Two common variants of the false cause fallacy are the slippery slope and scapegoating. The **slippery slope** fallacy takes the form of an argument that claims we must not make an even incremental step in a certain direction if we are to prevent a dramatic slide and decline into a terrible state of affairs. For instance, one very popular slippery slope argument takes this form: "we cannot allow even one handgun to be banned, because then we would inevitably end up completely

---

[15]For a discussion of causal inferences, see David Zarefsky, "The Role of Causal Argument in Policy Controversies," *Argumentation and Advocacy* 13 (1977), 179–191.

defenseless and unarmed." The warrant for this is: "a slight compromise on hand-
guns will produce a complete capitulation." The fallacy of this type of argument
is that it assumes an unstoppable domino theory of cause and effect that removes
human agency from the equation. The **scapegoating** fallacy takes the form of an
argument that claims that the reason some undesirable state of affairs has come
about is because of the existence or actions of a particular group of people who are
on the margins of society and are easy to blame. For instance, the argument that
"we need to deny health services and education to illegal immigrants if we want
to hope for a balanced budget" invokes the causal warrant "the presence of illegal
immigrants causes an excessive drain on the budget." What makes this argument a
fallacy is not that it makes the reasonable claim that state services go to illegal immigrants, but rather that this sole factor is responsible for the entire state's budget
crisis. In both cases, plausible causal sequences are exaggerated to such a degree
that they become fallacies.

Jonathan Edwards: "Look not behind you...lest you be consumed."

In rhetoric, causal arguments are consequentialist arguments; they tell us to adopt
or avoid a course of behavior based on the pleasurable or painful effects that are
assumed to result from them. In the rhetoric of religion, then, causal arguments are
typically those that rely on conceptions of heaven and hell, of salvation and punishment, to motivate an audience. The most famous of these types of religious exhorta-
tions in the American tradition is "Sinners in the Hands of an Angry God," a speech
first delivered by Calvinist preacher Jonathan Edwards in Enfield, Massachusetts
(now Connecticut), in 1741 but repeated many times afterwards. Edwards gradu-
ated as a brilliant intellectual from Yale and became a leader in the Great Awaken-
ing intended to revive enthusiastic faith in the God of the Puritans. This speech cast
aside the image of a loving, gentle God and tried to motivate an audience to faith out
of a desire to avoid eternal damnation in the pit of hell. Here is Edwards:

> O sinner! Consider the fearful danger you're in: 'Tis a great furnace of wrath,
> a wide and bottomless pit, full of the fire of wrath, that you are held over in
> the hand of that God, whose wrath is provoked and incensed as much against
> you, as against many of the damned in hell. You hang by slender thread, with
> the flames of divine wrath flashing about it, and ready every moment to singe
> it, and burn it asunder; and you have no interest in any Mediator, and nothing
> to lay hold of to save yourself, nothing to keep off the flames of wrath, noth-
> ing of your own, nothing that you have ever done, nothing that you can do, to
> induce God to spare you one moment...
>
> [But] now you have an extraordinary opportunity, a day where in Christ
> has thrown the door of mercy wide open, and stands in calling him crying with a
> loud voice to poor sinners; a day where in many are flocking to him and pressing
> into the kingdom of God. Many are daily coming from the East, West, North,
> and South; many that were very lately in the same miserable condition that you
> are in, are now in a happy state, with their hearts filled with love to him who
> has loved them, and wash them from their sins in his own blood, and rejoice in
> hope of the glory of God. How awful it is to be left behind at such a day! To see

many others feasting, well you are pining and perishing!... Therefore, let every one that is out of Christ, now awake and fly from the wrath to come. The wrath of Almighty God is now undoubtedly hanging over a great part of this congregation: let everyone fly out of Sodom: "Haste and escape for your lives, look not behind you, escape to the mountain, lest you be consumed."[16]

Most of the speech does not actually consist of specific arguments. Mostly, it simply describes all of the graphic details associated with the causal warrant that "God will bring great suffering upon all those who do not accept Christ as their Savior, no matter how virtuous they are." Only at the very end is a causal argument actually made. Reworded, this argument makes the claim "Any of you who fears the wrath of God should accept Christ as your Savior" because of the grounds that "otherwise you will be consumed in the fires of hell." As long as the audience has embraced the causal warrant, compliance follows immediately to shouts of joy.

Discussion: What we often call "ideological" arguments many times appeal to shared assumptions of causation. To advocate for higher or lower taxes, for more or less government regulation, all on the basis of assumed positive consequences that will result, is to argue from shared causal warrants. Can you think of some of these causal warrants that are commonly employed in ideological partisan discourse on both sides?

PRINCIPLE

Argument by principle draws on widely shared maxims, definitions, and norms either to categorize something or to justify a response to something. A **principle** is defined as a universal law, doctrine, or definition that helps guide judgment in particular cases. Of all forms of argument, principle is by far the most common. The reason is that principles are the most available thing to access in any culture. We learn principles in school, in places of worship, in the home, amongst our friends, and from literature and works of art. Any maxim that is repeated in any of these places can be used as a warrant for an argument by principle. All one needs to do is identify the warrant and build a claim and grounds that called it forth without having to make it explicit. For instance, take the Golden Rule: "Do onto others as you would have them do unto you." To turn this into an argument, you first make a normative claim: "You should return the money to lost and found." Then you create a ground that invokes the Golden Rule: "Because you wouldn't want someone to take your money if you lost it." Because any culture usually advertises its principles widely and vocally, it is the easiest resource to draw upon when making arguments, particularly with unfamiliar audiences.

Principles are valuable because they answer two fundamental questions about a person, an event, or an object: "What is it?" and "How should I respond to it?" There are thus two basic types of argument by principle, definitional and practical. In the **definitional** type, I argue that a certain thing has certain qualities ("Y") because of its nature as a specific *type* of thing (an "X"). These qualities can be

---

[16]Reid and Klumpp, 73–8.

specific physical traits, such as "hot" or "rude," or simply general virtues, such as "good" or "undesirable." For instance, the argument "People must be so friendly there because you live in a small town" relies on the warrant "people who live in a small town are friendly." Definitional principles therefore organize our environment by categorizing things and attaching predicates to them that tell us what to expect of them. By contrast, in the **practical** type of argument by principle, I claim that we should *behave* in a certain way because it is a certain type of thing. For instance, "let's move to a small town because people are friendly there" now invokes the warrant "whenever possible, live in a place where people are friendly." Rather than simply describing what something *is*, as with categorical principles, practical principles tell me what to *do*. They are therefore moral maxims of the type that we learn in kindergarten in order to play well with others and do the right thing.[17]

Usually, these two types of principle go hand in hand. Whenever I encounter a situation, I first want to know *what* I am dealing with, and then I want to know *how* to deal with this type of thing. Both of these answers can be given by principles. For instance, before women had the right to vote, a woman might have been told the following statements at a voting booth: "You shouldn't be at a voting booth because you are a woman" (the definitional warrant being "women cannot vote"), and "I should not let you vote because it is against the law for women to vote" (the practical warrant being that "people should not disobey the law"). The suffragists might then respond: "I have every right to vote because I am an American citizen" (the definitional warrant being "all American citizens have the right to vote") and "you should let me vote because your conscience tells you it is right" (the practical warrant being that "people should obey their conscience"). Once again, what defines an argument by principle is the invocation of a certain type of warrant that comes from the audience itself and is not explicitly identified by the rhetor.

The most common fallacies are those that are fallacies of principle. This is because the majority of our arguments invoke a warrant in the form of "All Xs are Y," a type of warrant that notoriously leads us to make broad and unjustified claims about a whole class of people or objects or events. Although there are numerous fallacies associated with argument from principle, the most common fallacy is **stereotyping**, which invites us to treat a diverse group of things as if they all were the same, thereby reducing a complex population to a simple and monolithic entity. For instance, if I say that "this waiter is going to be rude because he is French" I invoke the principle "all French waiters are rude." Most often, the origin of our stereotypes comes from a fallacy of overgeneralization in which a person encounters a single case (in this example, of a single rude French waiter) and then makes a universal overgeneralization from that experience (here, to include all French waiters). Stereotypes are thus the deductive application of an inductive overgeneralization. It is therefore a very common fallacy that is used to reinforce the biases of a community that are often based on very limited knowledge or experience.

---

[17]For more on argument by principle, see Chapter 4 of Richard M. Weaver, *The Ethics of Rhetoric* (Davis, CA: Hermagoras Press, 1985).

Another type of powerful fallacy of principle, the **either/or** fallacy, takes a different form. Instead of taking the form of "All Xs are Y," it says that "Either X or Y must occur." Importantly, this fallacy denies the possibility either that there is a third option or that some elements of both X and Y might occur together. Usually this fallacy is used in the context of polarization, in which a clear "us" and "them" has been established, and where a rhetor wishes to force people in the uncommitted middle to take sides without demanding compromise. For example, a speaker might argue that "we must support an aggressive war policy if we are not to simply choose complete capitulation to the enemy." The warrant for this argument is "war and capitulation are mutual exclusive alternatives." The effect of this type of argument is to make those who were seeking a diplomatic solution appear to be weak-kneed capitulators. The either/or fallacy appears similar to the slippery slope fallacy, but it differs for two reasons: (a) rather than warning us what not to do, it tells us what we have to do; and (b) the justification is not based on negative consequences but rather the preference for one choice over another. Usually, however, the two fallacies work together to increase the level of polarization in a deliberative atmosphere, as when one might make the slippery slope argument "if we agree to only one of our enemy's demands, we will soon find ourselves completely under their heel." Each of these fallacies is persuasive because they force people into hasty decisions based on fear and exaggeration, but more often than not these types of decisions have negative long-term results because they are done out of impulse rather than forethought.

Jonathan Winthrop: "We shall be as a city upon a hill."

In rhetoric, the principles that go unsaid are often more revealing about the character of the speaker and the audience than what is made explicit. For if a thing does not need to be said, it is so deeply ingrained in a person's character as to become part of that person. Therefore, by constructing arguments that call forth such deeply held principles, the speaker provides a rewarding sense of identification in an audience. Consequently, arguments by principle are particularly effective when trying to define the character of a particular nation or society. This problem of self-definition was particularly acute for the Puritans, led by John Winthrop, who left Britain for the shores of North America, where they had to forge a new identity in a strange land. This identity was based on a shared belief that they were servants of God who were on a divine mission to purify the church and combat the forces of the Antichrist. Their duty in New England was to establish a society that embodied all the elements of God's glory and thus function rhetorically to shame and to inspire others to follow their example. In his speech "A Model of Christian Charity" delivered in 1630, Winthrop draws on the preexisting principle that New England society is blessed by God and ends on this dramatic conclusion:

> The Lord will be our God, and delight to dwell among us, as His own people, and will command a blessing upon us in all our ways, so that we shall see much more of His wisdom, power, goodness and truth, than formerly we have been acquainted with. We shall find that the God of Israel is among us, when ten of us shall be able to resist a thousand of our enemies; when He shall make us a

praise and glory that men shall say of succeeding plantations, "May the Lord make it like that of New England."

For we must consider that we shall be as a city upon a hill. The eyes of all people are upon us. So that if we shall deal falsely with our God in this work we have undertaken, and so cause Him to withdraw His present help from us, we shall be made a story and a by-word through the world. We shall open the mouths of enemies to speak evil of the ways of God, and all professors for God's sake. We shall shame the faces of many of God's worthy servants, and cause their prayers to be turned into curses upon us till we be consumed out of the good land whither we are going.[18]

The first paragraph makes no formal logical arguments, but only states a series of claims (left ungrounded) concerning the relationship between New England and the God of Israel. The core argument by principle occurs at the beginning of the second paragraph, although it makes more logical sense in a different order. The claim is actually "The eyes of all people are upon us" and the reason for this, the ground, is that "We shall be as a city upon a hill." The warrant is that "all people turn their eyes upon a city on a hill." Winthrop is certainly brazen enough to declare the tiny colony of New England to be a city on a hill, but what he leaves unsaid is more significant. He assumes that his audience takes for granted the fact that all people in the world look upon God's chosen city as a model of virtue. But this, of course, is an assumption rooted in a particular Puritan reading of the Bible that views society in terms of the chosen and the fallen while assuming that all human beings aspire to perfection in the eyes of the Christian God. His subsequent warnings about what will happen should they not attain perfection are causal arguments that follow from this principle (i.e., "failure of God's chosen people to attain perfection will result in the corruption of the world"). By leaving these warrants unsaid, Winthrop shows how powerful the perfectionist impulse was in the Puritan audience, and how the natural result of perfectionism was the incredible burden of guilt.[19]

Discussion: When we say that we take a *principled stand* on something, we often mean that we do so from allegiance to a principle that stands in contradiction to some utilitarian causal argument. When have you taken such a stand in your life? Do you regret doing so based on the perceived benefits you might have gotten from using a causal argument?

---

[18]Ronald Reid and James Klumpp, *American Rhetorical Discourse* (Long Grove, IL: Waveland Press, 2005), 24.
[19]For more on Puritan rhetoric, see Patricia Roberts-Miller, *Voices in the Wilderness: Public Discourse and the Paradox of Puritan Rhetoric* (Tuscaloosa: University of Alabama Press, 1999).

KEY WORDS

SUMMARY

In rhetoric, logos represents not only the art of reasoning, but also the art of crafting one's arguments to make those reasons persuasive. Perhaps the most important aspect of this art is to know what to leave out. More often than not, amateur speakers put in too much rather than too little. They pile arguments on top of arguments as if persuasion occurred by the sheer weight of argumentation. However, a good speech will actually include only a few actual arguments, with each argument in effect representing a main point. The rest of the speech will then focus on providing backing for those arguments in various ways, including resources from ethos, pathos, and style. But the core persuasive intent of the speech is always expressed in specifically crafted arguments that can be quoted to answer the question "What was that speech about?" If there are not a couple of distinct sentences that can be directly quoted in your speech to answer that question, then the logos of that speech is usually faint to nonexistent.

The most important thing to remember about a good argument from logos is that it consciously leaves out the warrant that serves to bridge the claim and the grounds, and that this warrant has been chosen specifically because the speaker knows it will be subconsciously granted by the audience without it having to be made explicit. Although this point has been made numerous times, it bears repeating that the warrant is not an extra argument or defense of the claim. It does not add a great deal of "new" material.

It simply acts as a basis of inference that allows us to connect a claim with its grounds in a way that makes sense to us. For instance, we do not agree with the argument "I decided to put on my jacket because I was hot" not because we know anything special about that situation, but because we reject the causal warrant "wearing a jacket makes one cool" on logical grounds. By saying a warrant acts as a "bridge," it simply means it gets us from one side of the argument to the other on the basis of an inference that is stable enough to stand on. The art of crafting arguments is to therefore appeal to those premises that the audience already believes and are eager to use to help a speaker establish his or her claims. This means that a good argument from logos begins with an understanding of the audience, proceeds to making explicit the premises that they will readily assent to, and then finally to building arguments that invoke those premises without needing to verbalize them.

Let us take, for example, a woman who is advocating for universal health care and is speaking to a variety of different audiences:

- First, she first speaks to a Catholic audience who she knows respects the authority of the pope. She makes the argument: "I believe health care is a right, just as the pope has recently expressed in a speech," invoking the warrant from *authority*: "One should trust what the pope has to say."

- Second, she speaks to a group of college graduates who she knows are anxious about being on their own. She makes the argument: "Without universal health care we are all at risk, as we have seen in the story of one student who was forced to abandon her long-term career goals because of the debt incurred by the injuries caused by an uninsured motorist," invoking the warrant from *generalization*: "This recent graduate represents the possible fate of all recent graduates."
- Third, she speaks to a group of economists who are mostly concerned about the effect of universal health care on long-term economic growth. She makes the argument: "We are headed down an economic spiral without health care, as we have seen from the rise in personal debt and bankruptcy caused by health costs," invoking the warrant from *sign*: "Increased debt and bankruptcy are signs of future economic decline."
- Fourth, she speaks to the executives of multinational corporations familiar with different forms of health care across the globe. She makes the argument: "The American system needs to move to a single-payer system because of the success we have seen in European nations," invoking the warrant from *analogy*: "We can treat the American health care system like we treat the European health care system."
- Fifth, she speaks to a group of working parents concerned about both costs and securing the future of their children's health. She makes the argument: "Universal health care is absolutely necessary if we are to avoid condemning our children to a life of poverty simply because they had the bad fortune to get sick while looking for a job," invoking the warrant from *cause*: "Universal health care will help keep children out of poverty."
- Last, she speaks to a group of constitutional scholars familiar with the Bill of Rights and the Declaration of Independence. She makes the argument: "We cannot shirk our responsibilities to cover those who become sick because that is a violation of the right to life," invoking the principle from the Declaration of Independence that "all human beings should be guaranteed the right to life."

One should think of arguments from logos as establishing an initial bond between speaker and audience in which the speaker provides a framework that the audience completes by filling in the missing warrant. This generates a sense of participation that does not have the same effect as when the speaker spells out every single part of an argument. By leaving essential aspects out that the audience can contribute on their own, it makes them more willing to consider the subsequent backing for that claim that constitutes the rest of the speech.

Speakers slip into fallacies when they use warrants that appeal to misinformation or stereotypes that do not effectively or logically bridge the claims to the grounds. Fallacies, in other words, take the form of logical argumentation without providing the substance. Fallacies can take two forms. On the one hand, they might appeal to blatantly false warrants. To borrow an example from Plato, a candy maker might reason with a group of children that "they should not eat fruits and vegetables because they taste bad," invoking the warrant from principle that "one should not eat any food that tastes bad." This is a fallacy primarily because the principle is simply false. On the other hand, they might construct arguments that simply make no sense if they are examined closely. A *non sequitur*, for instance, represents any type of argument that simply does not have any sense of coherence and "does not follow." For instance, that same candy maker might say "you should eat candy because I am dressed like a funny elephant." The only way this argument makes any sense is by authority, "you should always trust things told to you by someone dressed like a funny elephant." This hardly even makes enough sense to be comprehensible, yet it is the verbal parallel of most techniques of advertising to children by using cartoon characters to sell medicine. But this example also shows that fallacies can be very effective persuasive techniques if they appeal to the unthinking impulses and biases of an audience in the guise of reason.

CHAPTER 5 EXERCISES

1. Analyzing your rhetorical artifact selected in Chapter 1, which was the primary form of logical reasoning used to make a case? Give examples and explain why this form of reasoning was most appropriate to emphasize given the speech topic. Then read the speech to identify any possible fallacies.

2. In response to the question "Why did the chicken cross the road?" give an impromptu speech offering a reason by selecting one of the major forms of logical reasoning. Then try to argue why chickens should be prevented from crossing roads by selecting from one of the fallacies. After each speech presented in class, try to identify what form of logos was at work.

3. Find a full-length editorial in a newspaper and identify all the logical reasoning and fallacies it contains.

4. As a class, select a particular argument to make about a current event. Divide yourselves into six groups and assign one form of reasoning for each group without revealing your choice. Write a 10 sentence speech supporting a single argument. Give the speeches and try to identify the forms of reasoning used by other groups. Were they all used correctly?

5. Start with the claim "chickens should not cross roads" and then come up with a ground that you think is funny. Have everyone deliver his or her "joke" and then try to determine what the hidden warrant is that makes it funny. Which warrants made for funnier jokes?

6. Using the health care example as a model, come up with a new claim for speech and try to figure out different arguments that one might make for six different audiences, choosing from a list which reflects the diversity of the experiences of people in your classroom.

Pathos

This chapter explores the ways of constructing appeals to emotion based on charged descriptions of people, objects, events, or actions. Whereas logos persuades based on cognitive beliefs derived from claims of fact, pathos persuades based on affective orientations derived from feelings of like and dislike, desire and fear, and pain and pleasure. The concepts employed thus come in opposite pairs relating to the attractive (+) and repulsive (–) spectrum of emotions, and they are organized according to their relationship to people (saint and sinner), objects (idol and abomination), events (utopia and wasteland), and actions (virtue and vice). The goal of this chapter is to demonstrate how, within certain problematic situations, to attract people to certain things that are beneficial while repelling them from others that are harmful. If logos persuades an audience as to what is the best course of action based on belief, pathos motivates them to actually pursue that course of action out of fear or desire.

In the Greek rhetorical tradition, **pathos** refers to the use of emotional appeals to persuade an audience. Whereas *ethos* persuades by the character and *logos* persuades by reasoning, *pathos* persuades by producing an emotional response in an audience that makes it favorable to one thing and unfavorable to another. In his *Rhetoric*, Aristotle offers a definition of emotions (*pathē*) that remains an important resource for understanding their function in rhetoric. He writes:

> The emotions are those things through which, by undergoing change, people come to differ in their judgments and what are accompanied by pain and pleasure, for example, anger, pity, fear, and other such things and their opposites. There is need to divide the discussion of each into three headings. I mean, for example, in speaking of anger, [one should describe] what is their state of mind when people are angry, and against whom are they usually angry, and for what reasons.[1]

Emotions, for Aristotle, are those psychological feelings of pain or pleasure we associate with things in our environment about which we must make a judgment. To understand someone's emotions, according to Aristotle, we only need to ask that person to describe three things: (a) his or her state of mind; (b) the people, objects, events, or actions that produce the state of mind; and (c) the reasons he or she feels this way. Once we know these things, we can then reproduce these emotions in others by speaking about those same people, objects, events, or actions in such a way that brings about that state of mind.

---

[1]Aristotle, *On Rhetoric: A Theory of Civic Discourse,* trans. George Kennedy (Oxford: Oxford University Press, 1991), 1378a.

In other words, emotional appeal does not simply tell us: "be angry at this thing." It describes the type of thing that makes a certain audience, for example, angry and the emotion is evoked on its own.

Although often maligned as an "irrational" means of persuasion, emotional appeal is an inevitable and necessary part of any persuasive act. Although people's emotions can certainly be manipulated for irrational ends, the use of emotion in persuasion is no more or less ethical than the use of credibility or logic. Indeed, the relative importance of *pathos* in rhetoric is exemplified by the fact that Aristotle, despite his apparent reservation about excessive use of emotional appeals and persuasion, nonetheless felt the need to spend almost a third of his book defining what he considered the most important emotions, including calmness, anger, friendship, enmity, fear, confidence, shame, shamelessness, kindness, unkindness, pity, indignation, envy, and emulation. This is because, far from "distorting" our judgments, emotions are what make judgments possible by giving us the motive to prefer one thing over another. Without emotional involvement in our surroundings, all the reason and credibility in the world would not encourage us to expend the least bit of energy to accomplish a task. That is why people who are "apathetic" (or "without pathos") are those who have an incapacity to make a judgment.

One way to understand the nature of emotion is to compare it with "feeling." Whereas a feeling can simply be a sensation (such as the feeling of being burned when touching a hot stove), an emotion is something more complex that relates to our entire reaction to that sensation (such as fear of being burned). In other words, emotions are different from feelings because they are tied up with our likes and dislikes, our hopes and fears, and our senses of self and other. **Emotions** are dramatized feelings that orient us to things within our immediate environment that stand out as significant. Calling them "dramatized feelings" recognizes that emotions are still related to feelings insofar as emotions either produce or anticipate sensations of pleasure and pain. When we look forward to a vacation, we both "feel" pleasure in the moment and also look forward to the feeling of the sand and the sun and the water. But the emotion is not simply these feelings. They are *dramatized* feelings because we play them out in our imaginary narratives in which we envision either how we will relate to something in the future or how something happened in the past. Emotions are therefore always objective and dramatic; they involve our active relationship with things either in the real world or in our imaginations.[2]

It is because of the "dramatic" character of emotions that they are tied so closely to our capacity for judgments. According to John Dewey, a sense of judgment always lurks behind any emotion because "emotions are attached to events

---

[2]This makes emotions different than **moods**, which tend to be pervasive qualities of a person's personality that affect his or her cognitive processing in all situational contexts (as when a "depressed" person always interprets things differently than one who is an "optimist"). Emotions, by contrast, are always specific. We love some*body* and we fear some*thing*. Emotions do not simply exist in a void. They are always responses to some aspect of our environment. Richard J. Davidson, "On Emotion, Mood, and Related Affective Constructs," *The Nature of Emotion: Fundamental Questions,* ed. Paul Ekman and Richard J. Davidson (Oxford, UK: Oxford University Press, 1994), 51–55.

and objects in their movement... toward an issue that is desired or disliked."[3] Emotions arise in the midst of objective situations and tell us how to orient ourselves to particular parts of that situation (as when we enter a strange room and try to determine who is a possible ally and who is an antagonist). Furthermore, we tend to feel the strongest emotions in those situations that are in flux and uncertain. He goes on:

> The rhythm of loss of integration with environment and recovery of union not only persists in man but becomes conscious with him; its conditions are material out of which he forms purposes. Emotion is the conscious sign of a break, actual or impending. The discord is the occasion that induces reflection. Desire for restoration of the union converts mere emotion into interest in objects as conditions of realization of harmony.[4]

Put another way, emotions are intelligent insofar as they inform us of ruptures in our environment and signal their possible restoration. Emotions tell us what we need to support, what we need to reject, what we need to be concerned about, and what we can trust. It is thus the ethical function of rhetoric to try to direct emotions toward the right objects in the right way in order to bring about a "realization of harmony."

As indicated by Dewey's remark about liking and disliking, because emotions always involves a dramatic relationship between ourselves and other things, they can be effectively divided into emotions that *attract* us to things (and therefore have a positive orientation) and ones that *repel* us from them (and therefore have a negative orientation). **Attracting emotions** draw us closer to somebody or something; we associate such attracting emotions with love, curiosity, pity, generosity, envy, trust, respect, obsession, or greed. Clearly, not all attracting emotions are "good" ones. Sometimes we are attracted to the wrong things for the wrong reasons. The mark of an attracting emotions is simply that, when something is present, people tend to want to "get closer" to it and to preserve it. **Repelling emotions,** by contrast, push us negatively away from somebody or something; we associate such negative emotions with anger, fear, shame, guilt, embarrassment, anxiety, disgust, or cowardice. The characteristic response of a repelling emotion is something like a "fight-or-flight" reaction in which we either try to avoid something or decide to face up to it in order to get rid of it. Of course, emotions do not always demand immediate action. Often we may love somebody and yet never talk to them, and we may be angry at those whom we must, by necessity, obey. But the lasting presence of such repelling emotion usually makes us try to get out of that situation; just as attracting emotions usually push us toward something over time.[5]

The power of rhetorical discourse is often based upon its ability to harness this motivational power of emotions to encourage new beliefs and actions. The

---

[3]John Dewey, *Art as Experience* (New York: Perigree Books, 1934), 20.
[4]Dewey, *Art as Experience*, 41.
[5]For a review of different perspectives on emotion, see Randolph R. Cornelius, *The Science of Emotion: Research and Tradition in the Psychology of Emotions* (Saddle River, NJ: Prentice Hall, 1996).

first step is to connect the right emotion to the right things. A rhetor who wishes an audience to reject something will inspire repelling emotions, while attracting emotions will be directed toward the object of the rhetor's preference. Usually, both of these effects are produced by loading up certain objects with positive or negative feelings. One of the basic strategies of advertising, for instance, is simply to show a product in association with pleasurable sensations (attractive people, a clean house, fresh breath, a healthy body) while associating its competitor with negative sensations (ugly people, a dirty apartment, bad breath, disease). These feelings then are bundled together in a particular way to make us desire or fear certain products and consequences. We then imagine ourselves owning this product through an imagined drama that culminates in us being popular, powerful, healthy, and wealthy. Our emotional attachment to this vision then leads us to buy a product.

After relating certain emotions to certain things, the second step is to either amplify or diminish the salience, or relative strength, of our emotional response. **Amplification** increases salience by exaggerating something and making it "larger than life" so that it stands out as important and demanding of our attention. This can be done both to attract us to something and to repel us from something. For instance, nations that go to war inevitably amplify the great virtues and material rewards that will come from victory, promising both glory and riches in order to attract soldiers to the battlefield. By contrast, pacifist critics amplify the inevitable consequences of war, including the death of civilians, the traumatic effects of war on soldiers, and the rise of militarism at home, in order to repel us from war. Likewise, **diminution** reduces something, pushes it into the background, and makes it insignificant and trivial. Naturally, diminution has an inverse relationship to attraction and repulsion than amplification. To encourage attracting emotions, diminution actually seeks to reduce the level of threat in order to make something seem benign and therefore harmless. For example, investors in a controversial plan for a nuclear energy plant to be built next to a nature preserve will diminish the possible impact of the plant on the environment (while amplifying its economic benefits). By contrast, to encourage repelling emotions, diminution will downplay the benefits in order to make an alternative not very worthwhile to pursue, as a critic of nuclear power might do when showing how the energy benefits are meager over the long term compared to a more sustainable investment in wind and solar energy.

Pathos works in rhetoric, then, by dramatizing feelings and amplifies or diminishes aspects of our environment in such a way that we are actively attracted to or repelled by four categories of things—people, actions, events, and object. **People** represents both individuals and groups (George Washington, the American people, the human race); **actions** refer to conscious behavioral choices made by people (eating fast food, declaring war, philosophizing); **events** stand for time-bound, complex, moving situations that have a beginning, middle, and an end (a car accident, the Middle Ages, the Apocalypse); and **objects** represent entities (both physical and conceptual) that can be understood and named as discrete things (trees, laws, atoms, Dante's *Inferno*). To make us feel something strongly about something, then, a rhetor must make it stand out from our general environment and endow it with particular qualities that make it worthy of our attention and concern. That is why pathos is necessary in rhetoric. Out of the infinite aspects of our environment, a rhetor must select those things that are vital to address in any effort at a successful resolution. One must necessarily *amplify* and *exaggerate* these things in order for them to stand out and attain salience. Poor efforts at pathos will simply name emotions and tell us to feel them, as if emotions could simply be brought forth on command; effective uses of pathos will call them forth without needing a name. Rhetoric uses graphic examples to inspire emotions that make an audience turn away from one thing and toward another.

In other words, the essence of pathos is vivid description, not logical exposition. Whenever one gives formal reasons, detailed accounts, or logical analysis, one is using logos; the appeal is to one's cognitive belief structure based in propositions and facts. Pathos, by contrast, gives "life" to those beliefs. For example, a speaker can use logos to give a formal cost-benefit analysis for why addressing poverty helps people's lives at the same time that it improves the economy and cuts crime. But one can also describe the squalor of living in a slum, the diseased skin of a hungry child, the lost potential of dying addicts, and the success story of a person who escaped the ghetto through the help of a teacher. Pathos thus incorporates elements of narrative and style to sculpt powerful images that live in people's imaginations and make them *feel* ideas that logic can only *explain*. The best rhetoric, then, will always balance the use of pathos with a more reasonable logical analysis. There is nothing wrong with exaggeration when it is done for the purposes of getting an audience engaged and enthusiastic about an issue that it may have otherwise thought important. One must simply supplement this enthusiasm with the kind of practical judgment that can be produced only through long and careful forethought and analysis.[6]

Fortunately, a good narrative can easily combine reason and emotion in such a way to reconcile the tension between logos and pathos. As many of the examples used in this book have shown, public speakers rarely restrict themselves to making explicit claims that are grounded in empirical data and warranted by logical reasoning. More often than not, their claims are embedded in narrative stories. These stories may be personal, moral, historical, fictional, or demonstrative, but *as stories* they all share in a common aim—to give meaning to ideas by showing how they function over time in people's lives and in the environment in a way that is both pleasing as a story and plausible as an account. A narrative is thus more than a mere stringing together of events in chronological order. Even the timeline of someone's life, insofar as it has a beginning and an end, is not a narrative. A **narrative** is a dramatic story that creates a desire in an audience and then fulfills that desire by describing the interaction among agent, scene, act, purpose, and agency in such a way that brings about an emotional and cognitive unity.

The rhetorical aspect of narrative becomes clear once we are forced to choose between the validity of competing narratives about the same situation. In our interpersonal lives, we are constantly faced with this choice whenever we find ourselves caught in a dispute between mutual friends. Political situations are no

---

[6]For the relationship between reason and emotion, see John M. Cooper, *Reason and Emotion: Essays on Ancient Moral Psychology and Ethical Theory* (Princeton, NJ: Princeton University Press, 1999).

different. When faced with competing narratives, an audience must decide which narrative is more "rational" to follow. Recall that in Chapter 1 we distinguished between **narrative fidelity** or how accurately a narrative represents accepted facts, and **narrative probability,** or the coherence of the narrative as a story apart from the actual facts. The most effective narrative from a rhetorical standpoint should have both high narrative probability *and* high narrative fidelity. By presenting an argument in a form of a story that accurately represents reality in a coherent, engaging, and powerful manner, a speaker invites an audience to vicariously participate in a new vision of reality. Especially when narratives are broad in scope, these narratives can completely alter an audience's basic worldview. The narratives we tell of our common histories have particular power in structuring our social organizations, our self-conceptions, and our relationships with other groups. Logical rationality plays a crucial role in structuring these things as well, but more often than not they begin and end in narratives whose lasting impact is usually emotional.

The strategies in this chapter are therefore based on the premise that pathos is most persuasive when a rhetor attaches an attracting or repelling emotion to a specific type of "target" (a person, action, event, or object) and then amplifies that emotion through a dramatic narrative. Each of these strategies has been given a name, as follows:

Target of Pathos	Attracting Strategy (+)	Repelling Strategy (–)
People	Saint	Sinner
Actions	Virtue	Vice
Events	Utopia	Wasteland
Objects	Idol	Abomination

In each of the strategies, a rhetor has embedded a person, action, event, or object and made it a central factor (for good or evil) in dramatic narrative that has both fidelity (insofar as it reflects reality) and plausibility (insofar as it tells a good story). Combining both fidelity and plausibility within a narrative is no easy task. A narrative that has fidelity without plausibility tends to reduce to an uninspiring recounting of details, whereas a narrative that has plausibility without fidelity is interpreted as a merely entertaining fiction. Only when an audience receives our stories as being both realistic and well told do they bring about the pathos that becomes a motive for action. It is therefore an ethical responsibility on the part of the speaker to create stories that actually represent a state of affairs and do not to slip into easy exaggeration and melodrama that play to the biases of an audience for the sake of short-term persuasive victory.

Discussion: A major component of the art of interviewing is being able to amplify one's good qualities and diminish one's negative qualities, thereby bringing about attracting emotions in the interviewer concerning your status as a future employee. What was one of the most successful narratives that you told about yourself in an interview context? What was amplified and what was diminished? And what type of response did you get that told you it had been a success?

UTOPIA

A utopia is a vision of a perfect event, understood as a state of affairs. This event can be personal and momentary, such as the moment parents witness the birth of their first child; it can be shared and historical, such as one's memories of a Golden Age; and it can be shared and futuristic, such as one's visions of the Promised Land. In all cases, the event is portrayed as the culmination of hopes and desires that we yearn to recapture in memory or in actuality. To employ **utopia** is to use the power of an ideal to reveal the limitations of one's actual situation and inspire hope that future "perfect" events will occur. Ronald Reagan, for instance, was famous for referring to the United States in such utopian terms, referring to it as a "Shining City on a Hill." Whenever rhetors engage in this form of amplification in which they outline some noble dream for the future or nostalgia for the past, they are engaging in utopia.

This is not to say that utopia is always employed for noble sentiments. Some of the worst crimes in history have been perpetrated by those who use the power of utopia to justify acts of terror and oppression. Hitler used utopia when he went into ecstatic praise of his vision of a Third Reich that would last 1,000 years, and the medieval church used utopia when it inspired its Children's Crusade. Yet to abuse a tool does not condemn the tool. The speeches of the most adored and humane leaders of the twentieth century, such as Gandhi, Martin Luther King, Jr., and Nelson Mandela, equally make use of utopia to liberate and empower. By creating a sense of dissatisfaction with one's present state of affairs and inspiring hope for the future, utopia is one of the most powerful manifestations of pathos. There is no social movement at any time that has not inspired its followers by envisioning a perfect state of affairs that will be brought about through struggle and effort on the part of the people. Consequently, although utopia can be something that spurs on the powerful to seek more power, utopia actually has the most direct impact for oppressed audiences that confront the direst of situations. When people feel they have nowhere to go but up, utopia inspires in them the hope that they can finally lift themselves up out of their conditions. Similarly, as Aristotle pointed out, utopia tends to be more effective with younger audiences who have not had the life experience that typically provides the skepticism (healthy or unhealthy) that comes with age. In cases where audiences believe that the best times are past, utopia usually operates nostalgically as a consolation and a reason not to put forth a lot of effort in changing things in the present.

Mary Elizabeth Lease: "We shall have the golden age of which Isaiah sang."

In the late nineteenth century, small farmers were losing their land to large corporate interests as the high costs of mechanization brought them deeper into debt. The Populist movement responded to this problem by trying to organize small farmers into a collective political force. One of its leaders was Mary Elizabeth Lease, who offered her audience a utopian vision of the future in a speech given at the Women's Christian Temperance Union in 1890. Based on a Christian belief that "the teachings and precepts of Jesus of Nazareth" will help "enact justice and equity between man and man," Lease combined a utopian vision of the past ("We seek to bring the nation back to the constitutional liberties guaranteed us by our forefathers") with a utopian prediction of the future that will emerge as soon as dedicated Americans bind together and seek justice through political action. When that day arrived, a sequence of events would unfold that would bring forth an era of peace and beauty. She prophesizes:

> Crowns will fall, thrones will tremble, kingdoms will disappear, the divine right of kings and the divine right of capital will fade away like the mists of the morning when the Angel of Liberty shall kindle the fires of justice in the hearts of men. "Exact justice to all, special privileges to none." No more millionaires, and no more paupers; no more gold kings, silver kings and oil kings, and no more little waifs of humanity starving for a crust of bread. No more gaunt-faced, hollow-eyed girls in the factories, and no more little boys reared in poverty and crime for the penitentiaries and the gallows. But we shall have the golden age of which Isaiah sang and the prophets have so long foretold; when the farmers shall be prosperous and happy, dwelling under their own vine and fig tree; when the laborer shall have that for which he toils; when occupancy and use shall be the only title to land, and every one shall obey the divine injunction, "In the sweat of thy face shalt thou eat bread."[7]

Part of what makes this utopia powerful is that in the midst of it appears a repulsive image of greedy kings and wasted children. Not only is her audience headed toward a "golden age," but they are leaving behind an age of toil. This description of the terrible state in which they currently live represents the strategy of wasteland, which exaggerates events in order to bring about a sense of anger or contempt for indignation or disgust. This shows that as strategies, wasteland and pathos almost always appear together to heighten the dramatic tension.

Discussion: Vacation resorts rely on the strategy of utopia to attract vacationers through a promise of a "heavenly" experience through the course of the week on a beach, at a ski resort, or whatnot. When have you gone on such a vacation and experienced something different than what was promised? What were specific elements in that experience that were far from utopian?

WASTELAND

The opposite of utopia is wasteland. Instead of playing on hope, it draws its power from disgust and fear produced by amplifying qualities in events that we find repulsive. Specifically, **wasteland** portrays a horrific event or state of affairs that we either wish to escape (if we are in it) or to avoid (if we are not). In other words, if utopia envisions Heaven, wasteland dramatizes Hell. Not surprisingly, especially for anyone who has seen Michelangelo's *The Last Judgment* or read Dante's *Inferno*, portrayals of wasteland are more graphic, more violent, more dramatic, and generally more exciting than portrayals of utopia. This is because whereas utopia

---

[7]Mary Elizabeth Lease, available from http://historymatters.gmu.edu/d/5303/ (accessed 6 Sept. 2012).

presents a perfect state of affairs that typically has resolved all tensions, wasteland presents a state of affairs that is full of conflict and uncertainty. Thus, despite the fact that we yearn for utopia, when we are in it, there just isn't much to talk about. But we talk unendingly about our problems, which are full of suspense and shock and climax and struggle.

There are three types of situations in which wasteland is usually employed. First, as Lease demonstrates, wasteland can be used to motivate to action by portraying one's current situation as so terrible as to be intolerable. To live in a wasteland is by necessity to seek utopia. Second, wasteland can be used to inhibit a path of action much as the slippery slope fallacy functions in logic. By picturing a horrible fate should one adopt the wrong path, wasteland warns against certain routes of action that will result in destruction. Consequently, this second form of argument is most effective in the opposite situations of the first. In these cases, wasteland most appeals to audiences who either are content with the current situation or are wary of making the wrong decisions because they have much to lose. Third, wasteland can be used to describe a past situation from which we have escaped, thereby making us content with our current lot by comparison. The first strategy motivates us to change, the second makes us fearful of change, and the third makes us content with the status quo.

Mark Twain: "We see the terrified faces."

Take an example from the great American novelist and essayist Mark Twain. Although popularly known as a humorist who created much beloved characters like Huckleberry Finn and Tom Sawyer, Twain was also a biting social critic and vigorous opponent of U.S. military expansion. In 1899, the United States invaded and occupied the Philippines, resulting in the deaths of many civilians in a guerilla war, including the deaths of almost a thousand native Moros who had fortified themselves within an extinct crater. In his essay "Comments on the Moro Massacre," written on March 12, 1906, Twain uses graphic images to evoke a feeling of repulsion in his American audience that makes them confront the wasteland being produced in a far-off land:

> This incident burst upon the world last Friday in an official cablegram from the commander of our forces in the Philippines to our Government at Washington. The substance of it was as follows: A tribe of Moros, dark-skinned savages, had fortified themselves in the bowl of an extinct crater not many miles from Jolo; and as they were hostiles, and bitter against us because we have been trying for eight years to take their liberties away from them, their presence in that position was a menace. Our commander, Gen. Leonard Wood, ordered a reconnaissance. It was found that the Moros numbered six hundred, counting women and children; that their crater bowl was in the summit of a peak or mountain twenty-two hundred feet above sea level, and very difficult of access for Christian troops and artillery. Then General Wood ordered a surprise, and went along himself to see the order carried out...Our soldiers numbered five hundred and forty. They were assisted by auxiliaries consisting of a detachment of native constabulary in our pay—their numbers not given—and by a

naval detachment, whose numbers are not stated. But apparently the contending parties were about equal as to number—six hundred men on our side, on the edge of the bowl; six hundred men, women and children in the bottom of the bowl. Depth of the bowl, 50 feet.

Gen. Wood's order was, "Kill or capture the six hundred...."

They were mere naked savages, and yet there is a sort of *pathos* about it when that word children falls under your eye, for it always brings before us our perfectest symbol of innocence and helplessness; and by help of its deathless eloquence color, creed and nationality vanish away and we see only that they are children—merely children. And if they are frightened and crying and in trouble, our pity goes out to them by natural impulse. We see a picture. We see the small forms. We see the terrified faces. We see the tears. We see the small hands clinging in supplication to the mother; but we do not see those children that we are speaking about. We see in their places the little creatures whom we know and love.[8]

Twain's purpose in this paragraph is to point out how much more visceral are our images of death once the word "children" is used. Compare, for instance, how different Twain's account would sound if we simply traded the word "children" for "Nazis" or "terrorists." Or retain the word "children" but remove the graphic details of tears, terrified faces, small hands, and supplicant mothers. All of these details are crucial in bringing about the sense of horror, disgust, pity, and shame that Twain endeavors to bring about.

Discussion: One of the most famous political advertisements was produced by Lyndon Johnson against Barry Goldwater and portrayed a young girl picking petals off of a flower while an ominous voice counted down in the background, leading to a nuclear explosion. The purpose of the ad was to show how Goldwater's election would inevitably lead to a nuclear war. Can you think of other negative advertisements you have seen that have relied as heavily on wasteland?

VIRTUE

Whereas events are things that happen outside of our control, actions are things that we do with conscious intent. If one volunteers to throw a party, that decision and its subsequent performance is an action. But the party itself, with all its unpredictable happenings and complex interactions, is an event. Actions are thus more specific and have a much more limited scope than events. But this limitation is also an advantage. It is only because we can focus our attention on particular types of actions that we can also improve them through care and skill and practice. The strategy of **virtue** is thus employed to help us identify the nature of specific types of actions that we find worthy of praise and to generate passionate commitment to cultivating these virtues. Usually, speakers draw from numerous instances of these actions, performed by a variety of usually ordinary individuals, each of whom shows how a specific type of behavior brings about some good consequence both in

---

[8]Mark Twain, "Comments on the Morrow Massacre," available from http://www.is.wayne.edu/mnissani/cr/moro.htm (accessed 7 Sept. 2012).

practical life and in the development of character. For instance, the biblical parable of the Good Samaritan praises the virtues of courage and charity by embodying these praiseworthy actions in such a way that is both memorable and powerful.

Usually we encounter this rhetorical strategy in educational environments, first in childhood and then in various religious environments. However, virtue also has rhetorical significance when a particular type of virtue needs to be called upon in a specific exigence in order to produce the necessary change to solve an urgent problem. In this case, the virtue might be present in an audience, but only in latent form. The rhetor thus needs to call upon these "reserves" of virtue by showing how the only way to overcome an obstacle is by harnessing the power of a specific type of virtue whose performance can meet short-term challenges and/or accomplish long-term goals. For instance, if a previously oppressed population is suddenly called upon to stage a mass protest against a violent regime, they will most certainly need to have the courage to withstand the inevitable crackdown that will follow. However, if their revolution is successful, the short-term necessity for courage will need to be tempered by a more long-term commitment to patience and humility if the revolution is not to simply continue the cycle of violence. It is therefore a sign of practical wisdom to know which virtue is the most important to call upon in any particular problematic situation.

Louis Pasteur: "Worship the spirit of criticism."

The long-distance vision of virtue is evidenced in this speech by Louis Pasteur, a nineteenth-century French chemist largely responsible for our knowledge of "germs." Before Pasteur, nobody knew how contagious diseases were transmitted. Doctors often operated without sterile instruments, and many times successful operations would result in death by infection. Pasteur, however, discovered that contagious diseases are transmitted by germs, thus giving birth to the science of microbiology. To honor his success, France opened the Pasteur Institute in Paris in 1888, and he was invited on November 14 to give an address. In his speech, he praises not his own personal accomplishments but the virtue that he felt contributed to his discoveries. One of those virtues was the spirit of criticism, or the ability to look critically at one's own ideas for the sake of making them better:

> Worship the spirit of criticism. If reduced to itself, it is not an awakener of ideas or a stimulant to great things, but, without it, everything is fallible; it always has the last word. What I am now asking you, and you will ask of your pupils later on, is what is most difficult to an inventor. It is indeed a hard task, when you believe you have found an important scientific fact and are feverishly anxious to publish it, to constrain yourself for days, weeks, years sometimes, to fight with yourself, to try and ruin your own experiments and only to proclaim your discovery after having exhausted all contrary hypotheses. But when, after so many efforts, you have at last arrived at a certainty, your joy is one of the greatest, which can be felt by a human soul, and the thought that you will have contributed to the honor of your country renders that joy still deeper.[9]

---

[9]Louis Pasteur, available from http://www.archive.org/stream/lifepasteur00unkngoog/
lifepasteur00unkngoog_djvu.txt (accessed 3 Sept. 2012).

Pasteur picks out the virtue of criticism for special praise, but the way he praises this virtue signals something about the overall rhetorical strategy of virtue itself. As Pasteur points out, upholding a virtue in only one or two instances may not produce any lasting benefit. It is only a long and consistent commitment to a virtue that results in a better future—perhaps even a utopia.

Discussion: We commemorate different virtues in different practical contexts. Think of the various types of practical contexts in which we live—family, work, education, and leisure (among others). What do you think is the dominant virtue that we apply in each context?

VICE

The opposite of virtue is **vice**, a strategy that repels us from certain concrete actions by making them morally offensive and/or practically harmful. Even young children are familiar with the long list of vices that they are taught to shun by reading Aesop's Fables. From "The Boy Who Cried Wolf" (lying), to "Little Red Riding Hood" (disobedience), to "The Fox and the Crow" (vanity), each of these stories is meant to attach a stigma to certain types of actions in the hope that children will avoid the temptations that often culminate in self-destructive and socially condemned behaviors. Without such a consensus about vices (alongside necessary virtues), no society could hold together for very long. And like virtue, vice is also a strategy used to guide behavior in specific rhetorical situations. In these contexts, vice usually has two functions. First, it complements virtue by telling the audience what kind of actions they should avoid if they wish to meet the challenges of the hour. Usually this list includes such devices as selfishness, vengeance, pride, impulsiveness, and the like. Second, it creates motivation through polarization by condemning the vices of an opposing group; these vices almost always including some combination of arrogance, greed, corruption, and ignorance. Combined, these two strategies justify an audience's opposition to another group while instructing them on what actions to avoid if they are not to fall into the same vices as their opponents.

Not surprisingly, vice can be easily abused as a rhetorical strategy by all sides. As indicated in the discussion on polarization, nothing comes more naturally to social groups than the feeling of their own superiority and the inferiority of others. Just as those in power often see dissenters as ungrateful and disruptive agitators, those resisting power see themselves as noble martyrs standing up to the forces of evil. Consequently, it is extremely common to find two opposing parties accusing each other of the exact same vices. As with all rhetorical appeals, however, the ethics of the strategies is determined by the strength of their evidence and warrants. Pathos appeals, including even accusations of the most horrific vices, are ethical if they are backed by stories grounded in narrative fidelity, meaning that they come from legitimate sources and can be verified by third parties. Unfortunately, many of the most successful propaganda campaigns were based on stories of vice that were completely fabricated. In World War I, the British made great gains in public opinion through false stories of German soldiers who stabbed babies with bayonets and crucified Canadian soldiers on crosses. The sad irony is that the cynicism produced in the public by the realization that they had been manipulated made actual stories of even worse atrocities by the Nazis three decades later impossible to believe. There is, then, something to be said for the fable of the boy who cried wolf. The more we abuse the strategy of vice for short-term gain, the less effective it is when we must confront genuine "evils" in actual life.

William Smith: "They may gradually deceive themselves."

One of the most momentous deliberations that occurred in the history of the United States concerned whether or not to split from England. Far from being a spontaneous revolution, the war only came about after years of debate about the wisdom of such an act. On the side of the Loyalists, who sought to retain connection with Britain, was William Smith, who wrote a series of newspaper letters "To the People of Pennsylvania" using the name "Cato," referring to a figure from Roman history who had defended the Republic against Julius Caesar. The fact that these were letters, and not speeches, shows that deliberative rhetoric often expands well beyond the bounds of the oral context and into the literate public sphere, in which a reader can often dwell upon more detailed reasoning. In the third of these letters published on March 23, 1776, in *The Pennsylvania Ledger*, Smith defends the following position that hasty, one-sided decision making is a vice that leads to ruin:

> I have, in my second letter, freely declared by political creed, viz.—"That the true interest of America lies in reconciliation with Great Britain, upon Constitutional Principles, and that I wish it upon none else." I now proceed to give my reasons for this declaration. It is fit, in so great a question, that you should weigh both sides well, and exercise the good sense for which the inhabitants of these Colonies have been hitherto distinguished, and then I shall be under no apprehensions concerning the pernicious, though specious plans, which are every day published in our newspapers and pamphlets. The people generally judge right, when the whole truth is plainly laid before them; but through inattention in some, and fondness for novelty in others, when but one side of a proposition is agitated and persevered in, they may gradually deceive themselves, and adopt what cooler reflection and future dear-bought experience may prove to be ruinous.[10]

Smith goes on to give several reasons for maintaining political allegiance to Great Britain, including past loyalty, military protection, economic gain, and all the devastation that would be avoiding by choosing peace. However, what is important here is less the reasons he gives for defending his position than his justification for engaging in deliberation at all. Smith prefaces his remarks by arguing for the necessity of deliberation (as a virtue) in order to avoid ruinous folly by hasty action (as a vice) and to guarantee prudent decisions by having aired all points of view. This spirit of inquiry remains at the heart of deliberative rhetoric.

---

[10]Ronald Reid and James Klumpp, *American Rhetorical Discourse* (Long Grove, IL: Waveland Press, 2005), 131.

Discussion: When is something a virtue in one context and a vice in another? Name two situations in which this is the case. Do you think that it is possible to maintain the same virtues in all parts of life, or do we alter our virtues and vices depending on the situation?

SAINT

There is a subtle but important difference between praising a person and praising a person's action. When praise a type of action (a virtue), the *specific* person performing the action does not make that much difference. It only matters that the character has certain general qualities that make him or her a certain *type* of person. For instance, in the story of the tortoise and the hare, we only need to know that the tortoise is a slow creature and the hare is a fast one so that, when they race, we are able to learn that the slow and steady runner will always beat the fast and fickle one. Consequently, one of the indicators of the strategy of virtue is that the characters are easily replaceable by other characters with similar qualities. For instance, one might tell the story of the farmer and the Wall Street banker and learn the same lesson as from the tortoise and the hare, when after a few years the farmer develops a successful organic fruit company while the Wall Street banker makes and then loses $10 million in an insider trading scheme. In virtue, the person doing the action is merely a placeholder for the activity, and is effectively replaceable by other people with similar qualities.

To praise a person means to praise a specific individual (or a specific group of people acting as if they were an individual) with a unique combination of characteristics that makes him or her stand out as someone who cannot be replaced. The strategy of **saint** therefore holds up a particular person as worthy of our special attention, praise, and emulation both for its own sake as well as for our self-advancement. What makes the strategy of saint similar to that of virtue is that the reason we wish to honor this person is precisely because of his or her unique virtues. If we give a eulogy to one of our parents, we will highlight his or her acts of love and generosity and sacrifice and humor and courage that made that parent special. However, the point is not to praise any particular virtue or set of virtues; it is to highlight the manner in which a person embodied these virtues that was greater than the sum of its parts. In other words, there is something "ineffable" about our saints that makes them impossible to ever completely define. We cannot, for example, go to great length praising the Good Samaritan precisely because the only thing we know about the Good Samaritan is that he was a Samaritan who stopped to help an injured person by the road. The only thing we can do is praise the action. A person, therefore, is more than the sum of a couple of virtues. A person embodies an infinite number of unique details and a host of contradictions that make him or her irreplaceable in the world.

Rhetorically, saint is used for one of two purposes. First, saint is used to legitimate authority by creating heroic images of leaders who stand above and apart from the everyday citizenry. This function has existed since the most ancient human civilizations and has also provided the impetus to create some of the most enduring monuments, such as the Egyptian pyramids. Although democratic political movements have significantly undermined the legitimacy of such grandiose strategies, one still finds exaggerated efforts at turning leaders into saints any time one encounters a relatively closed society or institution. Second, and more commonly, saint is used as a strategy to create identification by praising a particular individual with whom an audience feels a connection as well as a possibility to emulate. This strategy is common to both families and to nations. Eulogies for beloved matriarchs or patriarchs of a large family perform the same function as eulogies to heroic or noble citizens who stood for the best that a country had to offer. Those who listen to such commemorative speeches are not made to feel that sense of divine awe, often combined with fear, that is produced by praising a superhuman leader; rather, they feel a unique kinship that comes with familiarity and affection, feelings that produce in an audience a desire to emulate this person and to be as much like them as they can.

William Graham Sumner: "Now who is the Forgotten Man?"

Sometimes saint doesn't even have to be a real person to work. We can "imagine" a saint or construct a hypothetical image of a type of person we want people to be. This was the strategy of William Graham Sumner, an academic who believed in *laissez-faire* economic policies that celebrated entrepreneurship and hard work. Sumner lived in the late nineteenth century, when the rise of industrialism sparked calls for governments to actively address issues of economic inequality through policies that regulated business practices and subsidized programs for the poor. For Sumner, however, these calls were little more than an effort by people to get something for nothing. In his 1883 lecture "The Forgotten Man," he makes the ethical argument that social welfare policies punish and take advantage of hard-working laborers who must then give their hard-earned money to others. For Sumner, the tragedy was that nobody ever heard a word of complaint from these hard workers, precisely because they were too virtuous and independent to be interested in exciting public sentiments. Portraying the honest laborer as a saint, Sumner contrasts him with those who seek government hand-outs:

> Now who is the Forgotten Man? He is the simple, honest laborer, ready to earn his living by productive work. We pass him by because he is independent, self-supporting, and asks no favors. He does not appeal to the emotions or excite the sentiments. He only wants to make a contract and fulfill it, with respect on both sides and favor on neither side. He must get his living out of the capital of the country. The larger the capital is, the better living he can get. Every particle of capital which is wasted on the vicious, the idle, and the shiftless is so much take from the capital available to reward the independent and productive laborer. But we stand with our backs to the independent and productive laborer all the time. We do not remember him because he makes no clamor; but I appeal to you whether he is not the man who ought to be remembered first of all, and whether, on any sound social theory, we ought not to protect him against the burdens of the good-for-nothing.[11]

---

[11]William Graham Sumner, "The Forgotten Man," http://www.swarthmore.edu/SocSci/rbannis1/AIH19th/Sumner.Forgotten.html (accessed 12 Nov. 2012).

In Sumner's account, the Forgotten Man is simple, honest, productive, independent, self-supporting, fair, quiet, and polite. This saintliness is contrasted with the character of those who are vicious, idle, and shiftless. Employing the either/or logic of polarization, Sumner splits workers into one of two categories in the hope of rewarding one and punishing the other. This "other" represents the sinner, discussed next.

Discussion: One of the most practical modern applications of saint is to make such individuals spokespersons for products. Who are some of the most successful "saints" in this regard? What practical effect does this kind of sponsorship have? And what happens to such saints when they fall from grace?

SINNER

The counterpart of saint is sinner. In **sinner**, another person (or group that we feel justified in treating as if it were an individual) is portrayed in a negative light in order to make that person repellent to an audience. The strategy of sinner is a component of all polarization strategies that seek to divide the sheep from the goats by portraying the character of a particularly bad goat. As with saint, the key to this strategy is to make the "sinner" as unique a character as possible in such a way that makes him or her stand out as particularly reprehensible (even amongst sinners!). If the person is not described in detail, the strategy ends up becoming one of vice and becomes focused on a type of action rather than person (or type of person). There is a big difference between condemning the vice of violent persecution and condemning Hitler. A vice is something that anybody can do; but Hitler is a person that only Hitler can be. It is this level of detail that makes sinner an interesting rhetorical strategy. That is why stories about Satan, particularly in Hollywood movies, are far more interesting to us than hearing warnings about vices. Although we know what a vice is and produces, one never quite knows what Satan is going to do.

The rhetorical function of sinner is the opposite of saint. First, sinner undermines the legitimacy of authority by portraying the so-called "saints" in power as corrupt, cruel, and stupid. In relatively closed and oppressive societies, these rhetorical expressions often take the form of underground literature or anonymous graffiti, whereas in relatively open and democratic societies, they take the form of ubiquitous negative advertising and political harangue. In both cases, however, the strategy is simply to de-legitimate current leadership. However, sinner is also used by the powerful to demonize the opposition, often through show trials and prosecutions that ideally force "confessions" by would-be sinners. Second, sinner is used for identification through polarization, creating specific images of the "not-us" so that groups know who they are fighting against and who they do not wish to become. In these cases, a particularly "bad apple" is held up as an example of the whole group and is often then, literally or proverbially, "hanged in effigy." As with all strategies using repelling emotions, the ethics of when to use sinner is very complicated. There are certainly times when a leader or representative of a group can be legitimately held up for condemnation and ridicule, but these times are usually rare. Most of the time, people are more mistaken than cruel, and attempts at understanding are usually more fruitful than melodramatic attempts to divide human beings into good and evil.

Emma Goldman: "They turned our office into a battlefield."

If we look to the athletic field for our saints, our sinners are more often than not found in the courtroom. It is in the courtroom that we put on display for public view those individuals whom we wish to condemn in order that we might know who we are "not" supposed to be. The problem is that it is never quite clear just who is the "real" sinner. The prosecution seeks to characterize the defendant as a person of deficient character who is a threat to society, whereas the defense attempts to turn the tables and show the prosecution, and those backing the prosecution, to be corrupt, malicious, and ignorant of the truth. During the buildup to the U.S. entry into World War I, for instance, the government wished to portray anyone who attempted to obstruct the draft or to in any way undermine the war effort as sinners, as people worthy of condemnation and conviction. Pacifists and anarchists like Emma Goldman and Alexander Berkman, who founded the No-Conscription League and distributed 100,000 copies of a manifesto declaring conscription to be a violation of liberty, were thus predictably arrested under the Espionage Act and put on trial. However, even more predictably, Goldman used her address to the jury on July 9, 1917, in a New York City court as a forum to condemn the government actions instead. But rather than simply offer general criticisms, she creatively focused on the specific character of the U.S. Marshal who arrested her in order to give a concrete "face" to the government using a burlesque form of humorous narrative:

> On the day after our arrest it was given out by the U.S. Marshal and the District Attorney's office that the "big fish" of the No-Conscription activities had been caught, and that there would be no more trouble-makers and disturbers to interfere with the highly democratic effort of the Government to conscript its young manhood for the European slaughter. What a pity that the faithful servants of the Government, personified in the U. S. Marshal and the District Attorney, should have used such a weak and flimsy net for their big catch. The moment the anglers pulled their heavily laden net ashore, it broke, and all the labor was so much wasted energy.
>
> The methods employed by Marshal McCarthy and his hosts of heroic warriors were sensational enough to satisfy the famous circus men, Barnum & Bailey. A dozen or more heroes dashing up two flights of stairs, prepared to stake their lives for their country, only to discover the two dangerous disturbers and trouble-makers Alexander Berkman and Emma Goldman, in their separate offices, quietly at work at their desks, wielding not a sword, nor a gun or a bomb, but merely their pens! Verily, it required courage to catch such big fish…They turned our office into a battlefield, so that when they were through with it, it looked like invaded Belgium, with the only difference that the invaders were not Prussian barbarians but good American patriots bent on making New York safe for democracy.[12]

Her words heavy with sarcasm, Goldman holds up Marshal McCarthy as the paradigmatic "sinner" who follows the orders of the U.S. government. McCarthy is

---

[12]Emma Goldman, "Address to the Jury," http://americanrhetoric.com/speeches/emmagoldmanjury address.htm (accessed 12 Nov. 2012).

not necessarily an evil man; he is simply a kind of stooge. He sees himself to be a warrior for a great cause fighting great enemies, when in fact he is simply deluded by heroic fantasies and bullying his way into the virtuous private lives of "good American patriots" (saints) like Goldman and Berkman. Her rhetorical purpose, therefore, is to amplify the negative emotions we feel about people like McCarthy so that we are both discouraged from being like them and from obeying them.[13]

Discussion: It is a universal fact of political life that one group's sinner is another group's saint. Usually we refer to these people as "polarizing figures" that we either love or hate. Who are some of the major polarizing figures in today's political world? How are they considered saints or sinners by their respective supporters and critics?

IDOL

When we refer to objects, we refer to any identifiable and tangible part of our environment that is stable and familiar enough to label with a noun. Objects, therefore, do not simply mean discrete *physical things* such as trees and tables and pencils; they also include *organizations* such as schools and parliaments, and *processes* such as recycling and judicial review. Anything that we can define as a class of thing, with certain predictable characteristics associated with a common name, is an object. To make an idol out of an object is therefore to invest a common class of things with extraordinary qualities and powers that make those things worthy of reverence and worship. For instance, when we think of idols, we think of golden statues that possess magical forces that can be harnessed and used by the ones who possess them. The rhetorical strategy that goes by the same idol effectively is that which makes us feel this worshipful attitude toward objects. **Idol** is the attempt to invest an object with such attractive qualities that an audience seeks to possess, preserve, and/or use that object. For example, ads that lead us to believe that a car will make us sexy, computers will make us powerful, energy drinks will make us athletic, and cell phones will make us worldly all make use of idol. But idol is also used to justify "family values" policies by idolizing the two-parent middle-class home, to respond to an economic downturn by idolizing progressive tax increases on corporations, or to defend military aggression against a dictatorial state by idolizing parliamentary government. Any time a type of "thing" is help up as a solution to a problem because of its unique properties, one finds the strategy of idol.

There are three rhetorical situations in which idol is effective. First, idol is vital to any preservationist argument that wishes to protect something from being undermined or destroyed by changes in society. Here, idol invests an object with enough *intrinsic* value that people will seek to protect it, thereby making it a crucial strategy to defend the existence of things that may not have immediate utilitarian value, including buildings, works of art, nature preserves, social organizations, and many cultural traditions. Second, idol imagines a type of perfect object that might

---

[13]For more on Goldman, see Martha Solomon, "Ideology as Rhetorical Constraint: The Anarchist Agitation of 'Red Emma' Goldman," *Quarterly Journal of Speech* 74, no. 2, 1988, 184–200.

be created by ingenuity and effort, much as one might imagine a space station on Mars or perfectly functioning democratic Congress. In this case, idol motivates us to action by setting forth the possibility that we might create something new in the world. Third, idol can be effectively used in rhetorical situations that require a choice from among objects that can be used as practical tools to achieve success. For example, debates over modern military strategy often come down to rhetorical battles over competing idols. Should we rely on *smart bombs, air power,* or *boots on the ground*? In politics, the Constitution often functions as an idol, as do institutions, political parties, and even bureaucratic procedures. Any time a *thing* (including laws and processes) is held up as a solution to some specific practical problem due to its instrumental value, one is employing idol to make a case.

John Muir: "The smallest forest reserve was in the Garden of Eden."

When we arouse emotions about idols, we do so to treasure and protect some part of our environment that we hold dear. If that environment is our childhood home, we will point out specific parts of that home that we hold dear and wish to leave unchanged because they are places that hold valuable memories that we do not wish to see disappear. It is natural, then, that arguments using the strategy of idol are pervasive in conservationist rhetoric that wishes to protect and preserve parts of pristine nature. For a lumber company, a tree is simply raw material to be converted into products. For an environmentalist, a tree is an idol not necessarily to "worship" but to respect, to admire, and to defend. This rhetoric was perfected by one of the most important founders of the environmental movement and first president of the Sierra Club, John Muir. Instrumental in the creation of the first national park in Yosemite, Muir was a tireless advocate of natural preservation, which he believed was a religious duty to preserve God's work. In this sense, the "idol" he made of nature actually did have religious significance, believing as he did that one could commune with the divine through the natural world. He makes this defence during a speech to a meeting of the Sierra Club held on November 23, 1895, in San Francisco:

> The Yosemite National Park was made October 1, 1890. For many years I had been crying in the wilderness, "Save the forests!" but, so far as I know, nothing effective was done in the matter until shortly before the park was organized.... Then a National Park was proposed, and I was requested to write some articles about the region to help call attention to it, while the *Century* was freely used for the same purpose, and every friend that could be found was called on to write or speak a good word for it....But no sooner were the boundaries of the park established, than interested parties began to try to break through them. Last winter a determined effort was made to have the area of the park cut down nearly one-half. But the Sierra Club and other good friends of the forests on both sides of the continent made a good defense, and to-day the original boundaries are still unbroken.
>
> The battle we have fought, and are still fighting, for the forests is a part of the eternal conflict between right and wrong, and we cannot expect to see the end of it. I trust, however that our Club will not weary in this forest welldoing. The fight for the Yosemite Park and other forest parks and reserves is by no means over; nor would the fighting cease, however much the boundaries

were contracted. Every good thing, great and small, needs defense. The smallest forest reserve, and the first I ever heard of, was in the Garden of Eden; and though its boundaries were drawn by the Lord, and embraced only one tree, yet even so moderate a reserve as this was attacked. And I doubt not, if only one of our grand trees in the Sierra were reserved as an example and type of all that is most noble and glorious in mountain trees, it would not be long before you would find a lumberman and a lawyer at the foot of it, eagerly proving by every law terrestrial and celestial that that tree must come down. So we must count on watching and striving for these trees, and should always be glad to find anything so surely good and noble to strive for.[14]

In this speech, Muir makes an idol of the forests by investing these objects with transcendent qualities, not just of beauty and purity but also of rightness and divinity. To destroy the idol is thus to offend God and to condemn oneself as a brute. Important also is the allusion to wasteland at the beginning of the quotation, in which he warns that the preserve is already being threatened, leading to its exploitation and destruction. After all, the definition of a wasteland is one in which all of our idols have been destroyed by sinners.[15]

Discussion: Take the case of college athletics. What are some common idols that are often praised as essential tools of victory by coaches and commentators? Name a physical thing, a procedure, and a concept that are considered idols in this regard.

ABOMINATION

The opposite of idol is **abomination**, which is the attempt to make an object seem so repellent that an audience ignores, shuns, discards, or destroys it. If the idol is what gives one special power by possessing it, an abomination is something that gives one a demonic power or actively drains power away from a person. A perfect example of an abomination in literature is the "One Ring" from JRR Tolkein's *Lord of the Rings* trilogy, a ring that promises its wearer great power while at the same time isolating and weakening its wearer until he or she becomes a mere wraith. Abominations are those special class of objects that often appear to us as benign or beneficial but in fact damage ourselves or our environment in their use. For example, cultural critics often define objects such as pop music, television, video games, pornography, and fast food as abominations that suck the life out of the young generation. Likewise, critics of political culture use abomination to categorize laws, governing bodies, corporations, political parties, or even symbols as things that impede human progress. An abomination, therefore, is not simply something that we don't like and that has distasteful qualities; it is a thing that is an active threat to our well-being and is seductive enough to warrant special condemnation.

Abomination performs the exact opposite rhetorical functions as idol. First, instead of attempting to preserve objects, it seeks to point out the things in our

---

[14]John Muir, "The National Parks and Forest Reservations," http://www.sierraclub.org/john_muir_exhibit/writings/nat_parks_forests_1896.aspx (accessed 12 Nov. 2012)..

[15]For more on Muir, see Christine Oravec, "John Muir, Yosemite, and the Sublime Response: A Study in the Rhetoric of Preservationism," *Quarterly Journal of Speech*, 67, no. 3, 1981, 245–58.

environment that need to be eradicated or at the very least controlled and regulated. It is an old story that the idols of the young generation are the abominations of the older generation, a story that is not soon to end. Second, abomination warns against pursuing certain goals because of what might be produced as a result. For instance, pursuit of cloning is not necessarily done by sinners or engaged in as a vice, as this research is done by scientists undertaking technical research in the hopes of scientific progress; but that particular line of research might end up with various "abominations," such as a father's daughter who grows up to look like his deceased wife. Third, abomination tells us to avoid using certain tools because of their disastrous effects, much as demonic idols, once used, take over the user and bring about devastation in the form of a wasteland.

Mark Twain: "We have some legislatures that bring higher prices than any in the world."

Whereas we wish to preserve idols, we wish to destroy abominations. Rhetorically, we accomplish this task indirectly by creating disgust for certain objects or institutions that we find reprehensible. One of the most political functions of humor is to evoke emotions of justice by holding certain things up to ridicule in a way that calls forth both anger and laughter. Of American writers, Mark Twain was known for his biting wit that, combined with keen analytical insight, created some devastating satires of American society. His planned remarks during a Fourth of July celebration in 1899 in London, England, demonstrate his ability to scan the landscape of the United States to identify and ridicule its various abominations before a foreign audience:

> This is an age of progress, and ours is a progressive land. A great and glorious land, too—a land which has developed a Washington, a Franklin, a William M. Tweed, a Longfellow, a Motley, a Jay Gould, a Samuel C. Pomeroy, a recent Congress which has never had its equal (in some respects), and a United States Army which conquered sixty Indians in eight months by tiring them out—which is much better than uncivilized slaughter, God knows. We have a criminal jury system which is superior to any in the world; and its efficiency is only marred by the difficulty of finding twelve men every day who don't know anything and can't read. And I may observe that we have an insanity plea that would have saved Cain. I think I can say, and say with pride, that we have some legislatures that bring higher prices than any in the world.
>
> I refer with effusion to our railway system, which consents to let us live, though it might do the opposite, being our owners. It only destroyed three thousand and seventy lives last year by collisions, and twenty-seven thousand two hundred and sixty by running over heedless and unnecessary people at crossings. The companies seriously regretted the killing of these thirty thousand people, and went so far as to pay for some of them—voluntarily, of course, for the meanest of us would not claim that we possess a court treacherous enough to enforce a law against a railway company. But, thank Heaven, the railway companies are generally disposed to do the right and kindly thing without compulsion. I know of an instance which greatly touched me at the time. After an accident the company sent home the remains of a dear distant old relative

of mine in a basket, with the remark, "Please state what figure you hold him at—and return the basket." Now there couldn't be anything friendlier than that. But I must not stand here and brag all night. However, you won't mind a body bragging a little about his country on the Fourth of July. It is a fair and legitimate time to fly the eagle.[16]

The abominations Twain lists are many—the base tactics of the U.S. Army, the incompetent jury system, the corrupt legislature, and the tyrannical railway system. What makes this list a strategy of pathos, however, is that it is not simply a list; it is a collection of stories and narratives in which we see how these abominations function and affect people's lives. The U.S. Army is starving Native Americans into submission, the jury system is exonerating Cain and his descendants, the legislature is taking bribes at the expense of good policy, and the railway system is recklessly killing innocent people and demanding our compensation. Each of these stories creates images in our imaginations that repulse us emotionally rather than simply prove a logical assertion. It is this active emotional movement that constitutes pathos.

Discussion: One of the most influential technologies in the past decade has been the rise of the cell phone and other handheld communication technologies. In terms of its overall use in society, for whom does this technology represent an idol or an abomination?

---

[16]Mark Twain, "Address on the 4th of July," http://americanrhetoric.com/speeches/mark twain4thofjulyspeech.htm (accessed 12 Nov. 2012)..

KEY WORDS

SUMMARY

Pathos represents a form of proof that legitimates our attitudes toward objects, events, people, and actions in our environment based on how we feel about them. Although often criticized for being "irrational" forms of persuasion, pathos arguments are both unavoidable and necessary. In the first case, they are unavoidable because our language is always loaded with emotional connotations and judgments that influence the way we describe our environment. It makes a world of difference, for instance, whether or not we introduce someone as a "friend" or a "boyfriend/ girlfriend." Both of these terms might be technically accurate, but our selection of one over the other carries with it significant emotional significance about how we feel about this person. Moreover, to think one can escape from pathos simply by speaking in purely technical jargon is not to leave pathos behind, but to show oneself as "apathetic," or without emotional concern— itself an emotional proof. In the second case, pathos arguments are necessary because we cannot form elaborate rational judgments based on statistically good evidence about every single thing in our environment. Most of our behavior toward the people, objects, events, and actions that we encounter in our world is guided by largely emotional judgments of liking and disliking rather than true and false. Without the complex of emotional judgments about our world, we would have no background framework to make the careful logical judgments that are required in specific affairs.

We generate proofs of pathos largely by constructing narratives that show the object of interest interacting in a situation that produces an emotional response. To say that "I met an evil man yesterday" does not produce pathos simply because one labels a person with the epithet "evil." One has to show how this man interacts with his world in order for us to form an emotional judgment about him. There is a big emotional difference, for instance, between a description of a man who is poisoning a stream because he carelessly discharges wastewater from his chemical factory and a man who poisons a stream because he wishes to kill all the people in a village. We may have warrant to label both men as being "evil," but the emotions are different based on the different narratives. We may feel that the first man is evil because he is greedy and indifferent to the pain of others, whereas the second person is evil because he is cruel and inhuman. Either way, the dramatization of the *way* in which we think he is evil is what produces the emotion, not the label itself. In fact, it is often better in pathos arguments to leave the "labeling" of the emotion or characteristic to the audience. This allows them to participate in the construction of the argument without simply following the words of the speaker.

Each pair of pathos arguments generates attracting or repelling emotions to a certain type of thing. *Utopia* and *wasteland* produce emotional responses about of discrete events or more enduring situations. In other words, we celebrate or condemn certain specific events in our lives, such as the moment we caught the touchdown pass or the day we heard about the death of a loved one, much in the same way that we celebrate or condemn whole eras in history, such as the Golden Age of Rome or the horrors of World War I. Each of these examples represents a certain state of affairs that we either wish to reproduce or hope never happens again, and has as its rhetorical function to validate or condemn certain courses of action that will produce these states of affairs. *Virtue* and *vice* share with utopia and wasteland a focus on activity, but these arguments emphasize the worthy or unworthiness of the action being performed by people rather than by the quality of the events produced by those actions. In virtue and vice, we either admire certain habits of action for their own intrinsic value or condemn habits of action for their complete lack of it, often regardless of the consequences. For instance, it is a virtue to courageously stand one's ground and it is a vice to always cowardly flee resistance, even if the first might kill you and the second save your life in specific situations. But we usually believe that virtue brings about long-term goods nonetheless, and that those goods include not just practical survival but the goods of feelings of self-worth and the development of character. Rhetorically, then, the power of virtue and vice is to help cultivate the types of practices that we find valuable in society and that we believe are necessary for the development of culture and civilization.

The third pair of pathos arguments differs from the first two because it focuses on our feelings about specific, tangible things rather than types of events or activities. With *saint* and *sinner*, we are encouraged to respect or condemn specific people or more general types of people who can be considered collectively as an individual. For instance, politicians during the Red Scare might praise Joseph McCarthy as a saint while condemning the generic "Communist" as a sinner, therefore justifying their allegiance to McCarthy as he attempts to identify the various "sinners" in the State Department. Rhetorically, the point of this strategy is to populate our environment with friends and enemies, to tell us whom to trust and whom to avoid, and generally to say whom we should emulate and whom we should condemn. Last, *idol* and *abomination* arguments perform the same function for the various "things" in our world, including not only physical things such as books and televisions but also procedural things such as laws and constitutions, and conceptual things such as evolutionary theory or Christianity. Anything we think we can describe as a discrete or general thing with stable qualities that we can define is an object. Rhetorically, idol and abomination therefore tell us what kinds of things we should think about and surround ourselves with in order to produce a good life and a good character.

Overall, then, the function of pathos is to make us feel like we are in a specific situation with specific types of people doing specific types of actions with specific kinds of objects. The more we can graphically dramatize the situation in which we are in, the more we feel an emotional connection to that situation and the more we are motivated to act or think in a specific way. Without emotions, we might be able to logically construct reasons for why things happen or what we should do, but these reasons are not intimately connected to us personally in a way that makes us care about them. These explanations would simply exist for us like any number of graphs or charts or line drawings or pictures. Pathos is what brings a situation to life and makes us passionate about it; the absence of pathos, then, is not "reason" but barrenness.

CHAPTER 6 EXERCISES

1. Analyzing your rhetorical artifact, selected in chapter 1, what forms of pathos are employed? Select specific language choices that were made to generate emotional feeling, and then describe the action that you believe is encouraged as a result.

2. As a class, choose a contemporary controversy familiar to everyone. Then select one *attractive* method of pathos and one *repelling* method that is not the pair of the first. Deliver an impromptu speech employing both methods.

3. Using the same controversy, choose one method of pathos and use it in conjunction with one form of logical reasoning. How does the argument change from the previous exercise?

4. Find a print ad that uses a striking visual image to convey pathos. Interpret this image using the concepts of this chapter.

5. Using one form of pathos, locate a historical person, event, object, or action that fits the category. Give an impromptu commemorative speech describing why the category applies.

Eloquence

This chapter defines the ultimate goal of a speech as the accomplishment of eloquence. It describes eloquence not as a quality so much of the speech but as the experience produced by the speech, an experience defined in terms of the ability to address the particular demands of a situation while also pointing to more universal values, goals, and truth that inspire people to greater thoughts and feelings. It then proposes two methods for producing eloquence. The first method is to structure the speech around an organizing symbol that provides a coherent and recognizable narrative form. Often making use of analogical reasoning, an organizing symbol draws parallels between a specific exigence and a more familiar character or situation in order to clarify its meaning and establish purpose. The second method is to use one of the major poetic categories of the heroic, the tragic, or the comic in order to try to give an overarching dramatic structure that helps portray characters and plot in a coherent way. The goal of eloquence is to combine all of the previous methods of persuasion into a powerful dramatic telling that advances a prudent judgment while encouraging the audience to look to broader horizons of meaning.

The mastery of eloquence is the culmination of the art of rhetoric. As it was introduced in the introduction to this book, eloquence is something more than just pretty-sounding words; **eloquence** is a type of experience produced when an oration achieves the heights of aesthetic form in such a way that carries an audience beyond itself while simultaneously bringing illumination to the particulars of the audience's situation. The way that eloquent rhetoric addresses us can best be explained by pointing to the speech that is consistently ranked as the greatest oration in American history, Martin Luther King Jr.'s "I Have a Dream" speech. What gave that speech such unique power was King's ability to take the particular challenge of civil rights reform in the United States and see it as part of a larger historical and spiritual journey of the nation toward universal freedom for all, all the while drawing from vivid metaphorical imagery that made his "dream" tangible to the audience's imagination.

Eloquence thus achieves more than simply confronting a particular rhetorical exigence with prudence and timeliness, as important and as necessary as is that function. All rhetoric involves advocating choices in moments of uncertainty and urgency. However, eloquent rhetoric attempts to expand the boundaries of meaning to encompass more than the immediate appearances that trouble us, thus moving us from a concern for immediate action to a capacity for reflective thought. This means eloquent rhetoric makes us look at the situation from a distance and see it in the light of history, of truth, of beauty, and of the higher values that inspire us to think great thoughts and perform great deeds. In summary, eloquence is the effect of great rhetoric that (a) emerges in a moment of uncertainty or contingency, (b) addresses the particular appearances at issue, and (c) appeals to the critical judgment and ordinary convictions of others, while at the same time (d) offering a breath of vision that inspires an audience to dwell in a more general sphere of thought, meaning, and reflection. For example, when King delivered his "Dream" speech, he spoke at a time in which segregation and racial violence remained a reality in the country and when the possibility of civil rights legislation was still unrealized. He addressed the particular "appearances" at issue when he addressed the sights, sounds, and feelings that constantly confronted African Americans at the time—police batons, jail cells, "whites only" signs, poverty, and the ghetto. He appealed to the critical judgment when he called upon Americans to condemn acts of racial injustice and support laws enforcing equality of opportunity. But most important, he offered a breath of vision that soared over the natural and social geography of the nation, its valleys and mountains and streams as well as its many diverse racial, ethnic, and religious communities, bringing all of these elements into a narrative whole that roused the appetites of the audience and carried them through a drama that satisfied their desire to envision and pursue a better world.

We have defined eloquence, in effect, as an ability to wed together particular realities and appearances with more universal meanings and possibilities. A **particular reality** means a discrete entity that is unique in the world, usually indicated by words like "this" or "that." For example, although there are many schools in the world, you may attend *this* particular school with all of its unique history and idiosyncratic qualities. A **particular appearance**, then, refers to a unique way in which a particular reality shows itself to a person at a particular time and place. "Appearance" is thus not the opposite of "reality," but rather signifies the way a reality reveals itself and encountered by someone. For instance, although the school is a particular reality, one might encounter it through multiple appearances, such as sitting in one of its classrooms, driving past it in a car, or finding its doors locked. By contrast, a **universal meaning** is an abstract concept, embodied in a language, that is used to interpret and conceptualize a large number of things. The word "school" is used to describe an infinite number of particular realities in order to define its general character as a place in which children are educated. A **universal possibility** is thus a shared general meaning that might not exist yet in reality but that we believe we might be able to achieve through imagination, cognition, and effort. For instance, at the time of King's speech, it was still only a possibility that black and white children could attend school together without the threat of violence.

Eloquence attempts to bring together in a single speech the particular and universal side of a situation without favoring one over the other. Thus, as with most definitions, we can grasp the meaning of eloquence by comparing it with two common types of speeches that fail to achieve it. On the one hand, many speakers bewilder and bore their audience by overloading particulars. Speeches that concentrate on the minutia of a situation, force the audience to listen to long list of facts and statistics, and limit their goals to the minor and short-term changes necessary to confront only the immediate problem may accurately disseminate information and present viable solutions to specific contingencies, but they do not rouse an audience to great heights of emotion. On the other hand, just as many speakers make failed efforts at inspiration by ignoring particulars entirely and choosing instead to cite clichés, quote poetry, and generally dwell in the realm of empty platitudes. The speeches assume that all that is required to create the experience of eloquence is to articulate grand universal possibilities that an audience can enter into as easily as walking through an open door. But just as facts without meanings are shortsighted, meanings without facts are impotent. In both cases, the speeches are uninspiring.

FORM

As discussed in the first chapter, great rhetoric is the product of form, in which form represents a dramatic progression that rouses an audience's appetites, gradually moves them through a logical and narrative structure, and cumulatively builds toward a resolution that satisfies their appetites. Usually this means beginning with the particulars of a situation, putting those particulars in relationship to other particulars, and then gradually showing how the interaction of these realities and appearances reveals more universal meanings and possibilities that open up a grander vision of a situation that had not been previously recognized. To better grasp the meaning of form, we can look at two types of form defined by Kenneth Burke in his discussion rhetoric:[1]

1. **Syllogistic form** is form of a logical sequence, each step leading to the next in predictable and causal order. Often associated with legal and scientific reasoning, syllogistic form is produced when a conclusion (E) is asserted in the introduction and then followed by a clear sequence of stages that "go from A to E through stages B, C, and D." In syllogistic form, the pleasure comes in using logical reasoning to trace out the consequences of an action or to determine the cause of why something came to be. In popular culture, the genres of the detective story and the crime drama make use of syllogistic form to show how all the pieces fit together in a series of "if-then" statements.

2. **Qualitative form** occurs when certain qualities in a work of art prepare the way for another quality that is emotionally satisfying, but without logical determination. This can best be understood by interpreting "quality" and "state of mind" to mean an emotional state brought about by experiencing a part of a work of art, as when a person opening a door in a horror movie brings about suspense and when the final encounter with the villain produces excitement. By qualitative form, Burke thus means an arrangement of scenes whereby each emotion prepares the way for the next one, as when suspense produces relief, relief gives way to calmness, calmness sets the stage for curiosity, curiosity prepares us for fear, and fear makes us ready for courage.

---

[1]For more on form, see Kenneth Burke, *Counter-Statement* (Berkeley: University of California Press, 1968).

The interaction of syllogistic and qualitative form in a work of art gives it logical coherence and emotional continuity, respectively. Syllogistic form puts the pieces in order so that we understand why one thing led to another thing and produced a final result. Qualitative form gives us emotional variety while at the same time giving it a "flow" that allows emotional transitions without jarring effects and gaps. In a speech, syllogistic and qualitative form carries us from the beginning to the end in a way that rouses and satisfies our curiosities and desires.

The challenge of eloquence is therefore to find a way to reveal universal significance within particular situations by rousing and satisfying an audience's appetites through the cumulative development and consummation of form. Although this task is a daunting one, it can be made more accessible by approaching it methodologically rather than by simply assuming that eloquence is a product of "genius." Eloquence does not spring ready made from the mind of genius. It is produced through hard work and a dedication to craft. This chapter will focus on two central methods of producing eloquence—the creation of an organizing symbol and the employment of poetic categories. These strategies are introduced in this final chapter because they require mastery of all the other skills beforehand. Until one has completely understood the nature of a rhetorical situation and the structure of ethos, pathos, and logos, attempts at eloquence will fall flat and reduced to one of the two types of failed rhetoric. Only after mastering the parts can we finally constitute a meaningful whole.

Thomas Jefferson: "We hold these truths to be self-evident, that all men are created equal."

Although this book has attempted to quote only oral performances by American citizens, we make an exception here to quote from the Declaration of Independence, a written document prepared by the man who would become the third president of the United States. There are three reasons for this exception. First, at the time he composed the declaration, Jefferson was less a statesman than a citizen-revolutionary. Second, although it was technically a work of writing, the Declaration was not drafted as a legal document intended to have "signers" that would then have the power of law. The Declaration, as Jay Fliegelman has shown, was initially designed for explicitly rhetorical purposes, and its publication as a broadside (a one-sided pamphlet produced on a printing press) was undertaken with the intent that people would read it out loud in public squares in order to create support for the revolutionary movement. Thus, the "public readings made the declaration an event rather than a document."[2] Or, put another way, the Declaration was a rhetorical manuscript rather than a formal document. (In fact, its initial publication included seemingly random quotation marks where speakers were supposed to pause for effect. The text included here contains the original marks, indicated by a ~ symbol. To grasp the full effect of its eloquence, then, the text should be read aloud.)

---

[2]Jay Fliegelman, *Declaring Independence: Jefferson, Natural Language, and the Culture of Performance* (Stanford: Stanford University press, 1993), 25.

Finally, the Declaration is commonly cited as one of the most eloquent expressions of the desire for political liberty ever written, and its words have continually been called upon by subsequent American rhetors to advocate for all manner of causes, not the least of which have been civil rights and women's rights. Not only eloquent itself, it has inspired innumerable acts of eloquence, both in the United States and internationally. One of the reasons for it eloquence is precisely its ability to create a meaningful and active relationship between a particular situation and universal meanings. Jefferson chooses neither to simply enumerate, in legalistic fashion, the specific injustices done by the King of England, nor to pronounce, in philosophical fashion, the abstract principles on which good government must be founded. Instead, he invokes radical universal principles in order to justify a specific act of revolution in response to an immediate exigence, thereby appealing simultaneously to our practical wisdom, which seeks prudent action in the present, and our contemplative reason, which aspires to grasp transcendent laws. Jefferson begins by defining the universal meanings and possibilities relevant to the situation:

> When in the Course of human events, it becomes necessary for one people ~ to dissolve the political bands which have connected them with another, ~ and to assume among the powers of the earth, the separate and equal station ~ to which the Laws of Nature and of Nature's God entitle them, ~ a decent respect to the opinions of mankind requires ~ that they should declare the causes which impel them to the separation.
>
> We hold these truths to be self-evident, ~ that all men are created equal, ~ that they are endowed by their Creator with certain unalienable Rights, ~ that among these are Life, Liberty and the pursuit of Happiness, ~ that to secure these rights, Governments are instituted among Men, ~ deriving their just powers from the consent of the governed, ~ that whenever any Form of Government becomes destructive of these ends, ~ it is the Right of the People to alter or to abolish it, and to institute new Government, laying its foundation on such principles and organizing its powers in such form, as to them shall seem most likely to effect their Safety and Happiness. ~ Prudence, indeed, will dictate that Governments long established should not be changed for light and transient causes; and accordingly all experience hath shewn, that mankind are more disposed to suffer, while evils are sufferable, than to right themselves by abolishing the forms to which they are accustomed. But when a long train of abuses and usurpations, pursuing invariably the same Object evinces a design to reduce them under absolute Despotism, it is their right, it is their duty, to throw off such Government, and to provide new Guards for their future security. ~ Such has been the patient sufferance of these Colonies; ~ and such is now the necessity which constrains them to alter their former Systems of Government. ~ The history of the present King of Great Britain is a history of repeated injuries and usurpations, all having in direct object the establishment of an absolute Tyranny over these States. To prove this, let Facts be submitted to a candid world.[3]

---

[3]Thomas Jefferson, "The Declaration of Independence," http://www.archives.gov/exhibits/charters/declaration.html (accessed 12 Nov. 2012).

The universal meanings are the radical principles that Jefferson set forth that he believes are applicable to all people at all times—that all men are created equal, that people have the right to abolish an oppressive government and institute a new one of their own choosing, and that the end of government is not simply security or material profit but life, liberty, and the pursuit of happiness. The universal possibilities he imagines grow out of these universal meanings. No government at any time, either at that point in history or today, has ever achieved such ends in their pure form, although one can argue that we have certainly approached a closer approximation. Nonetheless, believing that such possibilities can be achieved by any people with the courage to pursue them is inspiring, particularly when such possibilities are grounded in self-evident truths. Then, having lifted his audience to the height of universal perspective, Jefferson returns to the particular realities and appearances that confronted the colonists at that point in time and that Jefferson attributes to the direct actions of the King of England. Here are just a few of the more graphic examples he uses:

> He has abdicated Government here, by declaring us out of his Protection and waging War against us.
>
> He has plundered our seas, ravaged our Coasts, burnt our towns, and destroyed the lives of our people.
>
> He is at this time transporting large Armies of foreign Mercenaries to compleat the works of death, desolation and tyranny, already begun with circumstances of Cruelty & perfidy scarcely paralleled in the most barbarous ages, and totally unworthy the Head of a civilized nation.
>
> He has constrained our fellow Citizens taken Captive on the high Seas to bear Arms against their Country, to become the executioners of their friends and Brethren, or to fall themselves by their Hands.[4]

Once again, the difference between a particular reality and a particular appearance is merely one of degree. Particular realities are things that we know exist and are facts that we can confirm. That the King of England is transporting armies of mercenaries, that he has ordered colonists to work on English ships against their will, and that he has burnt buildings in certain towns are facts that can be proven true or false. Particular appearances are ways that realities appear to us when seen in a certain light. Through his detailed use of language, Jefferson makes the king of England appear to be a barbarous brute and dictator and calls up horrific images of colonists being forced to execute their brothers on the high seas because of the threat of death. Jefferson thus does not seek to enumerate the facts on the ground; he wishes these facts to appear to us in a certain way so that we are disgusted and repulsed by them, thereby calling forth pathos. The final rhetorical gesture appears in the conclusion, when he declares the United States of America free from Great Britain and makes a commitment on their behalf: "And for the support of this Declaration, with a firm reliance on the protection of divine Providence, we mutually pledge to each other our Lives, our Fortunes, and our sacred Honor." Here is a practical judgment made in a rhetorical situation in light of universal meanings and possibilities that inspire courage and faith.

---

[4]Ibid.

Discussion: Consider the shocking event in 1986 when the space shuttle *Challenger* exploded after liftoff, killing the entire crew, including teacher Christy McAuliffe. This was a shocking moment for the United States, particularly as it had been set up to be broadcast in schools across the nation. In President Reagan's response, he praised the courage of the crew and famously ended his speech by quoting a problem noted by a World War II pilot, saying that the crew had "slipped the surly bonds of earth to touch the face of God." Why was this particular speech considered eloquent? What particular realities and appearances, and universal meanings and possibilities, were present in this speech situation?

ORGANIZING SYMBOL

Although eloquence can occur without them, most eloquent speeches make use of an organizing symbol as their organizing principle. An organizing symbol is different than simply a common symbol. At its most *general* level, a **symbol** is anything that represents something other than itself to some other person who understands this representation. A rock on which one stubs a toe does not function symbolically; but a rock that is thrown through a window does. At this level, all words and popular icons operate as symbols insofar as they mean more than their sound or their marking. Of course, we often make a distinction between "mere words" and meaningful "symbols," as we might distinguish between the word "nation" and the American flag. But both are equally symbols insofar as they stand for something meaningful. To communicate anything to anyone is to use symbols. We are awash in symbols every day, from the most trivial to the most sublime, and as human beings it is virtually impossible to escape their influence. So to say that the use of symbols is important to public speaking is a truism; saying anything to anyone at any time or thinking of the most elementary thought requires the use of symbols.

Yet it is true that certain symbols are more important than others. They not only stand out in our minds but they do more work for us by acting as frameworks for understanding. The symbols are what we can term **organizing symbols** because they organize other symbols into coherent dramatic structures that establish relationships and help us interpret and regulate our world. Importantly, organizing symbols are different than simply large value terms (such as "justice") or powerful **icons** (such as the flag). An organizing symbol must embody some coherent dramatic formula that can be understood in narrative terms that give some sense of **scene** (where), **act** (what), **agent** (who), **purpose** (why), and **agency** (how) in the unfolding of a story. It is the difference between the symbol of the American flag and the organizing symbol embodied in the famous image of U.S. Marines raising the flag on Iwo Jima. The flag by itself can symbolize any number of virtues or ideals or people or things to any number of people; but the image of the line of U.S. Marines straining to raise the flagpole on Iwo Jima represents to Americans the culminating act of heroic self-sacrifice that shows how much individuals are willing to suffer in the name of a greater community and a higher ideal even when there is very little to gain beyond a piece of blasted rock in the Pacific Ocean.

For Burke, an organizing symbol therefore represents not a multiplicity of meanings but a specific *formula* that stands for a recognizable **pattern of experience,** by which he means a recognizable and habitual way of adjusting to a specific set of stimuli. For instance, the formula represented by the Iwo Jima image is something like "face overwhelming obstacles with courage and fraternity and be willing to sacrifice yourself for the greater good." As a formula, it encompasses a whole series of relations and adjustments to environmental conditions and thereby provides people equipment for dealing with their own particular situations. The symbol says to us, in effect, "if your situation is X, then apply the formula X − Y = Z to understand it and act appropriately in response to it."

For instance, one example of a popular symbol is "The King and the Peasant," which embodies the narrative formula about the relationship between a king who dresses like a peasant and a peasant who pretends he is a king. Employing this symbol thus embodies a certain formula for action, such that one seeks to disrobe illegitimate authority while granting moral authority to currently marginalized individuals or groups. Thus, the organizing symbol of "The King and the Peasant" would be useful to an ordinary citizen who wishes to confront and overturn established authority. By using this organizing principle, it constructs a situation in which the true "king" is speaking on a street corner and being bullied by police while the true "peasant" is sitting in the capitol building playing dress-up. An audience, upon hearing this organizing symbol, now understands precisely what pattern of experience they must adopt—unmask the false king as an imposter and put the true king upon the throne.

A helpful way to think about organizing symbols is in terms of analogical reasoning that draws from familiar narrative structures embodied in particular characters or genres. Organizing symbols ask us to treat a complex situation as if it was a more simplified situation, complete with familiar characters, attitudes, tensions, purposes, and plot developments. For instance, a common organizing symbol is the Christian martyr. This symbol is applicable whenever an individual, usually a leader of a minority social movement who stands by particular principles, is singled out for persecution and punishment by a more powerful group that is simply interested in maintaining material power. Calling forth the symbol of the Christian martyr allows the individual to suffer with dignity, to announce victory even if all other signs point to defeat, and to give courage to followers that losing the battle may yet win the war. The organizing symbol itself is the specific, identifiable word or phrase used in the speech that stands for a common understanding of something (whether it names a person, object, or event—in this case the "Christ figure"), and the formula represents the pattern of experience that is implied and called forth by the symbol (in this case to willingly give oneself up for punishment in the name of truth and virtue and love). Understanding the importance of one's choice of organizing symbol therefore becomes clear when one imagines other biblical symbols that might have been used to much different effect—Moses confronting Pharaoh, Joshua in front of the walls at Jericho, Daniel and Lion's den, or Christ throwing the money changers from the temple. In each case, the organizing symbol calls forth a much different pattern of experience that can be used as a guide for appropriate action. Using Burke's categorization, an organizing symbol should thus perform many of the following functions:[5]

1. *Produce "artistic" effects:* An organizing symbol should engage an audience with its sheer value as a work of creative invention. This explains how critics who disagree with a speaker's message may often applaud the way the speech was composed and delivered. An audience may reject a speaker's description of nonsmoking regulations as the return of Prohibition, but the symbol nonetheless livens up the speech.

2. *Interpret a situation:* In a rhetorical situation marked by confusion and uncertainty—an unclarified complexity—an organizing symbol can function to give it order and meaning. The important thing to keep in mind is that an *interpretation* is not simply a novel description. It must act to create order out of disorder—otherwise it only fulfills the artistic function of imaginative play. Thus, after the terror attacks of 9/11, it was common to try to make sense of that uncertainty by comparing it to Pearl Harbor, thus bringing clarity and direction to a situation marked by confusion and anxiety.

3. *Force acceptance of things we had previously denied:* This function can only occur when there is a *preexisting* undesirable or threatening aspect of a situation that many have refused to acknowledge in the hope that it will just go away. Reacting to a state of denial, an organizing symbol of this kind can therefore act to establish a relationship between the audience and the danger that it has ignored, usually by giving the audience a feeling of power it had not previously experienced. For instance, one might encourage a friend to face up to his or her alcoholism by making it seem a noble battle ("You are David to this Goliath"), or by humorously mocking the threat ("Your name is not Jack Daniel"). Either way, the effect of the symbol is to make him or her face up to reality.

4. *Reveal future possibilities that "correct" imperfections in the present:* After interpreting or accepting a problematic situation, an audience naturally wants to be offered a destination that will get it out of that situation. An organizing symbol can offer a vision of possibility that helps correct the imbalances of the present. For example, living a busy city life can lead one to dream about a comfortable rural life, and vice versa. The symbol as a corrective speaks to the utopian qualities of our imaginations, offering a vision of that might become real if we only strive for that goal. Martin Luther King, Jr., for instance, was famous for using "the Promised Land" (drawing from the biblical story of Exodus) as a **corrective symbol** for racial segregation in the present.

5. *Encourage the expression of "submerged" emotions:* Organizing symbols allow people to express powerful emotions that they would otherwise suppress. These symbols often have the power to arouse deep emotions, either as symbols of cruelty and horror or as symbols of hope and love. As with all

---

[5]For more on symbols, see Burke, *Counter-Statement.*

aspects of pathos, these emotions can be both negative and positive. To use the symbols of a "crusade" or "jihad" inspires its followers to express their genuine love of divine justice at the same time that it generates often violent hatred against a demonized foe.

6. *Legitimate certain types of action:* Last, organizing symbols have the unique power to invert our moral codes, thus making the better into the worse and the worse into the better. By using symbols, behavior otherwise thought immoral and shameful can come to be seen as noble and courageous in a new light. Reminiscent of the symbol of the king and the peasant, symbols that emancipate action show the hypocrisy and shallowness of what is thought "high" while valorizing that which was once thought "low." For instance, the symbol of Henry David Thoreau in prison legitimates individual acts of civil disobedience to laws in the name of a higher code of morality.

To grasp the function of an organizing symbol, a comparison with the use of metaphor may be helpful. The difference between an organizing symbol and a metaphor is simply one of degree. A metaphor performs all the functions of an organizing symbol except that of scope and depth. Figurative metaphors are usually used to creatively define particular aspects of a situation and to engage people's imaginations. An organizing symbol is used to structure our view of an entire rhetorical situation, to guide action in the long and short term, to help "identify" both a speaker and audience as having a certain character, and, most important, to structure the organization of the entire speech from beginning to end. It gives audiences a single, coherent image that will stick in their memories after the oration is over. Ralph Waldo Emerson highlights this particular quality of eloquence:

> The orator must be, to a certain extent, a poet. We are such imaginative creatures that nothing so works on the human mind, barbarous or civil, as a trope. Condense some daily experience into a glowing symbol, and an audience is electrified. They feel as if they already possessed some new right and power over a fact which they can detach, and so completely master in thought. It is a wonderful aid to the memory, which carries away the image and never loses it…Put the argument into a concrete shape, into an image—some hard phrase, round and solid as a ball, which they can see and handle and carry home with them—and the cause is half-won.[6]

The organizing symbol is precisely this "glowing symbol" that compresses a complex situation into a concrete shape, a "hard phrase round and solid as a ball, which they can see and handle and carry home with them." In other words, an organizing symbol is a metaphor extended over the length of the speech because the speaker believes it grasps some essential aspect of the rhetorical situation that warrants such strategic simplification.

Many speeches, of course, do not have organizing symbols. They use a multiplicity of metaphors as seem appropriate to the specific argument at the time, and the speeches are structured using the conventional models as we defined in the

---

[6]Ralph Waldo Emerson, "Eloquence," http://www.rwe.org/complete-works/vii-society-and-solitude/chapter-iv-eloquence (accessed on May 7, 2010).

canon of organization. Eloquent speeches, however, seek to transcend the more rigid designs and allow a speaker to weave a more complex narrative story that follows the logic of the symbol rather than that of a template. Of course, beginning speechwriters cannot simply leap over mastering the logic of templates and all the specific strategies that go with them. Usually, such efforts result in a confusing mess. However, once these basic skills are mastered, one can begin experimenting with speeches that grow out of a more poetic sensibility that seeks not just to inform and persuade but also to bring about an experience of transcendence that is a rare accomplishment in the world.

Abraham Lincoln: "We here highly resolve that these dead shall not have died in vain."

As in the discussion of form, as an example used to demonstrate the function of an organizing symbol we will use one of the foundational texts in American history, the "Gettysburg Address" delivered by President Abraham Lincoln on the afternoon of November 19, 1863, during a dedication of the Soldiers' National Cemetery in Gettysburg, Pennsylvania, four and a half months after the defeat of Confederate forces at the Battle of Gettysburg. Although Lincoln's speech was just a few minutes long, dwarfed by the two-hour harangue delivered by the speaker who preceded him, the Gettysburg Address became famous because it embodied a powerful organizing symbol that spoke to the citizens of a war-weary Union, many of whom were questioning whether the bloody slaughter was worthwhile. This symbol was a simple one—the heroic soldier dying for a national cause. By using the symbol, Lincoln sought to give himself the opportunity to define precisely the nature of that cause and thereby show the nation what it was fighting for. The entire speech is dedicated to one thing: defining the principles on which the United States is based. That is why Lincoln begins the speech with the famous words that recall the founding of the nation:

> Four score and seven years ago our fathers brought forth on this continent a new nation, conceived in liberty, and dedicated to the proposition that all men are created equal.
>
> Now we are engaged in a great civil war, testing whether that nation, or any nation, so conceived and so dedicated, can long endure. We are met on a great battle-field of that war. We have come to dedicate a portion of that field, as a final resting place for those who here gave their lives that that nation might live. It is altogether fitting and proper that we should do this.
>
> But, in a larger sense, we can not dedicate, we can not consecrate, we can not hallow this ground. The brave men, living and dead, who struggled here, have consecrated it, far above our poor power to add or detract. The world will little note, nor long remember what we say here, but it can never forget what they did here. It is for us the living, rather, to be dedicated here to the unfinished work which they who fought here have thus far so nobly advanced. It is rather for us to be here dedicated to the great task remaining before us—that from these honored dead we take increased devotion to that cause for which they gave the last full measure of devotion—that we here highly resolve that

these dead shall not have died in vain—that this nation, under God, shall have a new birth of freedom—and that government of the people, by the people, for the people, shall not perish from the earth.[7]

In this speech, Lincoln takes the basic symbol of the "martyr for the national-cause" and flushes it out in more detail. The heroes are the brave Union soldiers, both living and dead, who struggled on the field of battle, and their cause is the continued existence of a free nation of the people, by the people, and for the people. For Lincoln's audience, both in attendance and those who would later read the speech as published in the press, the organizing symbol he creates performs four of the possible functions of a symbol. First, the carefully crafted language of the symbol has an artistic value all its own that draws our attention to the words and makes it a pleasure to repeat them and hear them. Second, the symbol interprets the situation by clarifying why, exactly, so many thousands of sons and brothers and husbands had to die and suffer on the field of battle—they died in the service of a grand experiment in freedom. Third, it forces our acceptance of the reality that war will go on and that more will have to die for this cause to be won. Lincoln promises no quick end to the war but rather calls for his audience to commit themselves to the great task that remains to be done. Last, the symbol provides a corrective to the bloody slaughter of the battlefield by pointing to a future in which a free popular government has continued to live and prosper because of the sacrifices of the martyred heroes.

The power of the symbol thus comes precisely from its compact and simple form, a form that allows it to be easily remembered, called forth, and applied in future experiences. The organizing symbol represents the essential, portable formula of interpretation that remains with an audience even after many of the details have been forgotten. It is the answer to the question "what was that speech about?" in a single, powerful, meaningful sentence that is not a statement of fact but a miniature narrative: "Lincoln told us how the soldiers struggled and died on the field of battle in order that a nation dedicated to popular freedom might live."

Discussion: Martin Luther King, Jr.'s "I have a dream" speech has continually been ranked the most eloquent speech in American history. Not surprisingly, one of the reasons for its eloquence is its heavy reliance on the organizing symbol of a "man with a dream." How do you see the "dream" performing the six functions of an organizing symbol? How do you think the speech would have been different had he chosen a different organizing symbol, such as Moses and Pharaoh or the "man against the mob"? What made his choice of symbol so effective?

POETIC CATEGORIES

Although rhetoric is not the same as dramatic art, an advanced public speaker is able to make use of dramatic resources in order to more powerfully deliver a message. These resources can be termed poetic categories. For Burke, a **poetic category** represents a way of telling a certain type of story that organizes the plot and characters in

---

[7]Abraham Lincoln, "The Gettysburg Address," http://myloc.gov/Exhibitions/gettysburgaddress/Pages/default.aspx (accessed 15 July 2012).

a certain predictable sequence and produces specific emotional responses. When we go to see a classical Greek tragedy on stage, for instance, we may not know which play we will see, but we can be assured that there'll be a great hero brought to ruin by some twist of fate, and when we see a Shakespearean comedy, we will know there will be a host of motley characters constantly scheming harmlessly against one another until chance brings everything into the open and people make up and fall in love. However, poetic categories are more than simply general templates for organizing fictional events and people into a coherent stage drama; they are also ways of interpreting actual events in real life. As Burke explains, a poetic category can be understood as a rhetorical way of making meaning of our lives in history. In other words, it makes a great deal of difference whether we write ourselves into tragedies or comedies as we try to play our role in the drama of existence.

Poetic categories are therefore similar to organizing symbols insofar as they represent a sort of formula for action. However, poetic categories are more general than organizing symbols, as they represent something closer to a genre than a specific pattern of experience. For example, even though both Macbeth and Hamlet are characters in Shakespearean tragedies, they represent different organizing symbols. Macbeth represents a pattern of experience whereby an ambitious hero brazenly kills all who stand in his way in order to retain power, whereas Hamlet represents a pattern of one who attempts to enact just revenge upon an enemy by employing overly intellectual and complicated maneuvering. Organizing symbols are therefore far more particular than poetic categories. At the same time, however, one's choice of organizing symbol often indirectly makes use of the resources of poetic categories. To choose, for instance, the symbol of the great European explorers as an organizing symbol for space exploration is also to make use of the poetic category of the heroic drama. The best speeches therefore often make use of both organizing symbols and poetic categories in concert to craft inspiring narratives. Of the many poetic categories that are available, we will look at three of the most important that frequently occur in rhetorical discourse—the heroic drama, tragedy, and comedy.

The Heroic

Perhaps the most common poetic category used in rhetoric is that of the **heroic**, which calls an audience to courageous and committed action in the name of some higher ideal that has been revealed through the actions of a hero, living or dead. Importantly, heroic dramas do not simply narrate and praise great and noble deeds, as one might think of ceremonies that praise the heroism of firefighters who run into a burning building or ordinary citizens who tackle a would-be murderer. When we talk about a "hero," we mean a particularly exceptional type of person who accomplishes deeds and achieves revelations that are unavailable to everyday people. According to Joseph Campbell, "a hero ventures forth from the world of common day into a region of supernatural wonder: fabulous forces are there encountered and a decisive victory is won: the hero comes back from this mysterious adventure with the power to bestow boons on his fellow man."[8] Interspersed in

---

[8]Joseph Campbell, *The Hero with a Thousand Faces* (Princeton: Princeton University Press, 1949), 23.

this journey are stages where the hero rejects his calling, then comes to accept it after a traumatic event and challenge, dies only to be reborn, and finds allies along the way to help him toward redemption and conquest. For instance, Luke Skywalker in the *Star Wars* movies follows the hero's journey on his way from being a mere mechanic on a desert planet to being the last Jedi who teaches the ways of the Force to the galaxy.

What makes these heroes important rhetorically is that their deeds give them ethos, which gives them credibility and an audience, whereas their revelations provide new principles of action, which their audiences are prepared to follow. According to Bill Butler, "among the chief characteristics of the hero is his right to establish the laws of Heaven on Earth, and the concurrent right to break any of those laws, including the most serious injunctions against murder, with impunity. For that is partially what a hero is: like the gods, both law-*maker* and law-*breaker*."[9] The paradigmatic biblical hero, for instance, is Moses, who journeys to the mountaintop to receive the Ten Commandments and then returns to the people to pronounce the new principles that shall lead them to the Promised Land. Essential to its rhetorical function, then, is the ability of the heroic drama to provide (a) an ideal vision of a better future, (b) new principles on which to act in the name of that future, and (c) courageous leadership to inspire collective action. Virtually any time groups feel they must strike out in new directions and confront new obstacles and/or enemies, some form of heroic rhetoric is not far behind. Already in this textbook one has seen numerous examples of heroic rhetoric, from Sojourner Truth to Eugene Debs to George Patton, and virtually any summer blockbuster will feature at least one character making a heroic speech in a time of crisis. Heroism is what inspires us to do things that we might not otherwise have the courage to do, and as a result it makes for great drama.

Walt Whitman: "Great poets will be proved by their unconstraint."

Although the idea of a hero tends to be mostly associated with the classic mold of adventurer-warrior in the model of the Homeric or Hollywood epic, a more common hero in popular culture is the inventor-creator. The American writer who established the mold for this kind of hero is Walt Whitman, the nineteenth-century poet, essayist, and journalist whose 1855 publication of *Leaves of Grass* created the first American epic written in free verse. Although a work of writing, Whitman clearly intended it to be read aloud, following as it does the cadences of the Bible. One of the dominant themes throughout the poem is the need for America to develop and encourage its own unique brand of heroism in which everyday people are free to break, bend, ignore, or transform the rules of tradition in the name of following their own creative impulses. One passage where he explicitly identified the hero reads as follows:

> The old red blood and stainless gentility of great poets will be proved by their unconstraint. A heroic person walks at his ease through and out of that custom or precedent or authority that suits him not. Of the traits of the brotherhood of writers savans musicians inventors and artists nothing is finer than silent

---

[9]Bill Butler, *The Myth of the Hero* (New York: Rider and Company, 1979), 9.

defiance advancing from new free forms. In the need of poems philosophy politics mechanism science behaviour, the craft of art, an appropriate native grand-opera, shipcraft, or any craft, he is greatest forever and forever who contributes the greatest original practical example. The cleanest expression is that which finds no sphere worthy of itself and makes one.[10]

For Whitman, a heroic person is one who freely and carelessly defies any and all resistance in order to express new ideas in new free forms. This applies not only to the poet and writer, but the one who advances new forms in any area of human endeavor, from politics to science, from philosophy to shipcraft, from engineering to opera. In other words, the hero is one who ventures into the sphere of the unknown in search of the new and returns to this world to give it form and share it with others, an expression of the "democratic" hero that remains one of the essential organizing symbols of political speeches and popular entertainment alike.[11]

Discussion: There are two basic types of heroic speeches, one type in which the speaker is the hero and the other in which one speaks on behalf of the hero. And sometimes these two speeches happen in sequence, as the hero rallies a courageous following only to be killed, thus opening a space for a new leader to step forward and carry on the fight. Can you think of a film in which this occurs? What was the nature of the speeches in the film? Now think in terms of politics. When have politicians or social activists acted as heroes or as spokespeople for past heroes? What is the difference in rhetorical effect?

The Tragic

Tragedy tends to arise in the opposite rhetorical situations as that of heroism. Heroic rhetoric is fitting for moments in which individuals or groups must ready themselves for a hard journey ahead to give them confidence in their success, despite sometimes even overwhelming odds. Tragic rhetoric, by contrast, almost always follows on the heels of disaster, after one's path has ended in pain, suffering, death, or failure. Whereas heroic rhetoric looks eagerly to a great future, tragic rhetoric reflects soberly upon an unfortunate past. The goal of tragedy, however, is not to lament one's fate and wallow in misery and pity. Quite the opposite, the goal of tragedy is to wrench meaning out of suffering to answer the lingering question, "why did this have to happen?" In tragedy, "one learns by experience" such that "the suffered is the learned."[12] *Tragedy* is therefore not synonymous with words like *horrific, violent,* or *sad,* despite its frequent usage. The unforeseen or accidental death of a loved one may be traumatic for those still living, but that does not make it tragic. A tragic death is one that, despite bringing intense suffering, also produces a kind of wisdom. For example, after learning of the death of Martin

---

[10]Walt Whitman, *Leaves of Grass.* http://whitmanarchive.org/published/LG/1855/whole.html (accessed 15 July 2012).

[11]For more on Whitman, see Peter Simonson, "A Rhetoric for Polytheistic Democracy: Walt Whitman's 'Poet of Many in One.'" *Philosophy and Rhetoric* 36, no. 4 (2003), 353–375.

[12]Kenneth Burke, *A Grammar of Motives* (Berkeley: University of California Press, 1969), 39.

Luther King, Jr., Robert Kennedy delivered his version of a quote from the Greek tragedy *Antigone*: "In our sleep pain which cannot forget falls drop by drop upon the heart until, in our own despair, against our will, comes wisdom through the awful grace of God."[13] This experience of gaining wisdom through suffering is the essence of tragedy.

The purpose of employing the poetic category of tragedy in rhetoric is to help an audience achieve **catharsis**, which Aristotle defined as the sense of wisdom that follows upon the purging of pity and fear brought about by the trauma of witnessing the suffering of others whom we love and respect. What an audience wants, in other words, from a tragic speech is not more images of trauma but the opposite—words that will help us overcome our traumas and their sufferings with dignity and wisdom and courage. Whereas the emotions of pity and fear focus our attention on particular people and things, tragedy expands our vision to a wider universe in which those things are embedded; tragedy thus purges pity and fear by turning our gaze from the object of suffering before us to the night sky above us, thus subsuming particular realities and appearances under universal meanings and possibilities.

One should not therefore confuse the meaning of tragedy with that of elegy. In poetry, the **elegy** is a mournful, melancholy, or plaintive poem, often presented as a funeral song or a lament for the dead. Like tragedy, elegy often focuses on the magnitude of human suffering; yet unlike tragedy, does not redeem suffering through wisdom or some higher purpose. The embodiment of the elegy is the perfected technique of complaint; it is a "wailing wall" that invites people to express their suffering in public in such a way that emphasizes how small they are in confrontation with immense forces. The goal of the elegy, in other words, is to condemn the magnitude of injustice in the world and appeal to some higher moral law to help the helpless and give strength to the powerless. In rhetoric, the elegy is often employed by individuals or groups who feel they have been unjustly oppressed by an illegitimate power. It expresses itself in a "Woe is me!" type of lament. Yet there is no catharsis in elegy. There is only lamentation and the reward of giving expression to one's pain.

The peculiar nature of tragic pleasure, by contrast, comes precisely from the act of bearing witness to universal truths about the world through particular images of traumatic suffering. That is to say, tragedy neither dwells on particular suffering nor simply ignores it by offering nice-sounding platitudes. Instead, tragedy goes *through* those particular appearances and tries to find the universal meanings within them. Most often, these meanings deal less with the individual who has suffered than with the environment that has brought about that suffering. The metaphor of the "night sky" really stands for a more expansive view of the world in which we live, including its moral laws and the degree to which our present reality fails to live up to them. The pleasure that accompanies catharsis is therefore the pleasure of having gained a greater wisdom and recognizing that such wisdom can only come through great suffering. It is the task of rhetoric to bring forth this wisdom and to produce a community of affiliation grounded in its acceptance.

---

[13]Robert Kennedy, "Eulogy for Martin Luther King, Jr.," http://www.eulogyspeech.net/famous-eulogies/Martin-Luther-King-Eulogy-by-Robert-F-Kennedy.shtml (accessed 12 Nov. 2012).

There are two types of tragic speeches, however, depending on the nature of the traumatic event. The first type is one that focuses on the suffering of a tragic hero. In Classical Greek tragedy, the one who suffers is the **tragic hero**, a larger-than-life individual who possesses great and noble virtues and who confronts mighty enemies, but who also possesses **hamartia**, or those fatal flaws in character that are simultaneously the cause of the individual's greatness and the cause of his or her destruction. Usually this hamartia is the sin of **hubris**, or overweening pride, which is both the virtue that allows one to accomplish great deeds and the vice that generates the blind spots and overconfidence that allow one to fall victim to the workings of fateful necessity. In other words, the tragic hero is a person we often have mixed feelings about. On the one hand, such heroes are dignified and almost superhuman individuals who espouse noble causes and heroically confront and disrupt the old order of things that has become stale and oppressive. On the other hand, they are often violent and dogmatic individuals who unintentionally bring harm to innocent people and ultimately fail in their goal because of their own flaws. Therefore, when the final traumatic failure of the tragic hero occurs, most often in death, it becomes the responsibility of the rhetor to wrest from pain a lesson of what is to be learned from the hero's flawed but virtuous struggle.

Henry David Thoreau: "He is not Old Brown any longer; he is an angel of light."

One of the most controversial tragic heroes of the nineteenth century was John Brown, whose speech to the court, following his failed raid at the federal armory at Harper's Ferry, we have already encountered in the chapter on logos. Brown, of course, cast himself in a familiar heroic mold, describing himself as being God's instrument on earth to lead and emancipate the slaves through violent insurrection. But his effort ended in failure, with Brown being captured and the raid resulting in the death of four soldiers and ten of his own men, including two of his sons. With his trial and eventual conviction and execution, Brown's story was right for a tragic reading. Here was a great man pursuing a noble cause, but one who was possessed by such hubris that he believed he could liberate millions of the slaves through a single raid with twenty men. For Abolitionists who believed in his cause, the task was to wrest universal meaning from this particular trauma and use Brown's immanent execution as an opportunity to gain wisdom. This was the goal of transcendentalist writer and philosopher Henry David Thoreau in his speech, "A Plea for Captain John Brown," delivered at Concord, Massachusetts, on October 30, 1859, just two weeks after the raid. After an extensive treatment of the press coverage on Brown, in which he was characterized as insane, a monster, and a monomaniac, Thoreau broadens the panorama to include Brown's principles and their relationship to conditions in the United States:

> It was his peculiar doctrine that a man has a perfect right to interfere by force with the slaveholder, in order to rescue the slave. I agree with him. They who are continually shocked by slavery have some right to be shocked by the violent death of the slaveholder, but no others. Such will be more shocked by his life than by his death. I shall not be forward to think him mistaken in his method who quickest succeeds to liberate the slave. I speak for the slave when I say that I prefer the philanthropy of Captain Brown to that philanthropy which neither shoots me nor liberates me...

I do not wish to kill nor to be killed, but I can foresee circumstances in which both these things would be by me unavoidable. We preserve the so-called peace of our community by deeds of petty violence every day. Look at the policeman's billy and handcuffs! Look at the jail! Look at the gallows! Look at the chaplain of the regiment! We are hoping only to live safely on the outskirts of this provisional army. So we defend ourselves and our hen-roosts, and maintain slavery. I know that the mass of my countrymen think that the only righteous use that can be made of Sharp's rifles and revolvers is to fight duels with them, when we are insulted by other nations, or to hunt Indians, or shoot fugitive slaves with them, or the like. I think that for once the Sharp's rifles and the revolvers were employed in a righteous cause. The tools were in the hands of one who could use them. The same indignation that is said to have cleared the temple once will clear it again.[14]

Although Thoreau casts Brown in a more "saintly" heroic mold than is typical of the conventional tragedy (at one point calling him an "angel of light"), he nonetheless displays here the essential rhetorical function of the poetic category—for Brown is clearly a flawed character, possessing many of the vices that less charitable newspaper editorialists attributed to him. What is important is not whether Thoreau acknowledges these flaws or not; what is important is that he acts as if these characteristics are irrelevant. What matters to Thoreau is that Brown acted on principle, nobly struggled for a cause, and failed in and suffered for that cause with a measure of dignity (thus following the general structure of the organizing symbol of the "man against the mob"). Furthermore, his failure in the immediate act nonetheless accomplished a greater goal, which was the illumination of the moral law ("that a man has a perfect right to interfere by force with the slave-holder, in order to rescue the slave") upon the wasteland that was slaveholding America ("Look at the policeman's billy and handcuffs! Look at the jail! Look at the gallows! Look at the chaplain of the regiment!"). His raid on Harper's Ferry may have been a foolhardy campaign by a zealot to accomplish an impossible task, but in its traumatic failure it revealed the true nature of slavery and injustice in America and produced a community of affiliation grounded in a commitment to freedom for all human beings.[15]

The deaths of tragic heroes are relatively rare occurrences, however. Far more common is the suffering of tragic victims. A **tragic victim** differs from a tragic hero because the victim does not bear any responsibility for his or her own suffering. Whereas the tragic hero consciously sets forth to challenge something and endures pain and failure partly as the result of his or her own flaws, the tragic victim often is a complete innocent who merely is in the wrong place at the wrong time. For instance, during the early stages of the civil rights movement in 1963, four young African-American girls were killed in a bombing at the 16th St. Baptist Church, an incident that shocked the nation with its indiscriminate terrorist violence. Nothing

[14]John Brown, "Address to the Jury," http://www.africa.upenn.edu/Articles_Gen/Plea_Captain_Brown .html. (accessed 15 November 2012).
[15]For more on Thoreau's praise of Brown, see Paul D. Erickson, "Henry David Thoreau's Apotheosis of John Brown: A Study of Nineteenth Century Rhetorical Heroism," *Southern Communication Journal* 61, no. 4 (1996), 302–311.

in the character of these children could be said to justify the punishment brought upon them. And yet, when Dr. King delivered the eulogy, he remarked with solemn hope that the tragic event would cause the South to come to terms with conscience. This hope is the product of catharsis, which can be produced only after pity for each individual child, and fear for one's own children, is replaced by a more expansive wisdom that comes from reflection on the meaning of suffering. In other words, rhetoric attempts to wrest meaning out of pain by showing how even the violent death of innocents can, like all tragic events, shed necessary light upon pervasive social conditions and make audiences aware of the principles of moral justice upon which future action must rest.

Dennis Shepard: "Good is coming out of evil."

Few things are more difficult to come to terms with than the violent death of an innocent child. Even worse is when this violence is personal, premeditated, and prolonged. On October 6, 1998, 21-year-old Matthew Shepard, a student at the University of Wyoming, got into a car with Aaron McKinney and Russell Henderson under the pretense that they would drive him home from a local bar. Instead, they drove Shepard to a remote, rural area where they robbed, pistol whipped, and tortured him, leaving him tied to a fence to die. He was discovered in a coma eighteen hours later by cyclist who mistook Shepard for scarecrow, and died six days later without ever having regained consciousness. The murder was horrific enough, but it was soon revealed that the reason for the torture was because the assailants discovered that Shepard was gay, and at the trial McKinney actually attempted to mount a defense based on the fact that they went temporarily insane due to "gay panic," which they suffered after Shepherd's alleged "advances." The day of their conviction, Matthew's father, Dennis Shepard, delivered a remarkable speech to the court that followed the pattern of tragedy:

> Matt officially died at 12:53 a.m. on Monday, October 12, 1998, in a hospital in Fort Collins, Colorado. He actually died on the outskirts of Laramie tied to a fence that Wednesday before, when you beat him. You, Mr. McKinney, with your friend Mr. Henderson, killed my son. By the end of the beating, his body was just trying to survive. You left him out there by himself, but he wasn't alone. There were his lifelong friends with him—friends that he had grown up with. You're probably wondering who these friends were. First, he had the beautiful night sky with the same stars and moon that we used to look at through a telescope. Then, he had the daylight and the sun to shine on him one more time—one more cool, wonderful autumn day in Wyoming. His last day alive in Wyoming. His last day alive in the state that he always proudly called home. And through it all he was breathing in for the last time the smell of Wyoming sagebrush and the scent of pine trees from the snowy range. He heard the wind—the ever-present Wyoming wind—for the last time. He had one more friend with him. One he grew to know through his time in Sunday school and as an acolyte at St. Mark's in Casper as well as through his visits to St. Matthew's in Laramie. He had God. I feel better knowing he wasn't alone.
>
> Matt became a symbol—some say a martyr, putting a boy-next-door face on hate crimes. That's fine with me. Matt would be thrilled if his death would

help others...My son was taught to look at all sides of an issue before making a decision or taking a stand. He learned this early when he helped campaign for various political candidates while in grade school and junior high. When he did take a stand, it was based on his best judgment. Such a stand cost him his life when he quietly let it be known that he was gay. He didn't advertise it, but he didn't back away from the issue either. For that I'll always be proud of him. He showed me that he was a lot more courageous than most people, including myself. Matt knew that there were dangers to being gay, but he accepted that and wanted to just get on with his life and his ambition of helping others.

Matt's beating, hospitalization, and funeral focused worldwide attention on hate. Good is coming out of evil. People have said "Enough is enough." You screwed up, Mr. McKinney. You made the world realize that a person's lifestyle is not a reason for discrimination, intolerance, persecution, and violence. This is not the 1920s, 30s, and 40s of Nazi Germany. My son died because of your ignorance and intolerance. I can't bring him back. But I can do my best to see that this never, ever happens to another person or another family again. As I mentioned earlier, my son has become a symbol—a symbol against hate and people like you; a symbol for encouraging respect for individuality; for appreciating that someone is different; for tolerance. I miss my son, but I'm proud to be able to say that he is my son.[16]

Like Thoreau's eulogy to John Brown, the speech by Dennis Shepard seeks that most tragic of all goals—to find the good that comes from evil and the wisdom that comes from suffering. Shepard mourns his son and condemns his attacker, but he also tries to find spiritual consolation in the fact that Matthew has become a symbol in death and graphically demonstrates how violent bigotry and intolerance remain a problem in this nation, not just concerning those who are gay but all those who are singled out for abuse because of trivial differences. In the immediate moment, his speech produces catharsis and the community of affiliation that follows in the wake of all tragic moments, and resonates with the common organizing symbol of the "Christ figure." But in the long term, his speech also set in motion a legislative movement that would result in the Matthew Shepard and James Byrd, Jr. Hate Crimes Act, which was signed into law in 2009, thus showing how tragic rhetoric often acts as the first episode in a drama that culminates in moral and political reform.

Discussion: Richard Weaver has written that "without rhetoric there seems no possibility of tragedy, and in turn, without the sense of tragedy, no possibility of taking an elevated view of life. The role of tragedy is to keep the human lot from being rendered in history. The cultivation of tragedy and a deep interest in the value-conferring power of language always occur together."[17] Behind this quote is a sense that rhetoric is always pushing us past conventional limits as we seek higher visions of ourselves, and that tragedy is the inevitable consequence of this lofty ambition. Speculate further on what you think he means by this passage.

---

[16]Dennis Shepard, "Statement to the Court," http://www.wiredstrategies.com/mrshep.htm (accessed 12 Nov. 2102).
[17]Weaver, *The Ethics of Rhetoric*, 23.

The Comic

Whereas the heroic is appropriate at the *beginning* of something and tragedy is appropriate at its *end*, **comedy** is the most appropriate while in the *middle* of something. Specifically, comedy always situates characters within a complex *deliberative* situation, in which **deliberation** means a communicative activity by which multiple parties, each with different perspectives, goals, and interests, attempt to come to a common practical judgment about some pressing issue. Obviously, then, comedy as it is being used here refers not to the art of making people laugh but a way of telling a dramatic story. Comedy, after all, was the counterpart of tragedy on the Greek stage. But instead of portraying the heroic suffering of individual heroes who were more noble and greater than ourselves, comedy portrayed the absurd antics of a multiplicity of exaggerated characters less virtuous and stupider than ourselves. In both Shakespearean plays and Hollywood films, the plot of a comedy usually revolves around an initial misunderstanding or deception that magnifies to absurd proportions until some chance event reveals what is truly going on to everyone involved, such that an amicable reconciliation between parties becomes possible. In comedy, the end does not come with the triumph of the hero over the villain (as in an epic) or with the noble death of the hero in his or her struggle for greatness (as in a tragedy); it comes with the resolution of misunderstandings made possible by humility and forgiveness.

The essence of dramatic comedy is therefore not the "joke" but the "situation." In both stand-up comedy and in dramatic comedy there is certainly **humor**, which can be defined as that burst of spontaneous laughter produced by the momentary violation of expectations and the absurd juxtaposition of incongruous things in such a way that also produces some new insight. For instance, it is funnier to throw a pie in the face of the king wearing ermine robes than it is to see a pie thrown in the face of a peasant child, precisely because the shocked expression of the king covered with cream reveals all the great trappings of royalty to be merely superficial covering on an ordinary person as capable of shock and embarrassment as the rest of us. With the child there is no such contrast, and hence this act would be interpreted merely as being cruel. The difference is that jokes bring about humor through condensed and usually stereotypical stories or phrases, whereas dramatic comedies bring forth humor by developing certain character types and showing how they interact with others in a complicated deliberative context. If a joke simply has us imagine a king getting hit with a pie, a dramatic comedy shows all the wild machinations that go into a group of oddball conspirators trying to bring about that event, inevitably resulting in a final scene in which all the characters are in the castle at the same time and end up in a pile laughing at each other and covered in cream pies.

In rhetoric, the poetic category of comedy is therefore most useful in deliberative situations that have become so polarized (usually by competing heroic narratives) that collective judgment has become virtually impossible. During these moments, comedy replaces a heroic narrative that pits good against evil with comic narratives in which multiple parties, each with the best intentions, are needlessly clashing with each other because they have not understood each other's perspectives and have exaggerated their own virtues and victimhood. Comic rhetoric is thus deliberative because comedy always portrays people as agents of change attempting to make the best judgment (often out of a bad situation) in collaboration or competition with many people unlike themselves.

In rhetoric, then, comedy is often used as a way of resolving disputes, easing tensions, and giving people broader perspective on issues through a combination of witty observations and enlightened interpretations. In comedy, one does not laugh *at* others but *with* them, often concerning foibles for which he or she is responsible. Consequently, comedy is often used in speeches of introduction, identification, enrichment, and administration in which the goal is a feeling of voluntary participation in a shared experience. Rather than seeking to magnify the glory of the end and the virtue of suffering, as with tragedy, comedy looks at suffering largely as the unnecessary consequence of ignorance, exaggeration, and narrow-minded partisanship and seeks to avoid it through mutual understanding and acceptance of differences. The reason that comedy is "funny," therefore, is twofold: first, it is funny to see how ridiculous people are when they take themselves too seriously; second, the most important way to overcome our own self-importance and try to work together with others (despite previous tensions) is to be able to laugh at ourselves.

Benjamin Franklin: "The older I grow, the more apt I am to doubt my own judgment."

The American "Founding Father" who possessed the most superior comic wit is undisputedly Benjamin Franklin. Not only did he continually publish witticisms in his "Poor Richard's Almanac," but he even found time to make jokes during one of the most crucial decisions in the nation's history, the decision to ratify the U.S. Constitution. On Monday, September 17, 1787, the last day of the Constitutional Convention, Pennsylvania delegate Benjamin Franklin wrote a speech with the intention of delivering it to the convention, although due to ill health he had it delivered by Pennsylvanian James Wilson. In this masterpiece, Franklin shows the rhetorical power of comedy during deliberative moments in which many uncertainties and disagreements still remain:

> I confess that there are several parts of this constitution which I do not at present approve, but I am not sure I shall never approve them: For having lived long, I have experienced many instances of being obliged by better information, or fuller consideration, to change opinions even on important subjects, which I once thought right, but found to be otherwise. It is therefore that the older I grow, the more apt I am to doubt my own judgment, and to pay more respect to the judgment of others. Most men indeed as well as most sects in Religion, think themselves in possession of all truth, and that wherever others differ from them it is so far error. Steele a Protestant in a Dedication tells the Pope, that the only difference between our Churches in their opinions of the certainty of their doctrines is, the Church of Rome is infallible and the Church of England is never in the wrong...In these sentiments, Sir, I agree to this Constitution with all its faults, if they are such...I doubt too whether any other Convention we can obtain, may be able to make a better Constitution. For when you assemble a number of men to have the advantage of their joint wisdom, you inevitably assemble with those men, all their prejudices, their

passions, their errors of opinion, their local interests, and their selfish views. From such an assembly can a perfect production be expected? ...

On the whole, Sir, I can not help expressing a wish that every member of the Convention who may still have objections to it, would with me, on this occasion doubt a little of his own infallibility, and to make manifest our unanimity, put his name to this instrument.[18]

One finds in this speech all of the elements of comedy. There are multiple parties coming together to make a decision, each with his or her own particular perspective that clashes with others, each with a certain sense of his or her own superiority, yet all of them equally flawed. Yet the comic response is not to reinforce one's own biases or to fight to the death, but to admit one's own limitations and to give grace to others in the knowledge that nothing is perfect, and yet something must still be done in the hope of a happy ending after all. The essence of comedy is not, therefore, riotous laughter—although that sometimes helps. It is rather the knowing and humble smile that comes from understanding that everyone is in the same ridiculous boat, just trying to keep afloat.

Discussion: If the heroic launches us on new expeditions and the tragic brings wisdom out of the inevitable suffering that such journeys bring, comedy helps us make our way day by day in the everyday world of human affairs. This is why comedians rather than heroes often make the best administrators. Can you think of ways that comedy is used as a conscious rhetorical strategy in our group deliberations in professional life? When is comedy an effective rhetorical strategy in such contexts? By contrast, when might an administrator (be he or she a CEO, a business owner, a middle manager, or a department chair) abandon the comic attitude to adopt a heroic or tragic approach to dealing with a rhetorical situation?

---

[18]Benjamin Franklin, available from http://www.usconstitution.net/franklin.html (accessed 7 Sept. 2012).

KEY WORDS

SUMMARY

Eloquence in a speech is not synonymous with pleasant-sounding words and delivery in a comfortable situation. Eloquence, rather, is produced when an audience within a rhetorical situation encounters a speech that is capable simultaneously of prudence and transcendence, in which **prudence** means the capacity to make a practical judgment about a particular matter of concern and **transcendence** means the capacity to move through the particular matter at hand and thereby experience meanings that are more grander and more universal than those that are immediately present. Importantly, transcendence does not mean ignoring the particular realities and appearances of the exigence and simply spouting maxims and clichés and grandiose abstractions. It means showing how universal meanings and possibilities are revealed *through* and *within* the specific events, people, actions, and objects that make up a rhetorical situation. This is why we feel that the words of the Declaration of Independence are thought to be eloquent:

> Despite the fact that they were written for a specific context, Jefferson managed to give universal expression to the desire of human beings to feel at home within a political system. The preamble deals neither with what

has been or what will be, nor with philosophical principles stated in the abstract. It deals with what exists within the common world we inhabit together through time, which includes infinity.[19]

In other words, Jefferson helped create a feeling of what it meant to be "American" by advocating a specific judgment of prudence in the moment—to declare revolution—while also revealing universal meanings and possibilities of a form of popular government based on the preservation of life, liberty, and the pursuit of happiness.

The first step in the construction of eloquent speech is therefore to identify a relationship between particular realities and appearances and universal meanings and possibilities. We identify *particular realities* when we simply define all of the specific people, events, objects, and actions that are significant in a rhetorical situation. Particular realities are all the definable "things" we must take account of. *Particular appearances* are the *ways* that we encounter all of these things. Appearances are the way a reality shows itself to us under a "certain light" and in a certain place and time. For instance, racial segregation certainly existed as a reality in the South, but it took many appearances, from segregated lunch counters

---

[19]Nathan Crick, *Democracy and Rhetoric: John Dewey on the Arts of Becoming* (Columbia: South Carolina University Press, 2010), 173–174.

to water fountains to school systems, and with those specific places looking different depending on how they were experienced and by what form of media they were represented. *Universal meanings* thus represent what more general types of things we can say about these particular realities as a way of categorizing them and broadening their significance. Even though Southern segregation was a particular reality in the United States, it also has general meaning as a form of oppression and violence that makes it a part of a larger history of the abuse of power. Finally, *universal possibilities* refer to general types of meanings or values that are not actually present in the particular situation but might nonetheless be valuable to us as ends-in-view, as guides for future action based on our hopes and imaginations. The irony of history is that we often glimpse universal possibilities through particular appearances of great suffering, as when children being sprayed with fire hoses makes us imagine what true freedom might mean.

Once we understand the relationship between the particular and the universal, we can then choose organizing symbols that give us a core "nugget," or narrative structure, that we can use to give order to the often chaotic complex of circumstances. The best organizing symbol is one that combines a recognizable common symbol with a familiar narrative formula. For instance, in college athletics (particularly the NCAA Basketball Tournament), sports commentators often make use of the "Cinderella story" to describe how a low-ranked team from a small conference has managed to triumph over higher-ranked teams to make it to the finals. The organizing symbol of the Cinderella story embodies the narrative formula by which a person without recognized status manages to find a way into an elite competitive environment (in this example, the "Big Dance" of the invitational basketball tournament) and ends up triumphing over more well-recognized competition to take the prize. We use organizing symbols all the time to create a bond between speaker and audience so that everybody knows what type of story is being told

and can follow along and participate. However, our choice of organizing symbol must be fitting to the actual situation. A Cinderella story is not an appropriate organizing symbol for merely a one-game upset, for instance, because it does not involve the kind of "party crashing" that is essential to its formula; rather, one would use a "David versus Goliath" organizing symbol to represent a single battle in which a seemingly weaker opponent triumphed over a "giant" through courage and mastery of technique.

Rhetors can also structure a speech using one of the major poetic categories that represents a certain genre of storytelling rather than a specific story itself. Although there are numerous poetic categories, the three major categories used in rhetorical speeches are the heroic, the tragic, and the comic. In the *heroic* category, a speaker attempts to rally an audience to courageous action by disclosing universal possibilities that will turn into a reality if they only follow a certain path that has been revealed to the speaker, usually by some higher authority. Heroic rhetoric thus accomplishes eloquence by showing how a particular obstacle must be overcome in order to achieve a universal possibility, usually in the form of a utopia, while making a saint of the leader. In tragedy, a speaker attempts to wrest meaning out of suffering, whether that suffering is by a hero or by a victim. Instead of advocating for heroic initiative, tragedy reflects upon past pain or failure in order to make sense of our particular suffering by revealing its universal meaning and perhaps even its universal possibility. In other words, when our heroic ventures fail, we look to tragedy to help us understand why they failed and what we can learn from that failure. Last, in comedy, a speaker tries to make the best of a complicated and contentious deliberative situation by helping all parties laugh at themselves just enough to make a limited judgment that benefits everyone. Unlike the heroic and the tragic, the comic tends not to dwell as much in the universal as it does in the particular, preferring prudence over transcendence. In this way, comic rhetoric often is not as "eloquent" as heroic or tragic rhetoric, but when done well it nonetheless can produce powerful feelings of relief, camaraderie, and optimism that produce their own sense of self-transcendence.

Finally, eloquence shows us the power and importance of public speaking even in our electronic age. It is difficult to experience eloquence sitting in front of a video screen or reading a newspaper. We experience eloquence when we are with others in a situation of uncertainty and urgency and when we hear words spoken to all of us with charisma, wisdom, and passion. These moments leave a lasting impression upon us that changes us in a way that other forms of communication find difficult to achieve. Human beings are social and political animals, born to live with others and to communicate with them using all of our bodily senses. Rhetorical public speaking at its best channels all of these energies and impulses and focuses attention on particular matters that require our agency to change. Of course, we cannot use a single speech to transform the globe—but neither can a single viral video, no matter how popular. History is written by an infinite number of particular acts by people pursuing the universal possibilities inherent within their own situations. The experience of eloquence is produced when we finally are able to break the bounds of our finitude and catch a glimpse of a meaningful world just beyond our reach yet potentially within our grasp. It is the responsibility of the engaged citizen to keep pushing those boundaries so that we can expand the horizon of human possibilities in a fragile and changing world.

CHAPTER 7 EXERCISES

1. Analyzing your rhetorical artifact, selected in Chapter 1, what was its organizing symbol? Did it use any of the poetic categories? If not, do you think that was a mistake?

2. Select a speech that has been traditionally classified as eloquent. Identify the particular realities and appearances and the universal meanings and possibilities that you think it addresses and explain the relationships.

3. Find a local news story about a particular happening of some kind that was out of the ordinary. Now act as if you were a reporter trying to write a better story than the one that had been published. Select a different organizing symbol by which to tell the story without significantly altering the actual facts but simply emphasizing different parts of the story. How is it different than the original? How many of the six functions does it perform?

4. Take a mundane event that happened to you today and retell it using a heroic, a tragic, and then a comic frame, exaggerating the events as necessary. What ended up being the rhetorical effects of telling the story in three different ways?

5. Find a popular movie that fits the genre of comedy. Inevitably, there will be a moment when one of the characters makes a speech that brings order to a situation that is about to spin out of control. Analyze the text of that speech using the rhetorical characteristics of comedy.

6. Compose your own tragic story of a fictional tragic hero. Then compose and deliver a tragic speech as a eulogy to the hero's death that will be meaningful even to those who do not know the "back story." Then ask the rest of the class to reconstruct the context of the speech based on its performance, including who they think the "audience" for the speech is supposed to be.

INDEX